Territory and Function

To Benton MacKaye, Lewis Mumford, Howard Odum,
Rexford Tugwell, and Harvey Perloff

Territory and Function

The Evolution of Regional Planning

John Friedmann and Clyde Weaver

University of California Press
Berkeley and Los Angeles
1979

University of California Press
Berkeley and Los Angeles, California

© John Friedmann and Clyde Weaver 1979

ISBN 0-520-03928-9

Library of Congress Catalog Card Number 79-64482

Printed in Great Britain

Contents

Prefatory note

This book is a collaborative work. The preparation of first drafts, however, was a divided task. Clyde Weaver is primarily responsible for chapters 2 and 3. The remaining chapters were written by the senior author.

Acknowledgments

The research and writing of this book were supported, in part, by the John Simon Guggenheim Foundation and with grants from the Academic Senate of the University of California at Los Angeles. The initial work was carried out while the senior author was a visitor to the Centre for Environmental Studies in London. To all these institutions we are greatly indebted.

In a more personal way, we are deeply appreciative of Ms Kitty Bednar who prepared the manuscript with extraordinary care. Her editorial suggestions were especially valuable and helped to give the manuscript its present form.

John Friedmann
Clyde Weaver

Chapter 1

Introduction and summary

Regional planning has come of age. In country after country, it has become part of the established machinery of government.[1] Teaching and research institutes have been set up.[2] Textbooks have been published in several languages.[3] Specialized journals have appeared.[4] And, since 1961, more than twenty international conferences concerned with regional planning have been held whose proceedings were subsequently published in English.[5]

These varied activities mark the arrival of a new professional field. Practice, teaching and research in regional planning, interlinked through key personalities and drawing on much the same stock of knowledge mixed with prejudice, have contributed to a growing consensus about theory and doctrine. Three recently edited books provide a striking illustration (Kuklinski, ed., 1975; Boudeville, ed., 1975; Gilbert, ed., 1976). Despite the large number of international contributions, they display astounding unanimity about basic principles, and the professional language is virtually the same. Even publications from centrally planned economies, such as Poland (Secomski, 1974) and Cuba (Rodriguez, 1973; Vidal Villa, 1973) reveal this agreement on fundamentals. The only significant departures are found in accounts of regional planning in the Soviet Union (Nekrasov, 1974) and Czechoslovakia (Schejbal and Zurik, 1975).

Mainstream doctrine thus seems secure enough. Yet, voices are beginning to be raised that question the established orthodoxy.[6] Much of this critique is of a technical nature, but there is also a growing literature examining regional doctrine from a neo-Marxist perspective.[7] Although lacking an explicit alternative, these critics have begun to undercut the self-complacent certainties of professional success.

Thus, at the very moment when regional planning appears to be accepted almost universally, established doctrine is being shaken at its very roots. For the past quarter century, regional planning was intended to reduce, and in the long run to eliminate, major inequalities of income among regions. The failure to score significant success along these lines has given credence to many of the critics' arguments (Stöhr and Tödtling, 1977). More fundamentally, the broad field of development studies of which regional planning is a part, is currently in the throes of a profound transformation of its own which is rendering much of the received planning doctrine obsolete. Among the new ideas that are beginning to replace the former simplicities, when economic growth was still regarded as the only thing worth striving for, are a growing awareness of the decisive role of natural resources in sustaining civilized life; a new ecological ethic; greater concern with questions of equity; a deeper understanding of the contradictions between the international division of labour and the territorial aspirations of new nation states; and a reassertion of the principle of self-reliance at all levels of territorial order. If it accomplishes nothing else, this reconstruction of the meaning of socio-economic development is forcing a serious re-examination of regional planning doctrine as well.

In the present volume, we have decided to adopt an historical approach. This, we hope, will help to throw regional planning doctrine into relief by revealing its origins, the options that were rejected, the influence of circumstantial events, alternative formulations that were neglected, and the new forms of doctrine that are beginning to emerge.

Our emphasis on doctrine is deliberate. The *practice* of regional planning usually involves an initiative on part of the state. Although it may take many forms, a specific method of procedure and a definite concept of development are always found to underlie it. The first is linked to *procedural planning theory* and the second to *regional planning doctrine*. Doctrine, in turn, feeds on a variety of theories in the social and environmental sciences which we designate as *substantive theories in regional planning*. Finally, both doctrine and theory are informed by certain *ideological assumptions* that change the contents of regional planning and determine its outcome. The internal relationships among these five major dimensions of regional planning and the underlying reality of socio-economic, political, and spatial organization, together with references to the relevant literature, are shown in Figure 1.1.

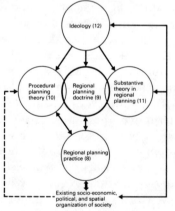

Figure 1.1   Principal dimensions of regional planning and their Interrelations

This relatively simple scheme hides the enormous complexity of what we are about to undertake. To illustrate: the only reason for looking at the history of regional planning doctrines is to gain a better understanding of variations in the actual practice of planning. Without practice, doctrine would remain a barren thing. In Great Britain, doctrine arose largely as a pragmatic response to problems encountered in reality (Hall, 1975). In the United States, however, doctrine came first and often continued to evolve independently of practice. Practice was the state bureaucracy's task – doctrine the task of academia. This institutional division produced considerable tension between applied and scientific work and often resulted in the virtual rupture between theory and practice. As a Polish author (Kolipinski, 1977, p. 153) has noted in a passage which also recalls American experience:

> The mutual penetration of theoretical and practical knowledge in Polish regional science seems to be insufficient. Theoreticians of space economy cannot even boast of any 'prototype' applications of their concepts in planning practice, to say nothing of any broad utilization of such concepts. The empirical experience of practical planning, on the other hand, is not utilized to enrich theoretical achievements as much as it might be, nor do planners use it as a material for learning from their own, and other people's mistakes.

Figure 1.1 shows a break between what we have called substantive theory and the practice of regional planning. The former is the work of geographers, economists, regional scientists, sociologists, and political scientists. *But only a minute proportion of these scientists has ever been exposed to, much less directly involved in, regional planning.* This gap would be closed only in non-market (socialist) economies.

The situation is somewhat better with procedural theory. Here again, a variety of academic subjects come together, including sociology, political science, organization theory, information theory, general systems theory, philosophy, and economics (Friedmann and Hudson, 1974). To the extent that procedural theory in planning is regarded as an academic subject, its removal from practice is as complete as with most substantive theory. But, in contrast to the latter, procedural theory often takes its cue from problems arising in the real world. It attempts to illuminate some of the major choices that need to be made in organizing the practice of planning. For instance, should planning be comprehensive or incremental, centralized or devolved to local decision units, technocratic or participatory, long-term or short-term, deterministic or aleatory?

These and similar choices pose major organizational and methodological issues that must be faced. Students of procedural planning theory cannot therefore ignore practice to the same extent that those who work the field of substantive theory are apt to do.

Finally, the ideological assumptions of both theory and doctrine in regional planning deserve attention. Reflecting underlying social relations in production, they tend to legitimate the existing distribution of power in society. As an activity of the state, actual planning practice is unable to go beyond the structural conditions that give rise to it. Radical planners are therefore reduced to unmasking the ideological biases and contradictions of existing practice. They cannot engage in planning without themselves becoming corrupted by power; radical planning is a contradiction in terms.

In light of this complexity, we have opted for a concentration on doctrine. Although doctrine combines the normative, procedural, substantive, and practical dimensions of regional planning, it is systematized to a degree that practice is not. Doctrine is the stock-in-trade of professional planners, the sum and substance of what they know and perpetrate upon the world. As such it serves not only to illuminate the practice of regional planning but to provide a focus from which the remaining dimensions of planning can be conveniently explored.

The American tradition: a summary

The close interweaving of ideology, doctrine, theory, and practice leads one to expect that the doctrine of regional planning will vary not only with national traditions in the practice of planning but also with ideologies and underlying socio-economic conditions. This tendency towards the national differentiation of regional planning is, however, counteracted by an opposing tendency towards the *normalization* of doctrines. This trend stems from cross-cultural technocratic approaches which dominate the field and reflect a strong bias for central resource allocation (Friedmann, 1978). All the same, some national variations of regional planning doctrine continue to exist.[13]

It is precisely because of significant differences in national tradition that we have chosen to focus our account on the United States. Our choice, however, should not be interpreted as a parochial view. American doctrine has become enriched by its extensive application overseas and its contact with other national traditions, especially the French. Carried abroad on the shoulders of American imperialism, its appeal enhanced by a fashionable claim to be 'scientific', it has become an *international* tradition which here and there has been extended to reflect specific national conditions (Boisier, 1976; Lo and Salih, 1976).

To anchor the history of regional planning doctrines in American experience, we need to go back more than half a century, to the mid-twenties, when regional planning doctrine was, for the first time, formally articulated (*Survey Graphic*, 1925; Sussman, ed., 1976). It was a very different doctrine then from what it would later become, and its immediate practical impact was negligible. All the same, it not only represents a significant chapter in American intellectual history, but it has also inspired recent efforts at rethinking the conceptual foundations of the field.

According to the original doctrine (chapter 2), regional planning was to create conditions that would establish a harmonious relationship between human beings and nature, grounded in a bio-ethics that would show a deep respect for the limits of human intervention in 'natural' processes and limit the 'cancerous' growth of cities. Lewis Mumford was the principal spokesman for this philosophy, which can be clearly seen in his critique of the Regional Plan of New York whose ten volumes had been a decade in the making (1921–31). Mumford's scathing criticism and Thomas Adams' reply (Sussman, ed., 1976, chapters 15 and 16) beautifully illustrate the perennial clash between utopian and practical reason.[14] Mumford's vision was of a territorial civilization that was scaled to human needs and constrained by humans' finite capabilities to control their social evolution. Adams, on his part, argued for the need to adapt regional structures to the requirements of an industrial civilization that was reaching maturity. More so than Mumford, he was conscious of planners' very limited capacity for controlling the physical outcomes of capitalist development. Or, perhaps, he was merely being more accommodating. In any event, Adams saw his job as shaping the cities of industrial capitalism. And he did it well.

Another 'giant' of this early period was Howard Odum, a University of North Carolina sociologist, whose path-breaking studies of American regionalism deserve far greater attention than they have received. Odum advocated a cultural regionalism that would withstand the onslaught of industrialism with its ruthless tendencies towards cultural levelling. He understood the threat which industrialism posed for territorially integrated regional societies, and he hoped to contain and move this force through what he called 'regional–national social planning'. The aim of such planning would be to shape an *organic territorial* structure in which history, natural resources, climate, and cultural traditions combined to form the varied landscapes of America. Odum actually took a minor part in some of the planning work of the New Deal. In retrospect, however, he was no more successful than Lewis Mumford in preventing the metropolitanization of America.

The 1930s saw the response of the New Deal to the social and economic crisis of the Great Depression. Utopianism gave way to David Lilienthal's 'Dreamers with Shovels'. The proving ground for the new doctrine was the Tennessee Valley. The utopians held out hopes that the Valley might become the cradle of a new civilization.[15] In reality this famous experiment simply became an extension, under state auspices, of monopoly capitalism into a remote and pre-industrial region (Shapley, 1976). The new doctrine promoted the *integrated development of natural resources for human use and saw the river basin as the most appropriate areal unit for this purpose* (chapter 3). Like Mumford's, it was a territorial vision, grounded, concrete, and palpable. But, unlike Mumford's, it was also a practical vision that made of the Valley simply another part of a growing America.

With World War II, regional planning receded in importance. The war had virtually obliterated interest in regional questions. For the first time the reality of an integrated national economy had been brought into being. America was becoming a world power, moving into the vacuum which had been created by the dismantlement of European empires abroad, and, in the mirror of the world, it saw itself as a unified nation. The United Nations, which had just been formed at the war's end, placed the question of growth and development on the international agenda. An era of expanding prosperity, realizing unprecedented rates of economic growth, seemed to promise a little share of happiness to everyone. The only problem was how to get launched into the trajectory of self-sustaining growth.

Regional planning became a part of these changes. Resource development, made popular by the dramatic example of the Tennessee Valley Authority, yielded to the more mundane planning for the location of manufacturing plants. Industrialization, it was assumed, would lead the way to ever-larger income streams and national wealth. As central governments became all-powerful (relative to local and regional authorities), the problem of territorial integration shifted from its previous focus on the river basin to the nation as a whole. The earlier planning had been geared to specific physical needs and so was bounded by these needs. The new thinking was unbounded and tied to an ever-expanding demand for goods and services in the market.

The new doctrine of regional planning came to be supported by a new theory, appropriately labelled *regional science*. Interest in the philosophical foundations of regional planning had dissipated; marching with the times, planning had become a 'scientific endeavour' (chapter 4).

The new doctrine of regional planning was bifurcated. Along one dimension, it emphasized the problem of *spatial organization*; accordingly, it was preoccupied with urbanization, industrial location, and the creation of stronger inter-city ties. The principal targets of this dimension were the newly industrializing, post-colonial countries. Here regional planning was associated with 'nation-building', central planning, and the spatial integration of the national economy. 'Growth centres' – i.e. induced urbanization through a combination of direct public investments and capital subsidies to private enterprise – emerged as the principal instrument of spatial policy. Agriculture would be drawn into the development process, it was thought, through the wave-like diffusion of 'spread effects' from the principal growth centres of the economy (chapter 5).

The second dimension of the new doctrine of regional planning concerned the problems of *backward regions* in industrially advanced economies. Backward meant poor, and poor almost always meant rural. Because migration to more prosperous areas was possible, however, regional policy for backward areas remained ambivalent. On the one hand, an effort was made to apply to them the 'growth centres' concept of induced industrialization. Yet the downward transition was also welcomed: let people seek their fortunes where they might! Funds for backward areas were thus regarded as a kind of public charity. The spotlight remained focused on the core regions of the national economy where, increasingly, regional merged with metropolitan planning (chapter 6).

The combination of an attractive doctrine and a scientific base proved irresistible. Regional planning became an established field of professional competence, teaching, and research. And yet, as the 1960s ended, a general sense of uneasiness spread among the profession. The early expectations had not been fulfilled. Growth centres did not grow, backward regions did not flourish, poverty continued to accumulate in cities, inequalities remained engrained as deeply as ever into the landscape. Received doctrines of economic growth were questioned, new concepts were advanced: employment and income distribution were added to economic growth as valid social objectives for planning. But beyond this limited change loomed altogether different approaches resting on the twin concepts of basic needs and self-reliance.

Within five years the first major criticisms were also being levelled at established doctrine for regional development. The growth centres strategy was losing its appeal. Its magic had not worked. Both technical and ideological reasons called for a drastic revision of doctrine (chapter 7).

Regional planning had to be brought in line with the newer thinking on development. The centrifugal forces of the international economy had to be controlled, corporate forces had to be subordinated to a territorial will. The term for this was *selective closure*; applied to a regional economy, it meant finding new ways of relating cities to rural areas and of overcoming the age-old contradictions between them. In the setting of poor, agrarian countries, a concept of *agropolitan development* was proposed. Chapter 8 elaborates this concept.

When we review the changing course of regional planning doctrines over the past half-century, two major forces of social integration appear to alternate with each other: territorial and functional. Intertwined and complementary to each other, they are nonetheless in constant struggle. The territorial force derives from common bonds of social order forged by history within a given place. Functional ties are based on mutual self-interest. Given inequalities at the start, a functional order is always hierarchical, accumulating power at the top. Territorial relationships, on the other hand, though they will also be characterized by inequalities of power, are tempered by the mutual rights and obligations which the members of a territorial group claim from each other (Table 1.1).

Although surely nothing more than sheer coincidence, in exactly fifty years we have passed through a complete cycle of territorial dominance, divided into two, roughly symmetrical, periods. The chapters which follow will tell the story in more detail.

Table 1.1   Epochs in the evolution of regional planning doctrine: 1925–75

1925–35	Utopian planning: bio-synthesis and a new culture; cultural regionalism	Territorial Integration
1935–50	Practical idealism: comprehensive river basin development	
1950–75	Spatial systems planning: A. Spatial development in newly industrializing countries (growth centres) B. Backward regions in industrially advanced countries	Functional Integration
1975–	Selective regional closure: the new utopianism? Agropolitan development	Territorial Integration

Notes

1. Acosta and Hardoy, 1971, 1972 (Cuba); Allen and MacLennan, 1970 (Italy and France); Barkin and King, 1970 (Mexico); Brewis, 1969 (Canada); Brutzkus, 1970 (Israel); Bugnicourt, 1971 (Africa); Cameron, 1970 (USA); Carrillo-Arronte, ed., 1975 (Mexico); Chisholm and Manners, eds, 1971 (Britain); Cumberland, 1971 (USA); Derthick, 1974 (USA); European Free Trade Association, 1974 (Western Europe); Fisher, ed., 1966 (Poland); Fisher, 1966 (Yugoslavia); Fried, 1975 (Italy); Hansen, 1968 (France); Honjo, 1971 (Japan); Instituto Nacional de Estudios del Trabajo, 1976 (Mexico); Kuklinski, ed., 1975 (world-wide); Lefeber and Chaudhuri, 1971 (South and Southeast Asia); Logan and Smith, eds, 1975 (Australia); Luttrell, 1972–3 (Tanzania); Mabogunje, ed., 1973 (Africa); McCrone, 1969 (Britain); Mann and Pillorgé, 1964 (France); Mihailovic, 1972 (Eastern Europe); Nekrasov, 1974 (USSR); O'Neill, 1971 (Ireland); Organization for Economic Cooperation and Development, 1970 (Western Europe); Rodriguez, 1973 (Cuba); Rodwin, 1970 (comparative); Rodwin *et al.*, 1969 (Venezuela); Safier, ed., 1970 (East Africa); Sant, 1975 (Great Britain); Schejbal and Zurik, 1975 (Czechoslovakia); Stöhr, 1975 (Latin America); Sundquist, 1975 (Western Europe); Vidal Villa, 1973 (Cuba); Weitz *et al.*, n.d. (Israel).
2. a. *UN-sponsored training and/or research centres* (see Perloff, 1966; United Nations Institute for Training and Research, 1972): United Nations Centre for Regional Development, Nagoya; Institute of Social Studies, The Hague; Settlement Studies Centre, Rehovot; Latin American Institute for Economic and Social Planning (ILPES), Santiago; United Nations Institute for Research in Social Development (UNRISD), Geneva.
   b. *Major university centres* (USA and Western Europe): Harvard University; Massachusetts Institute of Technology; University of California, Los Angeles; University of North Carolina; Cornell University; Lund University (Sweden); Erasmus University (Rotterdam); London School of Economics; Development Planning Unit, University College, London; Université d'Aix-Marseille III.
   c. *Research centres*: International Institute for Applied Systems Analysis, Laxenburg, Austria.
3. Alden and Morgan, 1974; Boisier, 1976; Boudeville, 1966; Friedmann and Alonso, eds, 1975; Funes, ed., 1972; Gillingwater, 1975; Glasson, 1974; Hall, 1975; Hilhorst, 1971; Hoover, 1971; Instituto Latinoamericano de Planificación Económica y Social y la División de Desarrollo Social de las Naciones Unidas, eds, 1976; Klaassen, ed., 1972; McLoughlin, 1969; Misra *et al.*, 1974; Perrin, 1974; Richardson, 1969, 1973, 1978; Rondinelli, 1975; Siebert, 1969; Testi, 1970; Unikel and Necochea, eds, 1975.

4. *Regional Studies; Espaces et Societés; Raumordnung und Raumforschung; Growth and Change: A Journal of Regional Planning; International Journal of Urban and Regional Research; Journal of Regional Science; Papers of the Regional Science Association; Urban Studies; International Regional Science Review.*

5. Banco Nacional da Habitação, 1974; Dunham and Hilhorst, eds, 1971; Hägerstrand and Kuklinski, eds, 1971; Helleiner and Stöhr, eds, 1974; Isard and Cumberland, eds, 1961; Japan Centre for Area Development Research, 1967, 1968, 1970, 1972; Kuklinski and Petrella, eds, 1972; Macka, ed., 1967; Organization for Economic Cooperation and Development, 1969; Polish Academy of Sciences, 1964, 1965, 1968; Robinson, ed., 1969; Safier, ed., 1970; Swain, ed., 1975; Thoman, ed., 1976; United Nations Centre for Regional Development, 1976a; United Nations Industrial Development Organization (UNIDO), 1969.

6. Friedmann and Douglass, 1978; Gilbert and Goodman, 1976; Hansen, 1975; Lo and Salih, 1976; Pred, 1976; Stöhr and Tödtling, 1976, 1977.

7. Coraggio, 1972, 1975; Holland, 1976; Rochefort, ed., 1975; Rofman, 1974a, b; Santos, 1974, 1975; Slater, 1975a, b; Stuckey, 1975a, b.

8. *Regional planning practice*: Hansen, ed., 1974; Hirschman, 1967; Manners, 1972; Rodwin and Associates, 1969.

9. *Regional planning doctrine*: e.g., Berry, 1973; Brutzkus, 1975; Friedmann, 1966; Friedmann and Douglass, 1978; Hansen, 1970; Johnson, 1970; Kuklinski, ed., 1972; Rondinelli and Ruddle, 1976; United Nations Institute of Training and Research, 1972.

10. *Planning theory (procedural)*: Faludi, 1973; Friedmann, 1973; Friedmann and Hudson, 1974; Gillingwater, 1975; Robinson, ed., 1972; Rondinelli, 1975.

11. *Regional planning theory (substantive)*: Berry, 1967; Berry and Horton, 1970; Borts and Stein, 1964; Chisholm, 1962; Dunn, 1954; Friedmann, 1972; Haggett, 1965; Hoover, 1948; Isard, 1956; Lösch, 1954; Moseley, 1974; Pedersen, 1975; Perloff *et al.*, 1960; Perloff, 1963; Richardson, 1973; Siebert, 1969; von Böventer, 1964.

12. *Ideological assumptions*: e.g., Chenery, 1974; Rostow, 1961; Weiner, ed., 1966.

13. a. *France*: Boudeville, 1966, 1970, 1972; Davin, 1964; Perrin, 1974; Ponsard, 1954.
    b. *Britain*: Hall, 1975; Alden and Morgan, 1974; Glasson, 1974.
    c. *South America*: Boisier, 1976; Instituto Latinoamericano de Planificación Económica y Social y la División de Desarrollo Social de las Naciones Unidas, eds, 1976; Unikel and Nechochea, eds, 1975.
    d. *USSR*: Nekrasov, 1974.
    e. *Poland*: Secomski, 1974.

14. Thomas Adams, the first administrator of Letchworth and founder of the Town Planning Institute, was the staff director of the *Regional Plan for New York and Its Environs*.

15. It was again Mumford who captured this vision in characteristically poetic language. The following excerpt is from the caption to a couple of photographs of the Tennessee Valley region (Mumford, 1938, pictorial insert VII):

> The Tennessee Valley project, with its fundamental policy of conservation of power resources, land, forest, soil, and stream, in the public interest, is an indication of a new approach to the problems of regional development: an advance in certain ways over those already initiated in New York and Wisconsin. The river valley has the advantage of bringing into a common regional frame a diversified unit: this is essential to an effective civic and social life, and has been overlooked in many schemes of regional development that are erected on a basis of purely homogeneous resources or interests. Regional unity is partly an emergent: a cultural product: a result of co-operative political and economic action. Upland areas, from the Alps to Norway, from the Cascade Range to the Appalachians, are scenes for neo-technic planning with electric power and decentralized industry. In the Tennessee Valley and kindred areas, like the Upper Connecticut Valley, a basis can be laid, not merely for more efficient industrial order, but for a new social order and a new type of urban environment, provided the

requisite political courage and social imagination are collectively brought to bear.

Upland area in Tennessee: potentially the scene of a more intensive settlement that will conserve rather than blot out the natural foundations for a good and durable social life. Sun, wind, cloud, earth, grass, forest, farm, garden – these are constants in human life that only shriveled imaginations would displace by mechanical substitutes: but the finer utilization of these gifts of nature are themselves a product of a higher type of scientific and technical organization. Airplanes and electric lights are the beginnings: the sun-accumulator and the solar engine are already in embryonic existence: we await, among other things, an efficient electric accumulator, light and powerful, to displace the gasoline-driven engine, and a localized domestic method of sewage disposal which will convert sewage into fertilizer. Domestic hothouses capable of supplying fresh vegetables and fruits throughout the year should soon be available where power and fuel are cheap: these things promise a diminishment of wheeled transportation except for travel and association.

Many of Mumford's visionary images have come true. But is our life a better one as a result? Physical vision and social reality appear to contradict each other.

Bibliography

Acosta, Leon M. and Hardoy, J. E. 1971: *Políticas urbanos y reforma urbana en Cuba*. Caracas: Síntesis 2000.

1972: Urbanization policies in revolutionary Cuba. In Geisse, G. and Hardoy, J. E., editors 1972, 167–78.

Alden, J. and Morgan, R. 1974: *Regional planning: a comprehensive view*. New York: John Wiley & Sons.

Allen, K. and MacLennan, M. C. 1970: *Regional problems and policies in Italy and France*. Beverly Hills, California: Sage Publications.

Banco Nacional da Habitação 1974: *Symposium on urban development*. Rio de Janeiro: BNH.

Barkin, D. and King, T. 1970: *Regional economic development: the river basin approach in Mexico*. Cambridge University Press.

Barkin, D. P. and Manitzas, N. R., editors 1973: *Cuba: the logic of revolution*. Andover, Mass.: Warner Modular Publications.

Berry, B. J. L. 1967: *Geography of market centers and retail distribution*. Englewood Cliffs, New Jersey: Prentice-Hall.

1973: *Growth centers in the American urban system* 1. Cambridge, Mass.: Ballinger.

Berry, B. J. L. and Horton, F. E. 1970: *Geographic perspectives on urban systems (With integrated readings)*. Englewood Cliffs, New Jersey: Prentice-Hall.

Boisier, S. 1976: *Diseño de planes regionales: métodos y técnicas de planificación regional*. Madrid: Colegio de Ingenieros de Caminos, Canales y Puertos, Centro de Perfeccionamiento.

Borts, G. H. and Stein, J. L. 1964: *Economic growth in a free market*. New York: Columbia University Press.

Boudeville, J. R. 1966: *Problems of regional economic planning.* Edinburgh University Press.

  1970: *Les espaces économiques.* Collection Que sais-je? No. 950. Paris: Presses Universitaires de France.

  1972: *Aménagement du territoire et polarisation.* Paris: Génin, Lib. Technique.

  editor 1975: Regions et villes. *Économie appliquée* **28**, Nos. 1–3.

Brewis, T. N. 1969: *Regional economic policies in Canada.* Toronto: Macmillan of Canada.

Brutzkus, E. 1970: *Regional policy in Israel.* Jerusalem: Ministry of Interior, Town and Country Planning Department.

  1975: Centralized versus decentralized pattern of urbanization in developing countries: an attempt to elucidate a guideline principle. *Economic Development and Cultural Change* **23**, 633–52.

Bugnicourt, J. J. 1971: *Disparités régionales et aménagement du territoire en Afrique.* Paris: Lib. Armand Colin.

Cameron, G. C. 1970: *Regional economic development: the federal role.* Washington, DC: Resources for the Future.

Carrillo-Arronte, R., editor 1975: *Desarrollo regional.* Número especial de *Ecopolítica* **1**, No. 1.

Chenery, H., *et al.* 1974: *Redistribution with growth.* Oxford University Press.

Chisholm, M. 1962: *Rural settlement and land use.* London: Hutchinson University Library.

Chisholm, M. and Manners, G., editors 1971: *Spatial problems of the British economy.* Cambridge University Press.

Coraggio, J. L. 1972: Hacia una revisión de la teoría de los polos de desarrollo. *Revista Latinoamericana de estudios urbano regionales* **2**, 25–40.

  1975: Polarization, development and integration. In Kuklinski, A., editor 1975, 353–74.

Cumberland, J. C. 1971: *Regional development: experiences and prospects in the United States.* The Hague: Mouton.

Davin, L. E. 1964: *Économie regionale et croissance.* Paris: M. Th. Génin.

Derthick, M. 1974: *Between state and nation: regional organizations of the United States.* Washington, DC: The Brookings Institution.

Dunham, D. M. and Hilhorst, J. G. M., editors 1971: *Issues in regional planning. A selection of seminar papers.* The Hague: Mouton.

Dunn, E. S. 1954: *The location of agricultural production.* Gainesville: University of Florida Press.

European Free Trade Association 1974: *National settlement strategies: a framework for regional development.* Geneva: EFTA Secretariat.

Faludi, A. 1973: *Planning theory.* Oxford: Pergamon Press.

Fisher, J. C. 1966: *Yugoslavia: a multinational state. Regional differences and administrative response.* San Francisco: Chandler Publishing Co.

  editor 1966: *City and regional planning in Poland.* Ithaca: Cornell University Press.

Fried, R. C. 1975: Administrative pluralism and Italian regional planning. In Friedmann, J. and Alonso, W., editors 1975, 695–711.

Friedmann, J., editor 1964: *Regional development and planning.* Special issue of *Journal of the American Institute of Planners* **30**.

1966: *Regional development policy: a case study of Venezuela.* Cambridge, Mass.: The MIT Press.

1972: A generalized theory of polarized development. In Hansen, N. M., editor 1972, 82–107.

1973: *Retracking America: a theory of transactive planning.* New York: Doubleday/Anchor.

1978: The Epistemology of social practice: a critique of objective knowledge. *Theory and Society* **6**, 75–92.

Friedmann, J. and Alonso, W., editors 1964: *Regional development and planning. A reader.* Cambridge, Mass.: The MIT Press.

editors 1975: *Regional policy. Readings in theory and applications.* Cambridge, Mass.: The MIT Press.

Friedmann, J. and Douglass, M. 1978: Agropolitan development: towards a new strategy for regional planning in Asia. In Lo, F.-C. and Salih, K., eds, *Growth pole strategy and regional development policy. Oxford:* Pergamon Press.

Friedmann, J. and Hudson, B. 1974: Knowledge and action: a guide to planning theory. *Journal of the American Institute of Planners* **40**, 2–16.

Funes, J. C., editor 1972: *La ciudad y la región para el dessarrollo.* Caracas: Comisión de Administración Pública de Venezuela.

Geisse, G. and Hardoy, J. E., editors 1972: *Regional and urban development policies: a Latin American perspective.* Vol. 2: *Latin American urban research.* Beverly Hills, California: Sage Publications.

Gilbert, A., editor 1976: *Developing planning and spatial structure.* London: John Wiley & Sons.

Gilbert, A. G. and Goodman, D. E. 1976: Regional income disparities and economic development: a critique. In Gilbert, A., editor, 1976, 113–42.

Gillingwater, D. 1975: *Regional planning and social change.* Lexington, Mass.: Lexington Books.

Glasson, J. 1974: *An introduction to regional planning.* London: Hutchinson.

Hägerstrand, T. and Kuklinski, A., editors 1971: *Information systems for regional development. A seminar.* General Papers. Lund: Royal University of Lund, Department of Geography.

Haggett, P. 1965: *Locational analysis in human geography.* London: Edward Arnold.

Hall, P. 1975: *Urban and regional planning.* London: Penguin Books.

Hansen, N. M. 1968: *French regional planning.* Bloomington: Indiana University Press.

1970: *Rural poverty and the urban crisis. A strategy for regional development.* Bloomington: Indiana University Press.

editor 1972: *Growth centers in regional economic development.* New York: The Free Press.

editor 1974: *Public policy and regional economic development: the experience of nine Western countries.* Cambridge, Mass.: Ballinger.

1975: An evaluation of growth center theory and practice. *Environment and Planning A* **7**, 821–32.

Helleiner, F. and Stöhr, W., editors 1974: *Proceedings of the Commission on Regional Aspects of Development of the International Geographical Union 2. Spatial aspects of the development process. Meeting held at the University of Western Ontario, London (Ont.), Canada, 2–7 August 1972.*

Hilhorst, J. G. M. 1971: *Regional planning: a systems approach.* Rotterdam University Press.

Hirschman, A. O. 1967: *Development projects observed.* Washington, DC: Brookings Institution.

Holland, S. 1976: *Capital versus the regions.* London: Macmillan.

Honjo, M. 1971: *Trends in Japanese development planning.* MS.

Hoover, E. M. 1948: *The location of economic activity.* New York: McGraw-Hill.

1971: *An introduction to regional economics.* New York: Alfred Knopf.

Instituto Latinoamericano de Planificación Económica y Social y La División de Desarrollo Social de las Naciones Unidas, editors 1976: *Ensayos sobre planificación regional del desarrollo.* Mexico: Siglo Veintiuno.

Instituto Nacional de Estudios del Trabajo 1976: *Mercados regionales de trabajo. Projecto: desarrollo regional y urbano Mexico.* Mexico City: INET.

Isard, W. 1956: *Location and space economy: a general theory relating to industrial location, market areas, land use, trade, and urban structure.* Boston: The Technology Press of MIT and John Wiley & Sons.

Isard, W. and Cumberland, J. H. 1961: *Regional economic planning: techniques of analysis for less developed areas. Papers and proceedings of the first conference on problems of economic development organized by the Economic Productivity Agency,* Bellagio, Italy. 19 June–1 July 1960. Paris: Organization for European Economic Cooperation.

Japan Center for Area Development Research 1967: *The papers and proceedings of the international symposium on regional development.* Tokyo: JCADR.

1968: *The second international symposium on regional development.* Tokyo: JCADR.

1970: *The third international symposium on regional development.* Tokyo: JCADR.

1972: *The fourth international symposium on regional development.* Tokyo: JCADR.

Johnson, E. A. J. 1970: *The organization of space in developing countries.* Cambridge, Mass.: Harvard University Press.

Klaassen, L. H. 1965: *Aménagement économique et social du territoire: directives pour les programmes.* Paris: OECD.

  editor 1972: *Regionale economie: het ruimtelijke element in de economie.* Groningen: Wolters-Nordhoff N.V.

Kolipinski, J. 1977: Directions of research in space economy and regional planning. In Kuklinski, A., editor 1977, 151–66.

Kuklinski, A., editor 1972: *Growth poles and growth centres in regional planning.* The Hague: Mouton.

  editor 1975: *Regional development and planning: international perspectives.* Leyden: Sijthoff.

  editor 1977: *Regional Studies in Poland.* Bulletin of the Polish Academy of Sciences, Committee for Space Economy and Regional Planning. Special issue. Warsaw.

Kuklinski, A. and Petrella, R., editors 1972: *Growth poles and regional policies. A seminar.* The Hague: Mouton.

Lefeber, L. and Datta-Chaudhuri, M. 1971: *Regional development: experiences and prospects in South and Southeast Asia.* The Hague: Mouton.

Lo, F. and Salih, K. 1976: Growth poles and regional policy in open dualistic economies: Western theory and Asian reality. In UNCRD, 1976a, 191–246.

Lösch, A. 1954: *The economics of locations.* New Haven: Yale University Press.

Logan, M. I. and Smith, R. H. T., editors 1975: *Urban and regional Australia: analysis and policy issues.* Malvern, Australia: Sorrett Publishing.

Luttrell, W. L. 1972–3: Location planning and regional development in Tanzania. *Development and Change* **4**, 17–38.

Mabogunje, A. L., editor 1973: *Planificación regional y desarrollo nacional en Africa.* Buenos Aires: Ed. SIAP.

McCrone, G. 1969: *Regional policy in Britain.* London: George Allen & Unwin.

Macka, M., editor 1967: *Economic regionalization.* Prague: Academia.

McLoughlin, J. B. 1969: *Urban and regional planning: a systems approach.* London: Faber and Faber.

Mann, L. D. and Pillorgé, G. T. 1964: French regional planning. *Journal of the American Institute of Planners* **30**, 155–60.

Manners, G., *et al.* 1972: *Regional development in Britain.* London: John Wiley.

Mihailovic, K. 1972: *Regional development experiences and prospects in Eastern Europe.* The Hague: Mouton.

Misra, R. P., Sundaram, K. V. and Prakasa Rao, V. L. S. 1974: *Regional development planning in India: a new strategy.* Delhi, Bombay: Vikas.

Moseley, M. 1974: *Growth centers in spatial planning.* Oxford: Pergamon Press.

Mumford, L. 1938: *The culture of cities.* New York: Harcourt, Brace and Co.

Nekrasov, N. 1974: *The territorial organization of the Soviet economy.* Moscow: Progress Publishers.

O'Neill, H. B. 1971: *Spatial planning in the small economy: the case of Ireland.* New York: Praeger.

Organization for Economic Cooperation and Development 1969: *Multidisciplinary aspects of regional development.* Annual Meeting of Directors of Development Training and Research Institute, Montpellier, France, 7–12 September 1968. Paris: OECD Development.

1970: *The regional factor in economic development: policies in fifteen industrialized OECD countries.* Paris: OECD.

Pedersen, P. O. 1975: *Urban-regional development in South America: a process of diffusion and integration.* The Hague: Mouton.

Perloff, H. S. 1963: *How a region grows: area development in the US. economy.* Supplementary paper No. 17. New York: Committee for Economic Development.

1966: *Design for a worldwide study of regional development. A report to the United Nations on a proposed research-training program.* Washington, DC: Resources for the Future, Inc.

Perloff, H. S., Dunn, E. S. Jr, Lampard, E. E. and Muth, R. F. 1960: *Regions, resources, and economic growth.* Baltimore: Johns Hopkins University Press.

Perrin, J.-C. 1974: *Le développement régional.* Paris: Presses Universitaires de France.

Polish Academy of Sciences, Institute of Geography, 1964: *Methods of economic regionalization. Geographia Polonica* **4**. Warsaw: PWN.

1965: *Aims of economic regionalization. Geographia Polonica* **8**. Warsaw: PWN.

1968: *Economic regionalizational and numerical methods. Final report of the Commission on Methods of Economic Regionalization of the International Geographical Union.* Berry, B. J. L. and Wrobel, A., editors. *Geographia Polonica* **15**. Warsaw: PWN.

Ponsard, C. 1954: *Économie et espace.* Paris: Sedes.

Pred, A. 1976: *The interurban transmission of growth in advanced economies: empirical findings versus regional planning assumptions.* Research report 76–4. International Institute of Applied Systems Analysis, Laxenburg, Austria.

Richardson, H. W. 1969: *Regional economics: location theory, urban structure, and regional change.* New York: Praeger.

1973: *Regional growth theory.* New York: John Wiley & Sons.

1978: *Regional and urban economics.* Harmondsworth (England): Penguin.

Robinson, A. E. G., editor 1969: *Backward areas in advanced countries.* Proceedings of a conference held by the International Economic Association. New York: St Martin's Press.

Robinson, I. M., editor 1972: *Decision-making in urban planning: an introduction to new methodologies.* Beverly Hills, California: Sage Publications.

Rochefort, M., editor 1975: *Organisation de l'espace.* Special issue of *Revue Tiers-Monde* **16**.

Rodriguez, F. R. 1973: El papel de la planificación regional en la economía nacional. *Revista Interamericana de Planificación* **8**, 102–15.

Rodwin, L. 1970: *Nations and cities: a comparison of strategies of urban growth.* Boston: Houghton Mifflin.

Rodwin, L., *et al.* 1969: *Planning urban growth and regional development: the experience of the Guayana program of Venezuela.* Cambridge, Mass.: The MIT Press.

Rofman, A. B. 1974a: *Dependencia, estructura de poder y formación regional en América Latina.* Buenos Aires: Siglo XXI.

    1974b: *Desigualdades regionales y concentración económica: el caso Argentino.* Buenos Aires: Ed. SIAP-Planteos.

Rondinelli, D. A. 1975: *Urban and regional development planning: policy and administration.* Ithaca: Cornell University Press.

Rondinelli, D. A. and Ruddle, K. 1976: *Urban functions in rural development: an analysis of integrated spatial development policy.* Washington, DC: Office of Urban Development, Technical Assistance Bureau, Agency for International Development.

Rostow, W. W. 1961: *The stages of economic growth: a non-Communist manifesto.* Cambridge University Press.

Safier, M. S., editor 1970: *The role of urban and regional planning in national development for Africa.* Papers and proceedings of a seminar. Kampala: Milton Obote Foundation.

Sant, M. 1975: *Industrial movement and regional development: the British case.* Oxford: Pergamon Press.

Santos, M. 1974: Sous-développement et pôles de croissance économique et sociale. *Revue Tiers-Monde* **15**, 271–86.

    1975: Space and domination: a Marxist approach. *International Social Science Journal* **27**, 346–64.

Schejbal, D. and Zurek, O. 1975: Methods of achieving consistency between national and regional location plans. In Friedmann, J. and Alonso, W., editors 1975, 751–72.

Secomski, K. 1974: *Spatial planning and policy: theoretical foundations.* Warsaw: Polish Scientific Publishers.

Shapley, D. 1976: TVA today: former reformers in an era of expensive electricity. *Science* **194**, 814–18.

Siebert, H. 1969: *Regional economic growth: theory and policy.* Scranton, Pa.: International Textbook Co.

Slater, D. 1975a: El capitalismo subdesarrollado y la organización del espacio: Perú, 1920–40. *Revista Interamericana de Planificación* **9**, 87–106.

    1975b: Underdevelopment and spatial inequality. Approaches to the problem of regional planning in the Third World. In Diamond, D. and McLoughlin, J. b., editors 1975, 97–167.

Stöhr, W. 1975: *Regional development: experiences and prospects in Latin America.* The Hague: Mouton.

Stöhr, W. and Tödtling, F. 1976: Spatial equity: some antitheses to current regional development doctrine. MS. Vienna: Interdisciplinary Institute of Urban and Regional Studies, Wirtschafts-universität.

1977: *Evaluation of regional policies: experiences in market and mixed economies.* IIR-Discussion paper no. 1. Vienna: Interdisziplinäres Institut für Raumordung, Wirtschaftsuniversität.

Stuckey, B. L. 1975a: *From tribe to multinational corporation: an approach for the study of urbanization.* Ph.D. dissertation. School of Architecture and Urban Planning. University of California, Los Angeles.

1975b: Spatial analysis and economic development. *Development and Change* **6**, 89–101.

Sundquist, J. L. 1975: *Dispersing population: what American can learn from Europe.* Washington, DC: Brookings Institution.

Survey Graphic 1925, No. 7 (May).

Sussman, C., editor 1976: *Planning the fourth migration: the neglected vision of the Regional Planning Association in America.* Cambridge, Mass.: The MIT Press.

Swain, H., editor 1975: *National settlement strategies, East and West.* Selected papers from IIASA conference on National Settlement Systems and Strategies, Schloss Laxenburg, Austria, December 1974. Laxenburg, Austria: International Institute for Applied Systems Analysis.

Testi, A. 1970: *Sviluppo e pianificazione regionale: le teorie e le politiche.* Con una antologia della letteratura internazionale sull-'argumento. Turin: Einaudi.

Thoman, R. S., editor 1974: *Proceedings of the Commission on Regional Aspects of Development of the International Geographical Union.* Vol. I. Methodology and Case Studies. Meeting held in Victoria (E.S.), Brazil, 12–15 April 1971. Allister Typesetting and Graphics.

Unikel, L. S. and Necochea, V. A., editors 1975: *Desarrollo urbano y regional en América Latina: problemas y políticas.* Mexico: Fondo de Cultura.

United Nations Centre for Regional Development 1976a: *Growth pole strategy and regional development planning in Asia.* Proceedings of the Seminar on Industrialization Strategies and the Growth Pole Approach to Regional Planning and Development: The Asian Experience. Nagoya, Japan, 4–13 November 1975. Nagoya: UNCRD.

United Nations Industrial Development Organization 1969: *Report of the Interregional Seminar on Industrial Location and Regional Development,* 14–24 August 1968. Vienna: UNIDO.

United Nations Institute for Training and Research 1972: *The United Nations Programme in regional development: an introduction to sub-national planning.* New York: Social Development Division.

Vidal Villa, J. M. 1973: El concepto de la región económica y la planificación regional. *Revista Interamericanna de Planificación* **8**, 80–101.

von Böventer, E. 1964: Spatial organization theory as a basis for regional development. *Journal of the American Institute of Planners* **30**, 90–9.

Weiner, M., editor 1966: *Modernization: the dynamics of growth.* Voice of America Forum Lectures. Washington, DC: US Information Agency.

Weitz, R., *et al.* n.d.: *Regional cooperation in Israel.* National and University Institute, Rehavot (Israel), Settlement Study Centre.

Part I: Regionalism in America

Chapter 2
The search for regional balance in America

The social environment

American regionalism was a response to the far-reaching social and economic changes which occurred during the first half-century after the Civil War. Some of these changes were more or less generalized throughout the North Atlantic community; others were peculiar to the United States. In Figure 2.1 we have categorized them in a way that throws some light on the appearance of regional planners and their theories.

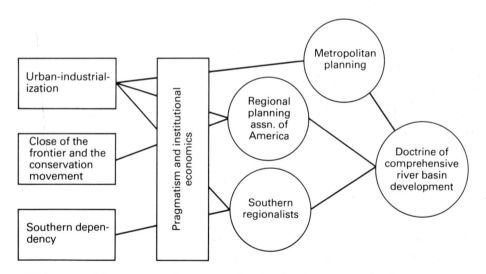

Figure 2.1   Influences on early regional planning doctrine

1. Urban industrialization

A major influence on early regional thinking in the United States was the recognition of the predominant role which urban-based industrialization was playing in national life. At the time of the Civil War (1861–5) most Americans still earned their livelihood from agriculture. A mere sixty years later, however, more than half of the population was found in cities, and nearly three-fourths of the country's wage-earners worked outside of farming. The fifteen largest cities accounted for nearly one-fifth of the total population and factories employed about forty per cent of all urban workers (Beard, 1924; US Bureau of the Census, 1960).

This change towards an urban focus of national life held profound implications. People who had lived within the confines of rural communities, and regulated their habits by the rhythms and folk wisdom of agricultural occupations, no longer set the pattern for national development. The functional relations of an urban-based industrial economy had replaced the more organic world-view and institutions of rural society.

By 1883 no less than four railroads spanned the American continent, linking city to city and facilitating the nation-wide marketing of farm commodities. While agriculture was being commercialized, technological innovations which made the industrial city both possible and necessary were coming into extensive use (Beard, 1924; Gunderson, 1976).[1] The open hearth blast furnace to convert pig iron into steel had been perfected in 1858. Wood-pulp paper and rotary presses (1860) made it possible to spread the gospel of urbanization. In 1879, electric lighting began to be introduced and, soon afterwards, electric urban railroads expanded the effective area of the metropolis. By the turn of the century, John D. Rockefeller's Standard Oil Company was providing kerosene for street lighting, asphalt for roads, lubricating oil for machinery, and gasoline for the revolutionary motor car.

Economic power was concentrated in a small number of corporations. Monopolies and trusts were already so powerful that 'trust-busting' became one of the main targets of progressive reformers (Schlesinger, 1941; Hofstadter, 1948). During the first decade of the new century, corporate enterprise employed over three-fourths of all American wage-earners, but a mere one per cent of all firms hired one-third of the country's workers and turned out nearly one-half of the total product (Beard, 1924).

The Captains of Industry were clearly in charge.[2] Across the country, territorial communities watched effective control over local production slip out of their grasp. Political power came to focus on the national level of territorial integration which, for the time being, effectively bounded the operation of most businesses.

Despite this creation of a national economy, and despite the concentration of power in the hands of both private entrepreneurs and the Washington government, the eighteenth-century doctrine of *laissez-faire* yielded only grudgingly. As late as the third year of the Great Depression, President Hoover still felt morally obliged to avow a policy of non-intervention in the 'natural' workings of the business system (Tugwell, 1932).

2. Resource depletion and the close of the frontier

Rapid urbanization was accompanied by other major changes. With the admission of Arizona and New Mexico to statehood in 1912, the celebrated 'frontier' had finally been filled in. This, along with the accelerating resource demands of an expanding industrial economy, gave Americans a new perception of their national destiny. A strange feeling of boundedness began to pervade the collective consciousness. A new era had begun.

The importance of the frontier in shaping American life was first asserted by Frederick Jackson Turner in 1893. Besides claiming that the moving frontier superimposed a rough democratic structure over the development of American political institutions, he argued that the ready availability of a 'second chance' for the dispossessed at the margins of existing settlement was a safety valve against the social pressures of excess labour. As long as the frontier beckoned, a subservient proletariat would be unlikely to arise.

Whatever the validity of Turner's claims, the disappearance of cheap farm land and the unprecedented spread of urban tenements was a rude shock. While Australia and New Zealand still offered untrammelled opportunities for immigration, the traditional refuge of Europe's unwanted millions was gone. The more than half a million people who had reached US shores each year since the middle of the nineteenth century were cut to an annual trickle of 150,000 by the Johnson Act of 1924 (Schlesinger, 1941).

From another perspective, while Europe had depended on overseas resources to stoke its industrial expansion, North America dug into its own rich storehouse of natural materials. The cornucopia seemed unlimited. But not long after the turn of the century, some people began to believe that the bottom had come into sight. Between the Civil War and World War I, the land in the public domain had been cut by half and harvested cropland more than doubled. The Great Plains were ploughed and sown; the seeds of the 'dust bowl' had been planted.[3]

Another striking fact which gained public recognition during this period was the retreat of the forests. They had been stripped since the beginning of American settlement, first to yield arable land and then for commercial timber. By the late 1800s, however, it had become apparent that unless efforts were made to treat forests as a renewable resource, the escalating demands of industry would soon mine them out of existence. After George Perkins Marsh's early recognition of this problem, it was brought to public attention by a massive conservation movement led by Theodore Roosevelt and Gifford Pinchot (Marsh, 1864; Hynning, 1939). Forest conservation became one of the principal concerns of progressive reform. Benton MacKaye made it a part of the evolving philosophy of regional planning.

3. **Southern dependency**

The political and economic dependency of the 'Old South' was another prominent feature of the American scene at this time. Throughout the nineteenth century the southeastern states had suffered, relative to the rest of the country, a continuing decline in terms of both economic development and political influence (Nicholls, 1960; North, 1961). After the Civil War, however, this situation was institutionalized by 'reconstruction', leaving the southern states at the mercy of an unsympathetic federal bureaucracy and open to systematic underdevelopment by northern financial interests (Cash, 1941). A detailed description of the structurally based exploitation of the South during reconstruction is beyond our task. We must note, however, that there were several characteristics of the post-bellum period which had a critical impact on regional planning. As in the case of Scotland in the United Kingdom and Brittany and Occitania in France, peripheral regions with a strong historical and cultural identity played an important role in the birth of modern regionalism and regional policy (Mumford, 1938).[4]

The American South had always been an agrarian society. Although most of its goods were produced for the market, its ante-bellum economy displayed certain traits which were clearly pre-capitalist in form (Marx, 1964; Schlesinger, 1950). Perhaps because of that, its culture exhibited a degree of regional unity which defied simple functional explanations (Cash, 1941).

With the war and the end of the chattel slavery, the economic structure of the South collapsed. Productive forces had to be harnessed within a different set of economic relationships to confront the reality of wage labour. The plantation system had been based on brutal exploitation and, without slave-power, immediate land reform was imperative. Two economically viable options seemed open: leasing or renting small plots of land to blacks and poor whites, or the outright sale of land in small quantities which could be worked by one or two hands. The former course was taken, with much of the land falling into the hands of suppliers and middlemen who acted as local agents of northern capital. Share-cropping became the new bane of the southern countryside, and this time it spread to poor whites as well (Beard, 1924).

The same sources of investment capital, working with newly forming regional elites, also began exploiting the South's growing pool of disenfranchised wage labour, which was put to work in factories that no longer seemed profitable in the North. The traditional cash crop economy of cotton and tobacco was supplemented by labour-intensive manufactures for export, such as textiles and shoes. Southern wage-earners multiplied ten times between 1860 and 1900, but low salaries provided only meagre income multipliers, and most of the profits went back to the northern investors who supplied the original cash.

There was little question, then, that by the early 1900s urban-based industrialization was drastically changing the traditional face of the South. By 1909 southern states had almost two-thirds as many wage-earners as the entire country had had at the opening of the Civil War. But politically the region continued to be disenfranchised, while its traditional culture – its last proud possession – was being destroyed by machine industry and alien lifestyles. It was a sudden intellectual awakening to these forces in the 1920s and 30s which created both the backward-looking Southern Agrarians and the more liberal-minded New South movement (Twelve Southerners, 1930). Regional planning was a major theme in the rhetoric of the new liberals (Odum, 1936).

Pragmatism and institutional economics

We need to make a short detour at this point because, in the United States, the great transitions of the 'Gilded Age'[5] were filtered through two peculiarly American intellectual constructs, John Dewey's pragmatism and the institutional economics of Thorstein Veblen (Parrington, 1930; Hofstadter, 1955). These movements played an important role in shaping both the substantive and procedural theories of regional planners. A number of commentaries have been written on both paradigms: our purpose here is merely to suggest how they helped to mould the emerging doctrine of regional planning.

1. Pragmatism

Pragmatism is a typically American invention. Much scorned by Europeans, it may nonetheless be judged, along with Marxism and existentialist philosophies, as one of the pivots of twentieth-century thought (Novack, 1966, 1975). Building on the work of his intellectual predecessors, Charles Pierce and William James, Dewey set out to reconstruct philosophy along lines he felt to be relevant to the experienced problems of everyday life (Dewey, 1917, 1920). Although its practical concerns should not detract from the importance of the enterprise, there is little question that the initial optimism and acceptance of prevailing social forms provided a framework compatible with the ideology of incremental liberal reform. In many ways, Dewey's methodology and subsequent proposals for change were precursors of the social learning theorists of today (Dunn, 1971; Heskin and Hoch, 1977).

In so far as Dewey's philosophy influenced regional planning, the following four aspects deserve consideration:

a. *Experience and knowledge.* Dewey argued that experience is the beginning of philosophy and, by involving a basic transaction between people and their environment, also the foundation of human inquiry. What is true for the broader relationship between society and the world of objects is doubly true for learning about society itself: valid knowledge comes about through a transactive process of experiencing present events and happenings. Knowledge is hypothetical, experimental and instrumental – something to be drawn from experience through social practice (Dewey, 1925; McDermott, 1973). In this process of inquiry, the dualism of theory and practice is collapsed into a problematic interaction, an ephemeral unity (Dewey, 1916a).

b. *Scientific method and experimental social planning.* The question of method becomes all-important if knowledge is ultimately to be drawn from experience. An efficient, systematic procedure for experimentation is required.

Dewey felt that the efficiency of learning about all realms of experience could be raised by application of the scientific method. In empirical science, problems are isolated, hypotheses are made explicit, experimentation is rationalized, and evaluation becomes a crucial, rigorous exercise. These propositions were thought to be as true for social learning as for the laboratory of the scientist. Society itself was to become a laboratory. Social problems would catch the public eye: they would then be learned about and ultimately solved through application of the scientific method (Dewey, 1927).

Like Karl Mannheim and Howard Odum, Dewey felt that social planning was the only course which could help democracy survive in an industrial age. A new order would have to be created in which industry and finance would be socially directed to provide the material basis for the cultural liberation and growth of individuals, bringing into being a new conception and logic of freed intelligence (Dewey, 1935).

c. *Education.* Dewey's third proposition was that institutional education was a way to organize for social planning. Through progressive education, based on systematic consideration of ordinary experience, people would learn how to apply the experimental method. Educational curricula should therefore be based on the principle of learning as a social experience. People trained to view situations from this perspective could be expected to speed the application of science to society (Dewey, 1900, 1916b, 1938).

d. *Reform and pragmatism.* To Dewey, liberal reform was the proper approach for dealing with the problems of capitalist urban-industrialization. Liberalism had to be founded on a pragmatic philosophy which concerned itself with ordinary experience. Knowledge about society's problems was to be gained through experimentation. Conflicts would be resolved through scientific social change.

It is easy to see why American advocates of planning leaned so heavily on Dewey's thinking. His arguments legitimized their calling. Pragmatism provided them with a philosophy which promised that they would be guardians of democracy.

2. Institutionalism

Institutional economics played a less global, though nonetheless decisive role in shaping the American approach to planning. As a coherent doctrine, it was the brainchild of the rustic son of Norwegian immigrants, Thorstein Veblen, whose views were frequently introduced into planning circles by his disciples, including Wesley C. Mitchell and Rexford G. Tugwell, both of whom were to be important contributors to Roosevelt's New Deal.

Veblen was a curious man. His ideas about economics were so thoroughly holistic and contextual, it is hard to separate them from other aspects of social life or, for that matter, from his personality (Dorfman, 1934; Mitchell, 1936, 1969; Riesman, 1953; Galbraith, 1977).

Trained at Johns Hopkins and Yale as a philosopher, Veblen became a cult hero in America; nevertheless, he had great difficulty finding acceptance within the economic fraternity. When, towards the end of his life, the reigning establishment finally offered him the presidency of the American Economics Association, he declined. According to Mitchell, he died a 'placid unbeliever', shortly before the Great Depression vindicated many of his unorthodox ideas.

The kernel of institutionalism seized upon by regional planners contains four principal elements:

a. *Economics and anthropology*. At the turn of the century, when Veblen came to general notice with publication of the *Theory of the Leisure Class* (1899), anthropology was still a new science, weaned on Darwinian ideas. In attempting to analyse the economic system, Veblen thought that the new anthropological perspective would be the most helpful. Accordingly, cultural evolution was to be treated as a linear, non-teleological process, without a trace of Hegelian 'contradictions'. Cultures move from 'savagery' to 'barbarism', said Veblen, and they transform their institutions as they go.

Such a view was obviously very much at odds with the doctrine of neoclassical economics which proposed the market, an institution beyond the pale of social evolution, as the natural arbiter of material well-being. Under its rules the factors of production – land, capital, and labour – and the sustaining commodities of life, competed in a struggle whose outcome was the inevitable harmony of interests. For Veblen, this scenario offered little insight into the workings of the actual economy. It was insufficiently historical.

b. *Institutions versus economic forces*. Breaking with the neoclassical tradition, Veblen proposed that economic *institutions* and their evolutionary transformation were the key to understanding the economic system. Influenced by the German historical school of economics and his Chicago colleague, John Dewey, Veblen insisted that social institutions governed economic behaviour, and that institutions could change, though not necessarily through conscious and directed effort (Veblen, 1919; Mitchell, 1969).

Considered a pragmatist. Veblen ridiculed pragmatic reform (Lerner, 1948; Riesman, 1953). As we will show in the next chapter, however, others of a less cynical disposition were to use his arguments to justify public institution-building as a way of planning the economy (Gruchy, 1939a, b).

c. *Technology, engineers, and monopoly.* Technology, for Veblen, was the energizing force behind institutional change. In an age of urban-based industrialization, technical know-how would hasten change and evolution. Engineers thus became the heroes of Veblen's scenarios of the future. Because of this attitude, and a growing bitterness with conditions after World War I, he came to cheer Soviet efforts to apply Frederick Taylor's notions of scientific management to planned industrialization. His writings applauded Soviet successes and called for a 'soviet of engineers' in other countries to overcome the wastefulness of the Captains of Industry. Such soviets, he thought, would help to spread 'the cultural incidence of the machine process' which he regarded as a truly revolutionary force.

On the other hand, Veblen was quite aware that the systematic application of machine technology would lead to bigness and the formation of monopolies. There is also the curious contradiction between Veblen's praise of the virtues of life in small-scale territorial communities (savagery) and his advocacy of the large-scale, functional (barbaric) organization of society. Such inconsistencies were apparently seen as inherent in the nature of things, and they undoubtedly contributed to Veblen's typically cynical view of reform.

d. *Industry versus business.* Now we come to one of Veblen's most fertile ideas, a concept that would heavily influence the thinking of the National Planning Board thirty years later. Veblen believed that there was a fundamental opposition between business and industry. Industry was supposedly driven by its 'machine discipline' to seek ever greater efficiency, while business was forced, in its concern to maintain profits, to create artificial shortages. This contradiction between the imperatives of production and distribution was seen to be at the root of the business-cycle problem. As the theme of his second classic book, *The Theory of the Business Enterprise* (1904), Veblen called it 'sabotage'.

For planners, the message was clear: play down the antagonistic role of business and promote the natural efficiency of industry through public institutions. Wesley Mitchell's lifelong empirical investigation of business cycles was conceptually based on Veblen's notion of this cleavage between business and industry (Tugwell, 1937b; Hill, 1957). And there is little room for doubt about Rexford Tugwell's position in his Veblenesque work,

The Industrial Discipline and the Governmental Arts (1933). Writing for an audience of planners, both Mitchell and Tugwell proceeded to apply Veblen's ideas in ways that his own inclinations would not have allowed.

The regionalists

The Progressive Era ended with the First World War. Muckraking, settlement houses, the urban planning movement, free education, feminism – all the liberal reactions to industrialism – seemed to have lost their vigour. According to Sussman (1976, p. 1):

> The 1920s were a decade-long intermission in Richard Hofstadter's 'Age of Reform': the Populists and Progressives on one side, the New Deal on the other. But while most reformers watched hard-won gains reversed in the twenties, one small and little-known group – the Regional Planning Association of America (RPAA) – voiced a wide-ranging and highly critical assessment of society.

To the dissent of the RPAA must also be added the liberal voices of the New South. Regional planning, especially the advocacy of *territorial values* by the Regional Planning Association of America and the Southern Regionalists at the University of North Carolina at Chapel Hill, was one of the last outliers of the progressive reform movement.

1. The Regional Planning Association of America

The RPAA was formed in 1923 by a group of architects and planners who met in New York City for regular discussions of urban problems. Its best known members were Clarence Stein and Henry Wright, the architects and new-town planners; Stuart Chase, a labour-union sympathizer and institutionalist; Benton MacKaye, the forester and conservationist: Edith Elmer Wood and Catherine Bauer, the housing advocates and, finally, Lewis Mumford. Mumford, who was to achieve world fame as an urbanist and social critic, described (Stein, 1957, p. 14) the group's intellectual foundations as:

> ... the civic ideas of Geddes and Howard, the economic analyses of Thorstein Veblen, the sociology of Charles Horton Cooley, and the educational philosophy of John Dewey, to say nothing of the new ideas in conservation, ecology, and geotechnics [which] all had a part in transforming the cut-and-dried procedures of the earlier planners.

At other times, Auguste Comte, Frederic Le Play, Henry Thoreau, George Perkins Marsh, Paul Vidal de la Blache, Elisée Reclus, Peter Kropotkin, and the English Fabians were also given credit as being 'among the precursors and intellectual perceptors' of the RPAA (MacKaye and Mumford, 1929).[6]

As an organization, the RPAA survived for ten years when its members began to drift off to work for the New Deal. The Tennessee Valley Authority, the Resettlement Administration, the United States Housing Authority and the Rural Electrification Administration were the primary recipients of their praise and talents.

The RPAA's important publications appeared over a three-year period between 1925 and 1928. The first, in May 1925, was the 'Regional Plan Number' of *Survey Graphic* magazine, edited by Mumford. It contained articles by most of the prominent members of the RPAA, and laid out their basic ideas for checking the spread of urban-industrialization and achieving internal regional balance through an environmental mix of wilderness and rural and urban habitats. This theme was developed the following year with the publication of the New York State Housing and Regional Planning Commission report (State of New York, 1926). Stein was the chairman of the Commission, and the report was written primarily by Henry Wright. It was the most significant piece of public planning work undertaken by members of the RPAA as a group. The last major statement to appear during the RPAA's brief corporate life was Benton MacKaye's *The New Exploration: a Philosophy of Regional Planning* (1928).

It was not until a decade later, in 1938, that the RPAA's approach to regionalism found an international audience.[7] Lewis Mumford's well-known essay, *The Culture of Cities*, wove the RPAA's interpretation of regionalism into an evolutionary history of Western civilization. Mumford explained the role of indigenous territorial society in creating urban culture and presented a strategy for using regional planning to create a new bio-technic social order.

The central arguments of the RPAA are best summarized under four general headings.

a. *Metropolitanization.* The Association was not a coven of 'anti-urbanists' (Goist, 1969). Its members conceived of the city as the locus of human culture, a bubbling retort distilling the cultural elements of civilization: art, literature, free debate, democratic government. But they also believed that the city could only survive in organic balance with the totality of its regional environment. City, countryside, and wilderness were all necessary – properly compartmentalized, in balance with one another. A fundamental unity of opposites formed the basis for a 'biotechnical' order that would 'recognize both the universalizing forces and the differentiating forces that are at work' (Mumford, 1938, p. 371).

Ascendance of urban-industrialization – the physical and spiritual spread of the metropolis – was upsetting the natural order of things. Regional life was being drowned in a flood of metropolitanism (Mumford, 1925; Stein, 1925). Led by finance capital, Veblen's malevolent businessmen were concentrating economic activities in a few large urban centres, agglomerations which were tied to the rest of the country only through exploitative functional relationships. In a protracted conflict between indigenous and metropolitan modes of organization, geographic regions were being reduced to the role of specialized economic links in a national system.

b. *Regions and regional balance.* According to the RPAA, the way to stop this invasion and destruction of the organic world order was through the reconstruction of the natural building blocks of human settlement, or 'balanced' regions (MacKaye, 1928). The intellectual concept of 'natural' regions (as well as 'regionalism' as a modern political movement) had nineteenth-century French origins (Dickinson, 1964; Charles-Brun, 1911). The RPAA drew heavily upon *la tradition vidalienne.*[8]

For most planners and regional scientists today, the region represents merely a taxonomic category, a functional subunit of national space. Regionalization appears as primarily a technical concern which, depending on the criteria employed, can result in a variety of abstract divisions.

None of these 'arbitrary lines', however drawn on maps, was satisfactory to Mumford and his colleagues. For them, a region was a real place, created by a particular group of people in interaction with their environment. The evolutionary product, Southern California or Brittany for example, was an actual locale, palpable to anyone who experienced it. The region became an ecological patch in the quiltwork of the cultural landscape.

In one of his many discussions of regionalization, Mumford (1938, p. 367) wrote:

> Rationally defined, the locus of human communities is the region. The region is the unit-area formed by common aboriginal conditions of geologic structure, soil, surface relief, drainage, climate, vegetation and animal life: reformed and partly re-defined through the settlement of man, the domestication and acclimatization of new species, the nucleation of communities in villages and cities, the re-working of the landscape, and the control over land, power, climate, and movement provided by the state of technics.
>
> In other words, the region, as a unit of geographic individuation, is given: as a unit of cultural individuation it is partly the deliberate expression of human will and purpose. The poles of these two aspects of regional life are the raw physiographic region and the city: they express the extremes of natural and human control. The human region, in brief, is a complex of geographic, economic, and cultural elements. Not found as a finished product in nature, not solely the creation of human will and fantasy, the region, like its corresponding artifact, the city, is a collective work of art. One must not confuse the region, which is a highly complex human fact, with arbitrary areas carved out to serve some single interest, such as government or economic exploitation. The country within fifty miles of a metro-

politan centre is not a region just because it is a convenience for a metropolitan advertising agency or newspaper or planning board to call it so. The discovery of the rough outlines and elementary components of the region in all its varied potentialities as a theatre of collective action is a task for democratic politics. The new regional disciplines complicate the task of finding and expressing political form; for they weaken faith in arbitrary simplifications: but in recompense, they promise a more durable pattern.

c. *Regional planning.* For the RPAA, regional planning was a method which could be used to contain metropolitan growth and re-establish what they called a regional balance. It was a self-conscious attempt to attain the good life for regional communities through large-scale physical planning. Moreover, it was to be a democratic, yet rational process, supervised by technicians and specialists.

Actual definitions of regional planning varied and ranged from the sophisticated philosophical statement to the mundane. A few examples will give the flavour of the Association's thinking. Beginning with the philosophical view, MacKaye wrote:

> Cultural man needs land and developed natural resources as the tangible source of bodily existence; he needs the flow of commodities to make that source effective; but first of all he needs a harmonious and related environment as the source of his true living.
> These three needs of cultured man make three corresponding problems:
> (a) The conservation of natural resources.
> (b) The control of commodity-flow.
> (c) The development of environment.
> *The visualization of the potential workings of these three processes constitutes the new exploration – and regional planning* [MacKaye, 1928, pp. 29–30, italics in the original].

In more specific terms, regional planning became what the French have more recently called *l'aménagement du territoire*.[9] It was:

> a term used by community planners, engineers and geographers to describe a comprehensive ordering of the natural resources of a community, its material equipment and its population for the purpose of laying a sound physical basis for the 'good life'. In America the term has also been used to describe plans for city extension over wide metropolitan areas; this type of planning should properly be called metropolitan planning. Regional planning involves the development of cities and countrysides, industries and natural resources, as part of a regional whole [MacKaye and Mumford, 1929, p. 71].

Mumford later elaborated on this definition and identified it with Dewey's concept of communal education:

Regional planning is the conscious direction and collective integration of all those activities which rest upon the use of the earth as site, as resource, as structure, as theatre. To the extent that such activities are focused within definite regions, consciously delimited and utilized, the opportunities for effective co-ordination are increased. Hence regional planning is a further stage in the more specialized or isolated processes of agricultural planning, industry planning, or city planning....

Regional plans are instruments of communal education; and without that education, they can look forward only to partial achievement.... [We] have still to invent that wider system of order which will assist in the transformation of our social relations: one of its symbols is the regional plan itself [Mumford, 1938, pp. 376–81].

Communal education through political action was conceived as a principal means for implementing regional planning. This was to come about through political mobilization, personal experience and institutional change:

All rational politics must begin with the concrete facts of regional life, not as they appear to the specialist, but as they appear first of all to those who live within the region. Our educational systems are only beginning to make use of the local community and the region as a locus of exploratory activities: but before the resources and activities of a region are treated as abstract subjects they should be understood and felt and lived through as concrete experiences [Mumford, 1938, p. 383].[10]

Only secondarily would more systematic, processed knowledge be brought into relation to these concrete experiences in 'the next step toward a rational political life' (*ibid.*, p. 384).

Once this more realistic type of education becomes universal, instead of being pieced into the more conventional system, we will create a whole generation that will look upon every aspect of the region, the community, and their personal lives as subject to the same processes: exploration, scientific observation, imaginative reconstruction, and finally, transformation by art, by technical improvement and personal discipline. Instead of an external doctrinal unity, imposed by propaganda or authoritarian prescription, such a community will have a unity of approach that will not need external threats in order to preserve the necessary state of inner cohesion. Science has given us the building stones of an orderly world. We need the further utilization of science, through the regional survey, regional exploration, and regional reconstruction if we are to increase the areas of political rationality and human control. Visual synthesis provides a foundation for unified creative activity [*ibid.*, pp. 385–6].

Mumford's ideas, drawn from the educational philosophy of Dewey and the civic activism of Patrick Geddes, predate the contemporary concept of *transactive planning* (Friedmann, 1973) by almost forty years. The emphasis on communal learning, common to all three as a means for combining personal and processed knowledge, can be traced to a shared territorial view of planning which accords to the members of a community the responsibility for creating their own future.

d. *Planning strategies*. The RPAA's goal was ecological reconstruction of the physical environment to promote high cultural development and a biotechnical economy. Their planning strategies were based on decentralization and resource conservation through technological improvements: highway construction, rural electrification and new towns. The notion of enhancing culture, ecology and social learning through technology may seem rather odd to us today, but it was obviously an idea in good currency during the 1920s.

It was argued that the metropolis could be defused, and the advantages of modern life extended to more people, by decentralizing employment in manufacturing and providing adequate public facilities and housing across the regional landscape. For the first time since the beginning of the industrial revolution this could be achieved, because of the technological advances described earlier in this chapter. Science both fuelled metropolitanization and was to be used to thwart it.

New-town building was the real focal point of the Association's philosophy, although their practical experiments seemed more closely related to metropolitan planning than their professed ideals. During their partnership, Henry Wright and Clarence Stein – following the inspiration of Ebenezer Howard – built several new communities. Their work at Sunnyside Gardens (New York) and Radburn (New Jersey) was seminal in the American context. They also contributed to the suburban new-town schemes of Rexford Tugwell's Resettlement Administration during the heady days of the 'first' New Deal (Stein, 1957; Myhra, 1974). Benton MacKaye's suggestion that new communities be used to absorb surplus labour and promote conservation after World War I found realization in Roosevelt's efforts to deal with the Great Depression (MacKaye, 1919; Tugwell, 1937a).

Dispersed industry, the economic base for the RPAA's projected garden cities, was to be made possible by the use of electric power. Electricity was also supposed to spread the possibilities of industrial employment to the farm and ease the the physical burdens of rural life (Chase, 1933). In sum, Kropotkin[11] and Veblen, *decentralization joined to modern technology*, were to play the leading roles in creating a regional environment where farm and factory, regional centre and garden city, wilderness and industry could form an intricate mosaic.

Highways, of course, were to contribute to the same end, connecting city to countryside in such a way that the historical contradictions between them would be laid to rest (MacKaye and Mumford, 1931).[12] The RPAA's faith in such measures, without having access to the power necessary for their implementation, was truly heroic. It is no surprise that when the TVA was created in 1933, embodying many of their basic proposals, they hailed it as a first step towards a new civilization (Chase, 1936).

2. The southern regionalists

Despite their espousal of decentralization and political education, the RPAA seldom escaped elitist frames of reference. Their concern for human settlements in their natural settings and self-realization through democratic action were approached from vantage points available only to the upper classes. For all their talk of learning about the concrete realities of regional life, they never seriously confronted the existence of widespread rural poverty nor developed the social implications of metropolitan financial dominance. Their interest in indigenous regional culture was basically a jumping-off point for pluralism in the arts. They were apparently incapable of transcending the influence of their own circumstances and the *beaux arts* traditions which had misdirected the earliest American efforts in urban planning.[13]

Howard Odum and the other southern sociologists who followed his lead did not have the high cultural aspirations of the RPAA. Their interest in regionalism was primarily political: they wanted to fend off the attack of northern industrial interests and metropolitan culture on southern rural values; they wanted to alleviate agrarian poverty and racism. They were rural-oriented, academic populists, not urban professionals, and their theories centred mainly around the problems of underdevelopment, marginal areas, and poverty.

Odum's key position among southern regionalists was unlike that held by any of the members of the RPAA.[14] His role seems more like Walter Isard's in the development of the Regional Science Association a generation later. Rexford Tugwell has said that Odum's school of thinking was the only 'real' regional theory during the 1930s. Tugwell thought Odum was a great man.[15]

There has never been an adequate investigation of Howard Odum's part in laying the foundations of American planning. Like the prejudice shown against most southern opinions and academic work until very recently in the United States, Odum's essential contributions have been all but passed over. In typical fashion, *The Encyclopedia of Urban Planning* (Whittick, 1974) discusses the work of Benton MacKaye, Lewis Mumford, Clarence Stein, Catherine Bauer Wurster, and Henry Wright – all members of the RPAA – but does not so much as mention Howard Odum. Mel Scott, in his history of *American City Planning* (1969), refers to Odum on five different occasions but never even hints at his major ideas or impact on regional planning.

Odum was a professor of sociology whose first professional interests had been public welfare and the role of blacks in southern society. Like most of the southern regionalists – T. J. Woofter, Katharine Jocher, Rubert B. Vance and Harry Estill Moore – he taught at the University of North Carolina at Chapel Hill. Odum was the motivating force behind the Southern Regional Committee of the Social Science Research Council, founder of the journal *Social Forces*, and eventually established North Carolina's well-known Department of City and Regional Planning. He also served as assistant director of research for the President's Research Committee on Social Trends, under the famous University of Chicago sociologist, William F. Ogburn.[16]

The southern regionalists were part of an intellectual movement which arose during the 1920s, proclaiming the need for a 'New South'. In an archetypal sequence which betrays the true cultural origins of regionalism, what began as poetry ended as politics: a literary style was soon transformed into a research paradigm (Odum, 1931) and later emerged as a debate over public policy issues (Odum, 1934).[17] The centrepiece of this debate became Odum's call for *regional-national social planning* which was meant to re-establish regional balance in America.

The southern regionalists' most important publications include the 'Toward Rural and Regional Planning Issue' of *Social Forces* (1934); Odum's *The Regional Approach to National Social Planning* (1935); Vance's *Regional Reconstruction* (1935); and Odum's and Moore's *American Regionalism* (1938). Even though the southerners' writings on regional planning began to appear somewhat later than the RPAA's, they had an immediate impact on the deliberations of the new Roosevelt administration. In the National Resources Committee's 1935 publication, *Regional Factors in National Planning* – the book which drew together the early doctrine of regional planning – Odum was the first authoritative source to be cited (in the preface).

a. *The problem-setting.* Like the RPAA, Howard Odum and his followers thought they could perceive the imminent decline of Western civilization. This was not a categorical imperative; it was an historical event, brought about by urban-industrialization, metropolitan dominance and regional imbalance. A rurally based folk society and culture were being destroyed by so-called *technicways*. Science and functional organization were supplanting regional folkways and territorial modes of social integration. Odum felt that technicways were drastically modifying traditional modes of human behaviour and replacing 'natural' evolutionary institutions with the dehumanizing social relations of urban-industrialization.

Perhaps nowhere are the extraordinary transformations of science, technology, and change more clearly marked than in the transition from rural culture to urban civilization, from agrarian life to industrial society. Indeed the world trend toward urbanization is changing the entire cultural landscape of the nation such that urbanization or megalopolitan culture has come to appear synonymous with the superlatives of technology [Odum, 1939, p. 86].

Odum thought that a major task faced American society: the reintegration of agrarian culture by ruralizing the city rather than by urbanizing the countryside, as had so often been advocated before.

Recognition of the 'megalopolitan' onslaught in the colonial relationship between the American North and South was the starting point of the southerners' analysis. They dubbed their viewpoint *regionalism*:

Regionalism ... represents the philosophy and technique of self-help, self-development, and initiative in which each areal unit is not only aided, but is committed to the full development of its own resources and capacities. This, on the one hand, is in contrast to dependency by any region upon the nation or to submarginality as compared with other regions; and on the other hand, to exploitation from any sources from without. It assumes that the key to the redistribution of wealth and the equalization of opportunity will be found in the capacity of each region to create wealth and, through new reaches of consumption of commodities, maintain that capacity and retain that wealth in well-balanced production and consumption programs [*ibid.*, pp. 10–11].

Thus, once again, we come across the notions of functional versus territorial organization, metropolis versus region, regional balance, and regional planning. Only this time the focus is not on physical planning but on institution-building to provide equal access to the basic needs of life: 'food, clothing, housing, tools, occupational opportunity'. This is a task of 'social reconstruction' rather than rehabilitation of the cultural landscape. And the appropriate concept of 'region' takes a different form as well.

b. *Regions and regional balance revisisted.* In their major attempt to synthesize the different schools of regional thinking, Odum and Moore (1938) tended to blur the distinctions between their own regional definitions and those of others, such as human geographers. The real contribution of the Chapel Hill group to the question of regionalization came in their earlier writings. They defined a region as an *historically* developed area, identified with a particular social group – a community of destiny – which was unified through culture and experience. The physical attributes of a region were important only in so far as they contributed to the regional evolution of folk culture and to the creation of opportunities for indigenous regional production and consumption.

The region is smaller than society yet is definitive of society. It is characterized by the joint indices of geography and culture and derives its definitive traits through action and behaviour processes and social patterns rather than through technological functions or areas. Even though a social region should coincide largely with a technological one, as in the case of a textile or mining or political region, it is important to emphasize the fundamental distinctions between the formal regionalism measured through technical processes at the top and the social or folk regionalism characterized and conditioned by the social processes at the bottom. These distinctions are equally important for the theoretical study of society ... or for the descriptive and 'practical' study of contemporary societies, or for the utilization of such study for social planning [Odum, 1931, p. 167].

For the southern regionalists the term 'regional balance' also had a whole collection of meanings: balance between cultures, balance between types of occupations, balance between city and countryside, and many more. Towards the end of World War II, after a decade and a half of writing on the topic, Odum attempted to summarize his views:

The heart of the problem [of balance] is found in search for equal opportunity for all the people through the conservation, development, and use of their resources in the places where they live, adequately adjusted to the interregional culture and economy of the other regions of the Nation. The goal is, therefore, clearly one of balanced culture as well as economy, in which equality of opportunity in education, in public health and welfare, in the range of occupational outlook, and in the elimination of handicapping differentials between and among different groups of people and levels of culture may be achieved [Odum, 1945, p. 36].

c. *Regional planning and its strategies*. Regional imbalances were to be overcome by social reconstruction. And this, according to Odum, was to be achieved through 'regional–national social planning'. The approach held several advantages. It provided for a full and knowledgeable inventory of the peoples and cultures of the various parts of the country. It held the potential for achieving total development of the unique resources and capacities of each region while taking into account their particular differences and problems. And finally, it promised a better opportunity for reconstructing an interregionally balanced social and political economy.

In a talk delivered at UCLA in July of 1934, Howard Odum focused his 'main hypotheses of regional planning strategy' around six major points of emphasis. The first two were global in nature, calling for a new national and regional consciousness. First, there was the need to bring about a change in attitudes towards planned society, regional inequities, racial discrimination, cultural adequacy, rural–urban conflicts, and federal/regional co-operation. Second, attitudes would also have to be changed towards regional participation in national affairs and the feasible extent of regional self-containment. Odum offered no concrete suggestions of how such basic changes in beliefs and values might be precipitated.

He simply listed them as the first and essential steps towards regional planning.

The next four strategies sound more familiar to regional planners today, but their details and radical political implications rest upon Odum's initial assumptions. First, a practical programme for reorganizing and developing southern agriculture was proposed. Its aim would be the production of commodities necessary for local consumption and as primary inputs into secondary industrial activities. A second strategy was the selected development of southern agricultural products for export. Third, a thorough-going reorganization of local government and fiscal policies would be necessary. And finally, Odum felt that a genuine effort to develop southern institutions of higher learning was absolutely essential in order to promote research and provide the leadership necessary to achieve the first three objectives.

In the agricultural sector, regional planning was to break the vicious circle of export-crop dependency, diversify food crops, and bring to an end tenancy and share-cropping. Odum wanted to reconstruct the tenant system, provide 'adequate' credit, diversify cropping patterns, increase access to consumption goods, increase technical support facilities, redistribute 'submarginal lands and people', and increase interregional trade and exports. This was all to be accomplished through 'a two-fold planning approach', first, an overall strategy of reconstructing the whole southern system of commercial agriculture, from production techniques through marketing and distribution, and second, a complete renovation of the prevailing land-tenure system, which, in effect, condemned tenants and small farmers to a submarginal level of existence.

At the operational level of projects to help the small farmer, Odum suggested a number of communal and collectivist measures: pooling rural labour for public service, pooling agricultural machinery on a county or community basis, special local industries to provide agricultural inputs, county plans for rationalizing agricultural land use, and co-operative arrangements for livestock breeding. Odum did not, however, elaborate on the implications of such schemes for ownership and effective control of the means of production.

Industry was to be expanded in support of agriculture and rural folk culture, through the same type of two-tier approach that was applied to agriculture. The higher level of policy would be aimed at the macro-economic factors in industrial expansion. While the lower level would:

> ...integrate the whole industrial region with the agricultural reorganization, including special planning for decentralized industry, for village and community industries, for a large number of new smaller industries, and for at least a six-year period of semi-civil or public works program looking towards the rehabilitation of farms and farm houses, of reforestation and erosion work, of housing deficiencies and especially for equalizing work and facilities for

Negroes in schools, health, sanitation, and the like [Odum, 1934, p. 21].

The fifth point of the strategy, reorganizing government and public administration, was mainly a matter of institutional experimentation to promote intergovernmental co-operation and, importantly, to integrate blacks into their rightful role in government. Odum hoped this last 'insolvable' difficulty could be approached through concrete technical procedures such as those just then being considered by the Tennessee Valley Authority.

Finally, Odum argued that the 'supreme' need for planning was in the field of 'higher education, science, and other cultural institutions'. So here too, like the RPAA, Odum came around to the advice of John Dewey and Thorstein Veblen – the megalopolis could supposedly be defeated by its own weapons: technology and education.

In the report undertaken by the Southern Committee of the Social Science Research Council in 1931 (Odum, 1936), Odum described how educational development would be integrated into regional planning. First, a limited number of *regional institutional centres* would be systematically strengthened. These universities would concentrate explicitly on advanced research, technological arts, and training for public service. The second approach Odum called a *functional framework of inquiry and action*. Here emphasis would be on investigating special deficiencies peculiar to the South, through a series of integrated work programmes. The third contribution of the educational establishment to regional planning Odum called *experimental units of work*. Through these problem-oriented work groups he envisaged that all levels of the educational establishment would be focused on solving some particular concrete problem, in which learning would take place through action and appraisal.

Regional planning doctrine: a preface

The regional planning theories of both the RPAA and the southern regionalists arose in response to the social changes and intellectual fashions of their times. Their ideas about regions, planning, and regional balance drew heavily not only on American experience but also on the formulations of European scholars, radicals, and reformers.

While we have tried to underline the differences between the concepts of these two groups, many of their fundamental notions and programmes were strikingly similar. They stood in basic opposition to the predominant trends in Western society: metropolitanization, rural decay, massive rural–urban migration, social polarization. They attempted to champion the territorial principle of social integration, which was quickly disappearing before a growing flood of market relationships.

Unlike the more recent theories of regional planning which we will discuss in later chapters, the prevalent concepts of the 1920s and 1930s did not start with the goal of economic growth. They did not encourage across-the-board urbanization. In fact, as we have seen, they advocated a counter position. Regional planning sought the recovery of ecological and social balance between city and countryside, folk culture and civilization, human life and nature. Planning was seen as a method to improve the cultural as well as material circumstances of regional communities: indeed, the two goals were held to be inseparable, on structural as well as epistemological grounds.

Starting in the mid-1930s with the domestic reform programme of the Roosevelt administration, the ideas of regional planners were synthesized along with those of other groups – notably the metropolitan planners – to form a coherent planning doctrine. This doctrine, *comprehensive river basin development*, provided the first generalized framework for regional development. Although along the way it lost much of its theoretical purity, it served as the prevailing model of development planning for almost three decades.

Notes

1. For a discussion of the relationships between the economy, technology, and the city see Harvey (1973), especially chapter 6.
2. 'Captains of Industry' was Thornstein Veblen's term to describe the leading entrepreneurs of the industrial era.
3. A seemingly endless drought which lasted from 1932 to 1936 converted vast areas of the Great Plains, from Texas to the Dakotas, into a veritable 'Dust Bowl'. Winds carried the ravished top soil as far east as Washington DC, and during the winter of 1935 'red snow' fell in New England. The dramatic exodus of farmers from Oklahoma to California in search of work is described emotionally in John Steinbeck's *Grapes of Wrath* (1939). Rexford Tugwell's suggestion of a Soil Conservation Service, to be housed in the Department of Agriculture, was largely in response to the Dust Bowl catastrophe.
4. We are grateful to Professor Derek Diamond of the London School of Economics for pointing out the United Kingdom example to us.
5. The 'Gilded Age' was a derogatory term used by intellectuals to characterize the materialism, political corruption and cultural vulgarity which went hand in hand with the development of American urban-industrialization. W. Somerset Maugham catches much of the spirit of Chicago during this period in his classic *The Razor's Edge* (1944).
6. This distinguished list of intellectual contributors to the thinking of the RPAA deserves a separate study to itself, but that would take us far beyond the scope of the present work. Auguste Comte, Frederic Le Play, Paul Vidal de la Blache, and Elisée Reclus were all Frenchmen. Their importance for the writings of the RPAA cannot be overstated, but their influence often came indirectly via such men as Patrick Geddes. Comte and Le Play affected the RPAA most directly through their ideas on political decentralization. Vidal, the founder of French university geography, gave them their idea of the region as a real, palpable entity. The other French geographer, Reclus, along with his Russian fellow anarchist Kropotkin, emphasized the economic and political viability of small-scale economic organization overcoming the contradiction between city and countryside. And the final two men, Marsh and Thoreau, were

Americans who spearheaded the early conservation movement. English Fabianism was a nineteenth-century socialist movement which worked towards the gradual replacement of capitalism by a more humane communal order.

For an assessment of the profound, formative influence of Patrick Geddes' thinking on the RPAA, see Kitchen (1975) and Boardman (1978).

7. In interviews with Professor Peter Hall of Reading University and Professor Leo Klaassen of Erasmus University, Rotterdam, both expressed the view that American regional planning ideas first found a wide European audience with publication of Mumford's classic, *The Culture of Cities*, in 1938.

8. *La tradition vidalienne* is the name usually given to the French paradigm of university geography, founded in 1898 when Vidal accepted a professorship at the Sorbonne. Vidal's school of thought was quickly disseminated throughout France, as his pupils, such as de Martonne, Demangeon, and Blanchard, accepted posts in various universities and continued his method of approaching the study of geography through regional monographs.

9. Synthesizing several French sources, Sundquist defined *l'aménagement du territoire* as:

'the search, in the geographical setting of France, for a better distribution of people' in relation to natural resources and economic activity. More than that, it was a search for a distribution that would best serve the welfare of the people in the noneconomic aspects as well – the living environment, the working environment, opportunities for recreation and for culture. . . . [I]ts objectives were to dam up the current that carries all the vital forces of the country toward the great centres; to re-create the sources of life in the regions whose resources are underutilized and which, despite rich possibilities, tend to become deserted; to restrain the development of the great agglomerations; to emphasize the underdeveloped zones of the country (Sundquist, 1975, p. 93).

10. It strikes us as very odd that although Mumford seems to be paraphrasing John Dewey's arguments about experience, education and planning, he never mentions Dewey here here or cites his writings (cf., especially, Dewey, 1935 and 1938). The lengthy annotated bibliography included at the end of *The Culture of Cities* does not contain a single one of Dewey's books, although several dealt explicitly with the relationship between education, planning, and social action.

11. Kropotkin's anarchistic theories for physical reconstruction were first presented comprehensively in 1899 as *Fields, Factories, and Workshops; or Industry Combined with Agriculture, and Brain Work Combined with Manual Work*. In *The Culture of Cities* Mumford commented on this piece bibliographically: 'Sociological and economic intelligence of the first order, founded on Kropotkin's specialized competence as a geographer and his generous social passion as a leader of communist anarchism. Able analysis and penetrating interpretation.'

12. An overall view of the RPAA's writings suggests that what they wanted to overcome were the exploitative aspects of city–county relations. Their ideas about the evils of metropolitanization and the need to compartmentalize the regional landscape point to their realization that both the regional city and the countryside – the functional and the territorial – were necessary for each other's existence.

13. See Murray Bookchin's attack on Mumford in *The Limits of the City* (1974), especially chapter 4 and also our discussion of the 'City Beautiful' movement in the next chapter.

14. Mumford's later prominence probably exaggerates his real significance as a member of the Regional Planning Association of America. He did not participate in any of their major planning projects, but served primarily as their chief editor and publicist.

15. Interview with Rexford Tugwell at the Centre for the Study of Democratic Institutions in Santa Barbara, California, on 29 April 1977.

16. This group, set up by Herbert Hoover in 1929, acted as a precursor to Roosevelt's National Planning Board. Its members included Wesley C. Mitchell, Charles E. Merriam, Howard W. Odum, and William F. Ogburn. Mitchell and Merriam went

on to belong to the NPB. Ogburn, a frequent colleague of Rexford Tugwell's, served under Tugwell in the Resettlement Administration. During the interview with Tugwell cited in note 12, above, Tugwell speculated that Odum was probably passed over for membership on the National Planning Board because of his advanced age and his southern origins.

Both Odum and T. J. Woofter contributed to the report of the Research Committee on Social Trends, *Recent Social Trends in the United States* (1933).

17. This seems to follow Charles Peguy's rule, cited in Graham (1967, p. 64), '*tout commence en mystique et finit en politique*'.

Bibliography

Beard, C. A. 1924: *Contemporary American History, 1877–1913*. New York: Macmillan.

Bookchin, M. 1974: *The limits of the city*. New York: Harper and Row.

Boardman, P. 1978: *The worlds of Patrick Geddes*. London: Routledge & Kegan Paul.

Cash, W. J. 1941: *The mind of the South*. New York: Alfred A. Knopf.

Charles-Brun, J. 1911: *Le régionalisme*. Paris: Bloud.

Chase, S. 1933: *The promise of power*. New York: John Day.

1936: *Rich land, poor land*. New York: Whittlesey House.

Dewey, J. 1900: *The school and society*. University of Chicago Press.

1916a: *Essays in experimental logic*. University of Chicago Press.

1916b: *Democracy and education*. New York: Macmillan.

1917: The need for a recovery of philosophy. In *Creative intelligence, essays in the pragmatic attitude*. New York: Henry Holt.

1920: *Reconstruction in philosophy*. New York: Henry Holt.

1925: *Experience and nature*. Chicago: Open Court Pub. Co.

1927: *The public and its problems*. New York: Henry Holt.

1935: *Liberalism and social action*. New York: G. P. Putnam's Sons.

1938: *Experience and education*. New York: Macmillan.

Dickinson, R. E. 1964: *City and region: a geographical interpretation*. London: Routledge & Kegan Paul.

Dorfman, J. 1934: *Thorstein Veblen and his America*. New York: Viking Press.

Dunn, E. 1971: *Economic and social development: a process of social learning*. Baltimore: Johns Hopkins University Press.

Friedmann, J. 1973: *Retracking America: a theory of transactive planning*. Garden City, New York: Anchor Press.

Galbraith, J. K. 1977: *The age of uncertainty*. Boston: Houghton Mifflin.

Goist, P. D. 1969: Lewis Mumford and 'anti-urbanism'. *Journal of the American Institute of Planners* **25**, 340–7.

Graham, O. L. Jr 1967: *An encore for reform: the old Progressives and the New Deal*. New York: Oxford University Press.

Gruchy, A. G. 1939a: Economics of the national resources committee. *American Economic Review* **29**, 60–73.

1939b: The concept of national planning in institutional economics. *Southern Economic Journal* **6**, 121–44.

Gunderson, G. 1976: *A new economic history of America*. New York: McGraw-Hill.

Harvey, D. 1973: *Social justice and the city*. Baltimore: Johns Hopkins University Press.

Heskin, A. and Hoch, C. 1977: The progressive era and contemporary theory. MS.

Hill. F. G. 1957: Wesley Mitchell's theory of planning. *Political Science Quarterly* **72**, 100–18.

Hofstadter, R. 1948: *The American political tradition and the men who made it*. New York: Alfred A. Knopf.

　1955: *The age of reform: from Bryan to F.D.R.* New York: Vintage Books.

Hynning, C. J. 1939: *State conservation of resources*. A report done for the National Resources Committee. Washington, DC: US Government Printing Office.

Kitchen, P. 1975: *A most unsettling person*. New York: Saturday Review Press.

Kropotkin, P. 1899: *Fields, factories, and workshops; or industry combined with agriculture, and brain work combined with manual work*. London: Hutchinson.

Lerner, M. 1948: *The portable Veblen*. New York: Viking Press.

McDermott, J. 1973: *The philosophy of John Dewey*. Vol. 1: *The structure of experience*. Vol. 2: *The lived experience*. New York: G. P. Putnam's Sons.

MacKaye, B. 1919: *Employment and natural resources*. Washington, DC: US Department of Labor.

　1928: *The new exploration: a philosophy of regional planning*. New York: Harcourt, Brace.

MacKaye, B. and Mumford, L. 1929: Regional planning. *Encyclopaedia Britannica*, 14th edition, **19**, 71–2.

　1931: Townless highways for the motorist. *Harpers Magazine*.

Marsh, G. P. 1864: *Man and nature*. New York: Charles Scribner's Sons.

Marx, K. 1964: *Pre-capitalist economic formations*. New York: International Pub.

Maugham, W. S. 1944: *The razor's edge*. New York: Doubleday.

Mitchell, W., editor 1936: *What Veblen taught: selected writings of Thorstein Veblen*. New York: Viking Press.

　1969: *Types of economic theory: from mercantilism to institutionalism* Vol. II, Dorfman, J., editor. New York: Augustus M. Kelly. From Lectures originally delivered at Columbia University during the academic year 1926–7.

Mumford, L. 1925: The fourth migration. *Survey Graphic* **54**, 130–3.

　1938: *The culture of cities*. New York: Harcourt, Brace.

Myhra, D. 1974: Rexford Guy Tugwell: initiator of America's greenbelt new towns, 1935 to 1936. *Journal of the American Institute of Planners* **3**, 176–88.

Nicholls, W. H. 1960: *Southern tradition and regional economic progress.* Chapel Hill: University of North Carolina Press.

North, D. C. 1961: *The economic growth of the United States, 1790–1860.* New York: W. W. Norton.

Novack, G., editor 1966: *Existentialism versus Marxism: conflicting views on humanism.* New York: Dell Pub. Co.

   1975: *Pragmatism versus Marxism: an appraisal of John Dewey's philosophy.* New York: Pathfinder Press.

Odum, H. W. 1931: Regional and folk society. *Social Forces* **10**, 164–75.

   1934: The case for regional-national social planning. *Social Forces* **13**, 6–23.

   1935: *The regional approach to national social planning.* New York: Foreign Policy Assn.

   1936: *Southern regions of the United States.* Chapel Hill: University of North Carolina Press.

   1939: *American social problems: an introduction to the study of the people and their dilemmas.* Revised edition, September 1947. New York: Henry Holt.

   1945: Regional quality and balance of America. In Odum, H. W. and Jocher, K., editors 1945, 27–43.

Odum, H. W. and Jocher, K., editors 1945: *In search of the regional balance of America.* Chapel Hill: University of North Carolina Press.

Odum, H. W. and Moore, H. E. 1938: *American regionalism: a cultural-historical approach to national integration.* New York: Henry Holt.

Parrington, V. L. 1930: *The beginnings of critical realism in America (1860–1920).* New York: Harcourt, Brace.

The President's Research Committee on Social Trends 1933: *Recent social trends in the United States.* New York: McGraw-Hill.

Riesman, D. 1953: *Thorstein Veblen: a critical interpretation.* New York: Charles Scribner's Sons.

Schlesinger, A. M. 1941: *Political and social growth of the American people, 1865–1940.* New York: Macmillan.

   1950: *The American as reformer.* Cambridge, Mass.: Harvard University Press.

Scott, M. 1969: *American city planning since 1890.* Berkeley: University of California Press.

Social Forces **12**, 1934; 'Toward rural and regional planning issue'.

State of New York 1926: *Report of the Commission of Housing and Regional Planning to Governor Alfred E. Smith.* Albany: J. B. Lyon.

Stein, C. S. 1925: Dinosaur cities. *Survey Graphic* **54**, 134–8.

   1957: *Towards new towns for America.* With an introduction by Lewis Mumford. Cambridge. Mass.: The MIT Press.

Steinbeck, J. 1939: *The grapes of wrath.* New York: Viking Press.

Sundquist, J. L. 1975: *Dispersing population: what America can learn from Europe.* Washington, DC: Brookings Institution.

Survey Graphic **54**, 1925: 'The regional plan number'.

Sussman, C., editor 1976: *Planning the fourth migration: the neglected vision of the regional planning association of America.* Cambridge, Mass.: The MIT Press.

Tugwell, R. G. 1932: *Mr Hoover's economic policy.* New York: John Day.
   1933: *The industrial discipline and the governmental arts.* New York: Columbia University Press.
   1937a: The meaning of the greenbelt towns. *The New Republic* **90**, 42–3.
   1937b: Wesley Mitchell: an evaluation. *The New Republic* **92**, 238–40.

Turner, F. J. 1893: *The significance of the frontier in American history.* An address read before the American Historical Association at their annual meeting in Chicago. New York: Henry Holt, 1920.

Twelve Southerners, 1930: *I'll take my stand.* New York: Harper Bros.

United States Bureau of the Census 1960: *Historical statistics of the United States, colonial times to 1957.* Washington, DC: US Government Printing Office.

United States National Resources Committee 1935: *The regional factors in national planning.* Washington, DC: US Government Printing Office.

Vance, R. B. 1935: *Regional reconstruction: a way out for the South.* New York: Foreign Policy Assn.

Veblen, T. 1899: *The theory of the leisure class: an economic study of institutions.* New York: Charles Scribner's Sons.
   1904: *The theory of the business enterprise.* New York: Charles Scribner's Sons.
   1919: *The place of science in modern civilization and other essays.* New York: Viking Press.

Whittick, A., editor 1974: *Encyclopedia of urban planning.* New York: McGraw-Hill.

Chapter 3
Metropolis and region

The Great Depression and the New Deal

The dissent of regional planners, such as the RPAA and the southern regionalists, was almost the only exception to the universal praise of the 'New Economic Era' (1921–9). After the short-lived recession of 1921, businessmen, government leaders and planners in the United States had nothing but applause for the accomplishments of urban-based industrialization. Profits were high, salaries rose, and there was a general glow of prosperity which seemed to transcend the boundaries of social class and region. The union movement suffered serious setbacks: the number of strikes fell from 3,400 in 1920 to 600 in 1928. Membership of the American Federation of Labor dropped from four million to less than three million between 1920 and 1929 (Schlesinger, 1941, pp. 492–3). Although functional integration went on at an intoxicating pace, there were fundamental problems at the roots of all this prosperity. Monopoly capital was creating a labyrinth of holding companies financed through 'watered' stock, and agriculture was so 'over-productive' that the selling price of a bushel of wheat plummetted from $1.82 in 1920 to 38 cents in 1932, the lowest price in American history (*ibid.*, p. 500).

The stock market crash of October 1929 was a consequence of this untenable situation. In its wake, millions of workers lost their jobs, and the ideology of free enterprise met its first serious challenge. The visionary and often conflicting dreams of a few utopian theorists and reformers were superseded by a spate of political promises and governmental programmes. Herbert Hoover's cautious attempts to re-initiate the processes of accumulation and 'top-down'* growth were judged inadequate by the American voters, and in 1932 Franklin Roosevelt was elected to the presidency with a temporary mandate for relief, recovery, and reform.

The whirlwind of legislation which Roosevelt pushed through Congress during his first hundred days in office has become a byword in American

---

* 'Top-down' economic growth refers to the idea that corporate expansion and increases in corporate profits will eventually lead to more jobs and higher living standards for people farther down the socio-economic ladder.

politics. His pragmatic interventionist policies set the course for liberal reform for three generations. The depression and Roosevelt's attempts to define a positive role for government in guiding the capitalist economy opened the door for national planning in the United States (Graham, 1976). Regional resource development became a major focus of public policy, and the doctrine of *comprehensive river basin planning* was one of its outgrowths. In this chapter we will show how this first doctrine of regional planning was forged through the fluctuating experiments of the New Deal, focusing mainly on the National Planning Board (NPB), the Resettlement Administration (RA), and the Tennessee Valley Authority (TVA).[1]

The impetus of planning

Upon taking office in March 1933, Roosevelt appointed Harold L. Ickes, a 'Bull Moose' Republican[2] from Illinois, as Secretary of the Interior. Unlike most old-school Progressives, Ickes was an active participant in, and supporter of, the New Deal (Graham, 1967). The choice of Ickes to head the department which was about to undertake a vast public-works programme to provide jobs for the unemployed was of critical importance. Ickes had been intimately involved in metropolitan reform and planning in Chicago and, on assuming his new duties, one of his first moves was to establish a National Planning Board within the Federal Emergency Relief Administration. The planning board's initial task was the allocation of funds to various projects in different parts of the country. What could have been an exercise in 'pork barrelling'[3] was from the beginning garbed in the concepts and institutional forms of rational decision making.

Active federal involvement in public-works construction and resource development, via the NPB and other agencies, was a sharp departure from American tradition and provided the entering wedge for the emergence of regional planning doctrine. The National Planning Board was composed of Wesley C. Mitchell, Charles E. Merriam and Frederic A. Delano, Franklin Roosevelt's uncle. Mitchell was the most influential of the second generation institutionalists, and Merriam and Delano were metropolitan planners from Chicago. Their early control of the board proved to be decisive for the later course of events. To understand the subsequent development of regional doctrine, we therefore need to summarize briefly the major themes of metropolitan planning, to show how it differed in its fundamental concerns and goals from regionalism.[4]

The metropolitan planners

Metropolitan planning – metropolitan regionalism, as it was sometimes called – grew up side by side with the city planning movement. In fact, many of the earliest urban planners argued forcefully for the development of a 'regional perspective'. They soon came to include entire metropolitan areas within the scope of their plans.

In substance, metropolitan planning was a mixture of four separate but overlapping elements, all reactions to urban-industrialization: housing reform, park and boulevard planning, the 'City Beautiful' movement, and local government reform. While advocates of the four different approaches were often allied and shared common concerns, their strategies for guiding metropolitan expansion were basically at odds. Housing the urban working class, designing monumental public architecture, and 'professionalizing' city government spring from very different motives and serve fundamentally different interests.

1. The housing movement

The housing movement was the first strand of metropolitan planning to manifest itself. As industrial cities grew in England, France, the United States and Germany, the outrageous living conditions of the new urban working class could not be overlooked. Cholera, typhoid fever and tuberculosis were rampant in tenement districts from Vienna to Chicago. And the blame clearly lay with overcrowded, unventilated living quarters, without proper sanitation, plumbing or sewage disposal. Fear of disease, philanthropy, and radical pamphleteering gradually stirred the middle classes to ameliorative action.

According to many observers, the worst living conditions in the industrial world were to be found in New York City.[5] Attention was apparently first drawn to this problem, and the relationship between bad housing and disease, by a report prepared in 1834 by the City Inspector of the New York City Board of Health. This was followed by several investigative commissions (1856, 1884, 1894) and a series of tenement house laws (1867, 1879, 1895, 1901).

In the United Kingdom, the Select Committee on the Health of Towns (1840) and the Royal Commission on the State of Large Towns (1844-5) recommended the creation of public health authorities at the local level to control living conditions and building standards. A number of acts by Parliament between 1848 and 1894 established a national board of health, set sanitary standards for local authorities to enforce, and finally brought about fundamental reform in local government.

Unlike the British, Americans made no generalized attempt to ameliorate the urban housing situation during the nineteenth century. At the First National Conference on City Planning, held in Washington, DC in 1909, housing reform was still a very controversial issue.[6] We can only grasp its importance, though, by viewing it from a more holistic perspective.

The housing questions provides, in its historical setting, a concrete example of the differences between metropolitan and regional planners. Metropolitan planners wanted to alleviate the social evils of congestion through planned expansion of the city; regionalists wanted to disperse population and economic activities over a broader geographic area. Radical socialists disavowed the workability of either of these reformist solutions.

Mrs V. G. Simkhovitch of Greenwich House in New York City summarized the metropolitan planners' solution to the housing problem at the national conference on city planning:

> ... we ought to make it impossible that any community now growing into a big city should repeat the errors which have been so costly for us in New York. To do this we must continue the educational campaign. We must also be clear that the housing question must be considered in its relation to congestion. Personally, I think that we should take the stand that congestion cannot be eliminated without some form of limiting the number of persons who can live within a given area. We can reduce the number of persons to an acre by lowering the limit on the height of tenement houses. This will in some cases result in its being unprofitable to build tenements on very valuable land, and will serve to force people out of cities [*Proceedings*, 1910, p. 104].

As a tireless settlement house worker, Mrs Simkhovitch's motives were above question. Like most other suggested reforms in working-class housing, however, density regulations were to bring additional hardships on the very people they were intended to help.

Regional planners, however, impressed with the anarchist ideas of Elisée Reclus and Peter Kropotkin, followed the example of British reformers such as Ebenezer Howard and Raymond Unwin. They suggested a scattering of free-standing new towns, 'Garden Cities', to provide jobs and housing for the urban population.

In 1925 Clarence Stein of the RPAA capsulized the regionalists' approach to the housing question:

> The real choice is not between the 'rent-barracks', as the Germans call the tenement, and the isolated House of our Dreams. The real alternative for most of us, as our wants become more complicated and as community costs go up, is between the rent-barracks and community planning.... Community planning ... is a method of achieving individuality by learning to work in common. The contrast ... between the rows of individual houses, done in the American style, and the spacious well-planned groups of the English garden city is essentially not a contrast between two countries, but between two different types of planning [Stein, 1925, p. 168].

Howard's two new towns, Letchworth (1903) and Welwyn (1919), were followed in the United States by Sunnyside Gardens, Radburn, Chatham Village, the Greenbelt and TVA towns, and Baldwin Hills. Like Becontree and Wythenshawe in England, however, these American ventures, shepherded into existence by RPAA members Stein and Henry Wright, fell far short of the garden city ideal. Except for the TVA towns (Norris, Wheeler and Pickwick Landing), they were basically residential suburbs. Much of the later terminological confusion about 'garden cities' and 'garden suburbs' or 'satellite cities' was a product of this dichotomy between theory and practice.

Radical socialists found both metropolitan and regional approaches to the housing question little more than sleight-of-hand. After reviewing an early German publication which contained accounts of both types of experiments, Friedrich Engels mocked: 'All that remains for us to do is to introduce the cottage system into the countryside and to make the workers' barracks in the cities as tolerable as possible.'[7]

Engels went on to dismiss all reformist solutions to the problem of working-class housing:

> On its own admission ... the bourgeois solution of the housing question has come to grief – it has come to grief owing to the *contrast between town and country*. And with this we have arrived at the kernel of the problem. The housing question can be solved only when society has been sufficiently transformed for a start to be made towards abolishing the contrast between town and country, which has been brought to its extreme point by present-day capitalist society. Far from being able to abolish this antithesis, capitalist society on the contrary is compelled to intensify it day by day [Engels, 1887, p. 51].

2. Park planning and the City Beautiful

The next two elements of metropolitan planning evolved directly from planning practice. Park and boulevard planning and the City Beautiful movement developed more or less sequentially and can be best described together.

While the working class was suffering in sub-human squalor, middle-class residents were yearning for a more refined, aesthetic environment. Georges-Eugene Haussmann's remarkable renovation of Paris for Napoleon III, starting in 1853, not only provided broad boulevards for the quick movement of troops and artillery, it also hid the sordid tenements of working-class people behind ornate façades which still today draw thousands of tourists to the city. Somewhat earlier, the bourgeoisie of Manchester had achieved similar, if more modest, results by lining all their major thoroughfares with shops which hid the swarming jungle of lower-class slums from the eyes of more fortunate passers-by.

At the same time that Haussmann was reconstructing Paris, Frederick Law Olmsted began the American tradition of metropolitan park building. Central Park in New York was followed by other Olmsted ventures, such as Fairmount Park in Philadelphia and Golden Gate Park in San Francisco, and led to his theory of connecting neighbourhood parks by boulevards to larger recreational areas, and finally to the open country-side. Chicago began the creation of a citywide park system in 1869, Minneapolis in 1883, Kansas City in 1890, and Boston created a permanent Regional Park Commission in 1893. This last effort led to a bill in the Massachusetts legislature in 1896 calling for a general referendum on creation of a countywide government, on the model of Greater London. The proposed law was too radical for its time in the United States, however, and was roundly defeated.

In a rather different vein, 1893 saw the opening of the first public play-ground in the Italian working-class district of Chicago, by Jane Addams, founder of Hull House. Hull House was undoubtedly the most famous of the settlement houses, and Addams' use of open space as an instrument of social reform was one of the first such instances on record in the United States.

But, for metropolitan planners, Chicago in the year 1893 meant something much more grandiose than minor philanthropic attempts to alleviate urban congestion. The year 1893 was marked by The World's Columbian Exposition, Daniel H. Burnham's 'White City'. This was indeed a much grander model. Its purpose was to show the middle class that America's cities, too, could aspire to be 'beautiful'. With a layout designed by Olmsted, the Chicago world's fair sat on the shores of Lake Michigan, displaying an incredible carnival of archaic architectural monuments. Its real importance was the stir it created for building fullscale repro-ductions of this make-believe world, and it started Burnham on the road to preparing one of the world's earliest metropolitan regional plans, the *Plan of Chicago* (Burnham and Bennett, 1909).

The year after the world's fair, Burnham started work on a plan for reconstruction of Chicago's southern lakefront, from the site of the fair northward to where the Chicago River flows into Lake Michigan. In 1896, he presented his ideas to a group of leading industrialists and businessmen, including such notables as Marshal Field and Philip D. Armour. But Chicago was not yet ready to undertake such a project, so the idea was shelved for over a decade. During the interim, Burnham worked on monumental architectural designs for Washington, Cleveland, San Francisco and Manila.[8]

In 1904, Burnham was approached by three members of the Commercial Club of Chicago, Charles Dyer Norton, Charles H. Wacker, and Frederic A. Delano, and asked to prepare a plan for the city, expanding on his original scheme for lakefront redevelopment. After some delay, work began on the plan in 1907, and two years later the grand opus emerged as a limited edition of magnificently illustrated volumes, selling for $25 each. By 1925 – the same year Mumford was editing the 'Regional Plan Number' of *Survey Graphic* – Chicago had spent some $300,000,000 to implement Burnham's plan. Like Haussmann's plan for Paris, Burnham's vision went a long way towards creating the city's contemporary ap-pearance.[9]

Burnham's plan was genuinely metropolitan in scope. Encompassing four thousand square miles, from Kenosha, Wisconsin to Michigan City, Indiana, it contained three major elements. The first was a system of regional ring-roads which created a series of concentric loops west of the city. These were connected with central Chicago by a network of radial highways and parkways. Additional electric railways and the re-location of several existing rail lines and terminals were also envisaged, following a scheme laid out earlier by Frederic Delano, then president of the Wabash Railroad.

The second element of the plan was an extension of the regional park system. Ranging from city parks to vast nature reserves, Burnham suggested that a total of 60,000 acres be set aside for recreational purposes. This was basically open space of the 'monumental' variety, however, and added little accessible parkland for the majority of the city's immigrant, working-class population.

The last major feature of the plan was an expansion of Burnham's original design for 'South Shore Drive'. Lakeshore Drive and the whole series of parks, marinas and airports that one sees today along the Chicago shoreline are the long-term result.

The shortcomings of the Chicago Plan were as monumental as its achievements. The plan hardly mentioned the concerns of social reformers, which had dominated the First National City Planning Conference only two months before its unveiling. Early releases from the Russell Sage Foundation's *Pittsburgh Survey* (Kellogg, P. U., editor 1914), which had set the tone for much of that conference, had shown that detailed analyses could be made of congestion, housing conditions, disease and unemployment. But Burnham's plan made no use of such information, nor did it make proposals for dealing with any of the fundamental problems of capitalist urban-industrialization. Expansion was its leitmotiv. In the best Haussmannesque fashion, it was a scheme to embellish the city and flatter its rulers. Ironically, as Veblen might have foretold, the lower classes were also impressed.

The high-water mark of metropolitan planning during the 1920s, however, was reached with publication of the *Regional Plan for New York and Its Environs* (Committee on Plan of New York, 1929–31). The New York project was started in 1920 by Charles Dyer Norton, the same insurance executive who had fathered the Chicago venture. When Norton died in 1923, his position as chairman of the Russell Sage Foundation's Committee on the Plan was taken over by a former Chicago colleague, Frederic Delano.

A list of the Committee's technical consultants and staff reads like a *Who's Who* of urban planning at the time. The staff's director was Thomas Adams: early secretary of Ebenezer Howard's Garden City Association (1901), first manager of Letchworth (1903–6) and founder of the British Town Planning Institute (1914). Raymond Unwin, designer of Letchworth, also came over from England, to consider the possibility of including garden city development as a part of the scheme. Other 'professional planners' such as Edward Bassett, Frederick Law Olmsted, John Nolen, and Harland Bartholomew contributed to the work. Housing and reform interests were represented by Shelby M. Harrison, graphics editor of the *Pittsburgh Survey*, and Russell Sage trustees Robert de Forest and Lawrence Veiller.

Of the ten volumes eventually published for the Committee, the first two, *The Graphic Regional Plan* (1929) and *The Building of the City* (1931), contained the bulk of their recommendations. The other eight volumes were taken up by surveys of various kinds. There is little doubt that this series of impressive volumes represented the most imposing metropolitan planning effort ever attempted. Its real departures from the earlier Chicago Plan, however, lay mainly in its extensive use of social statistics and in its emphasis, newly legitimized, of land use controls. The principal objective of the plan remained much the same: to promote the continued expansion of the metropolis by developing an ever greater land area, laced together by a network of highways.[10]

Perhaps the most important difference between the privately sponsored New York and Chicago plans was that the New York scheme was never really implemented. The Regional Plan Association of New York, founded in 1929 to promote the plan's acceptance, had only very limited success. Whether this was because of New York's greater governmental complexity, the onset of the Great Depression, or some other reason, is difficult to say. According to Lewis Mumford, this failure was really no loss. He characterized the plan as:

> In all, a mass of exhaustive statistical data (much highly useful), well-meaning half-truths, and contradictory plans and prescriptions, dignified by almost ten years of labour, a million dollars in expenses, and ten monumental volumes. The premises upon which the survey was conducted were sociologically unsound: continued population growth up to 1965 was treated as axiomatic and the economic stability of the metropolitan regime was taken for granted. The real task of transforming the inner area of the metropolis was shirked and the duty to prepare to receive larger increments of population in the immediate outlying areas was not even subjected to skeptical inquiry [Mumford, 1938, p. 541].

The trend of metropolitan planning had become all too clear. Parks, highways, and middle-class residential expansion were the order of the day. The housing question and social reform were left to the gentle ministrations of the market system.

3. Government reform

The last important aspect of metropolitan planning was a quest to reform urban government. It had two principal themes: 'de-politicizing ration' of personnel and procedures of local government and expanding the geo-

graphic boundaries of the city in order to reflect the new realities of metropolitan growth.

The first notion, ending 'boss rule' and professionalizing city official-
dom, was primarily the product of Progressive reform and the Muck-
rakers.[11] Its two characteristic institutional manifestations were the
council-manager form of municipal government and the city planning
commission. These were meant to elevate public affairs above the corrupt
domain of local politics.[12]

It is too far off course to go into the details of governmental reorganization; the basic ideas, however, behind the proposed
changes were straightforward.[13] Official channels of decision making were
to be rerouted from the traditional political hierarchy to a council of peers,
typically elected by popular vote from the city at large. The day-to-day
affairs of government were to be run by a professional manager above
the fray of politics. Recommendations concerning the physical development of the city were to be made a public function, but removed
entirely from the political arena and placed in the hands of a lay city-
planning commission. The commission's main task was the preparation
of a plan, modelled on the privately sponsored metropolitan plans discussed in the last section. Subsequent decisions pertaining to land development were viewed as a matter of technical interpretation of the intentions
of the plan. Similarly, general government expenditures were to be
handled through preparation of a municipal budget, which would make
the allocation of the city's funds among different functions and projects
primarily an exercise in technical judgment. It is here, with the subject
of metropolitan budgeting and the territorial expansion of municipal jurisdiction, that Charles E. Merriam enters the picture.

Along with Thomas H. Reed of the University of Michigan, Merriam
was one of the first American proponents of metropolitan government.
A political scientist at the University of Chicago, his interest in
metropolitan planning stemmed from a desire to rationalize the collection and expenditure of municipal revenues. His interests soon broadened,
however, to encompass the general field of intergovernmental relations,
and for six years he learned about the practical problems of city government as a member of the Chicago city council. Merriam's concern for
local governmental consolidation continued through the 1920s, and at
the end of the decade he served as a member of Hoover's Committee
on Recent Social Trends in the United States. This, along with his lengthy
experience as director of the Chicago Regional Planning Association,
made him a logical choice for membership on the National Planning
Board. He stayed with the board throughout its ten-year history and
played a major role in shaping its conception of regional planning.

Probably the best way to summarize the views on metropolitan planning
which Merriam brought with him to Washington in 1933 is to quote from
his preface to *The Government of the Metropolitan Region of Chicago* (Merriam
et al., 1933)[14] In describing the important themes of this book – part of a

larger research effort by the Social Science Research Committee of the University of Chicago – Merriam said:

> ... the special features of this discussion are as follows: (1) considera-
> tion of the governmental possibilities of the Region as a whole;
> (2) emphasis on the actual functioning of public agencies within the
> Area ... (3) emphasis on the principle of interlocking directorates
> as a means of obtaining consolidation; (4) attention to the importance
> of interstate agreements as a basis of regional organization; (5) dis-
> cussion of the possibilities of independent statehood as a means of
> metropolitan development; [and] (6) development of a system of
> central fiscal control over local governments without establishment
> of a new unit of government.

It is evident that Merriam had faith in the metropolis, as well as belief in a relatively high degree of governmental centralization. For him, metro-politan regionalism was a practical response to the fiscal and jurisdictional problems brought on by urban-industrialization.

The theory of metropolitan growth

Largely as a response to metropolitan planning, social scientists began searching for an explanation of metropolitan growth patterns. This was undoubtedly one of the major sociological contributions to the field of urban studies. Its early advocates came to be known as the 'Chicago school of urban ecology', and their ideas had a direct influence on the work of the National Planning Board during the 1930s.

Charles Horton Cooley of the University of Michigan was the most immediate predecessor of urban ecology. He took the view that society was best understood as an organic whole, and felt that the location of cities was primarily a function of transport facilities. (Not surprisingly, his ideas also influenced Lewis Mumford and the RPAA.) Urban ecolo-gists, like Cooley and many of his contemporaries, were deeply impressed with the notion of an organically integrated society. Unlike Veblen and Mumford, however, they applied the organic metaphor to the study of the metropolis. For them, ecological relations in an urban environment were for the most part reduced to a matter of the spatial interactions among various groups and activities, since most of the features of the natural habitat had already been eliminated by human intervention (McKenzie, 1924 and 1926).

The best known of the urban ecologists were Robert E. Park, who came to the University of Chicago as a young man in the fall of 1914, Park's student, Roderick D. McKenzie, and an early colleague of McKenzie at Ohio State University, Ernest W. Burgess, who later joined the staff at Chicago. Another Chicago sociologist who worked within the human ecology tradition was Louis Wirth. It was Wirth who had probably the longest and most intimate association with metropolitan planning, and who made a major contribution to the report of the National Resources Committee on the role of cities in the national economy.

The group's most important publications were Park, Burgess and McKenzie, *The City* (1925); Burgess, *The Urban Community* (1926); and McKenzie, 'The Rise of Metropolitan Communities' (1933). In these three works the authors developed the concept of human ecology as a separate discipline and the notion of the metropolis as the natural organic form of industrial civilization. They also argued for the concept of the neighbourhood unit or 'natural area' as the ecological building-block of the metropolitan community, as well as the idea of 'mobility' as the energizing force behind metropolitan expansion. The limits of metropolitan growth were thought to be a product of cyclical expansion, decay and rejuvenation, and could be little altered by the dictates of politicians or planners. In general, their work supported the proposition that metropolitan planning could function only as a watchdog to guide the 'natural' tendencies of urban-industrial expansion.[15]

The essence of their attitude towards planning is best captured in this early quote from Robert Park, the founder of the urban ecology approach:

It is because the city has a life quite its own that there is a limit to the arbitrary modifications which it is possible to make (1) in its physical structure and (2) in its moral order.

The city plan, for example, establishes metes and bounds, fixes in a general way the location and character of the city's constructions, and imposes an orderly arrangement, within the city area, upon the buildings which are erected by private initiative as well as by public authority. Within the limitations prescribed, however, the inevitable processes of human nature proceed to give these regions and these buildings a character which it is less easy to control. Under our system of individual ownership, for instance, it is not possible to determine in advance the extent of concentration of population which is likely to occur in any given area. The city cannot fix land values, and we leave to private enterprise, for the most part, the task of determining the city's limits and the location of its residential and industrial districts. Personal tastes and convenience, vocational and economic interests, infallibly tend to segregate and thus to classify the populations of great cities. In this way the city acquires an organization and distribution of population which is neither designed nor controlled [Park *et al.*, 1925, pp. 4–5].

Louis Wirth adopted a more activist stance towards metropolitan planning, but his ideas remained well within the bounds of ecological theory. At the 1942 National Conference on Planning, Wirth played an important role in discussing 'the metropolitan district as a planning unit'. In his argument, which we summarize below, his preference for dealing with the metropolitan region as a natural, inviolable unit comes across clearly:

> One of the first problems which confronts the planner is the delineation of the area to be planned.... It is a good rule here as elsewhere to start with the ideal of approximating the total situation.... Whatever else the city may be, in our kind of civilization it is first and foremost a human settlement resting upon an economic base with more or less widespread economic ramifications. If the planner therefore would delineate his planning area in such a way as to conform as nearly as possible with the definition of the region as an economic unit, he must take account of the interaction between the city and the outside world.... It is not the planners who have invented the new leviathan. But it is for the planners to recognize the actuality of the new leviathan that has been created by the economic, social and political forces of our time [Wirth, 1942, pp. 49–50].

Wirth's views echoed precisely the position taken by metropolitan planners from Burnham to Adams. And, characteristically, he held a much less positive attitude towards the broader notions of regionalism and regional planning espoused by Odum and Mumford. Although he clearly recognized the need for large-scale administrative districts, the concept of a 'natural' regional unit, larger than the metropolis, struck him as an idea of limited utility. Reviewing the regionalization schemes of the National Resources Committee during the previous decade, he warned: 'The best we can do is to make the most reasonable compromises we can invent.... It would be self-deceptive, however, to proceed as if the crude approximations we now make to an adequate regional arrangement were anything more than improvisations' (Wirth, 1951, p. 389). In summary, Wirth admonished: 'Regionalism as a dogma can easily degenerate into a cult' (*ibid.*, p. 392).

Without attempting to overplay the contrast, the very aspects of metropolitan growth which alarmed Mumford and the early housing reformers were seen as natural processes by Park and his followers. Inter-group competition was the ecologists' central hypothesis, and the industrial metropolis was the temporally dominant expression of that struggle. Invasion/succession, a set of concepts borrowed from plant ecology, described the process by which different 'natural' vocational groups and land uses replaced one another in the evolution of the city. Land values established by accessibility and land speculation were thought to be the *normal* ecological mechanisms by which location within the metropolis was determined. The available means of transportation and the vitality and breadth of the city's economic base set the bounds of metropolitan growth.

In his famous 1923 monograph Burgess attempted to model this process, based on his investigations of Chicago. Burgess argued that while earlier authors, such as Adna Weber (1899), had adequately described the process of urban *aggregation,* no one had given a theoretical explanation of the physical expansion of cities. He gave city planning and regional survey groups, like those then at work in New York and Chicago, credit for practical investigations of the problem and noted that it was in part for the benefit of regional planners that a proper theory of metropolitan growth was needed.

Burgess's original sketch is reproduced in Fig. 3.1.

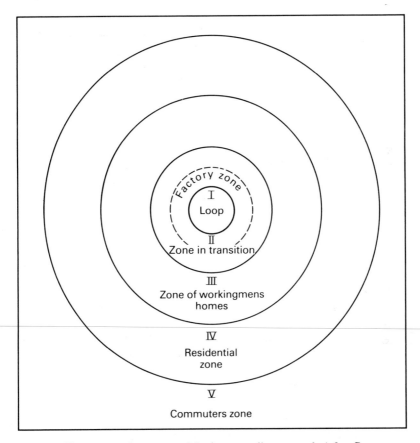

Figure 3.1   The concentric zone model of metropolitan growth (after Burgess, 1923, 1925, p. 51).

His own description of the model is probably still the most concise:

This chart represents an ideal construction of the tendencies of any town or city to expand radially from its central business district – on the map 'The Loop' (I). Encircling the downtown area there is normally an area in transition, which is being invaded by business and light manufacture (II). A third area (III) is inhabited by the workers in industries who have escaped from the area of deterioration (II) but who desire to live within easy access of their work. Beyond this zone is the 'residential area' (IV) of high-class apartment build-ings or of exclusive 'restricted' districts of single family dwellings. Still farther, out beyond the city limits, is the commuters' zone – suburban areas, or satellite cities – within a thirty- to sixty-minute ride of the central business district [Park *et al.*, 1925, p. 50].

In the model, expansion takes place through a process of disorganiza-tion and organization, in which the innermost zones invade the outlying ones, in a continuous cycle of extension and retreat. 'Mobility' is the mechanism which brings about the expansion of the city and, through the invasion/succession process, individuals and groups are sorted and relocated.

This differentiation into natural economic and cultural groupings gives form and character to the city. For segregation offers the group, and thereby the individuals who compose the group, a place and a role in the total organization of city life. Segregation limits development in certain directions, but releases it in others. These areas tend to accentuate certain traits, to attract and develop their kind of individuals, and so to become further differentiated [*ibid.*, p. 56].

Burgess's concentric zone model came in for much criticism which stressed his failure sufficiently to take into account the apparent tendency for various land-use areas to expand radially along major transport routes. Two other classic models of urban expansion were proposed to make up for the deficiencies of the concentric zone theory. They are shown in Figure 3.2.

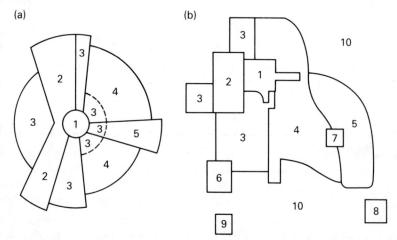

Figure 3.2 (A)   Hoyt's sector theory of urban growth; **(B)** Harris and Ullman's multiple nuclei theory of urban growth (after Dickinson, 1964, p. 128). The numbered districts represent: 1. Central business district. 2. Wholesale light manufacturing. 3. Low class residential. 4. Medium-class residential. 5. High-class residential. 6. Heavy manufacturing. 7. Outlying business district. 8. Residential suburb. 9. Industrial suburb. 10. Commuter zone.

The first of these, Homer Hoyt's 'sector theory' of urban growth, appeared in 1939. It was the product of an intensive study for the United States Federal Housing Administration. As can be seen in Figure 3.2(A), Hoyt accepted Burgess's contention that the city spreads outward in concentric zones from the central business district, but he stressed that 'growth along a particular axis of transportation usually consists of similar types of land use' (Harris and Ullman, 1945, p. 13). This was thought to be especially true for residential development, and it was argued that the axial trend of development for the whole city was determined by the direction of movement of upper-class residential areas.

The last of these seminal theories (Figure 32.2(B)), was suggested by two geographers, Chauncy D. Harris and Edward L. Ullman, in 1945. Like Burgess, they had based their model on empirical observation of Chicago. Its major innovation was that it acknowledged the fact that large metropolitan areas tend to be conurbations which have grown up around several different centres or nuclei. They presented the 'multiple nuclei' theory as a hybrid of the two earlier models, but, in fact, the growth patterns portrayed were not dissimilar from the result that might be expected from an overlapping series of Burgess's concentric zones. In his monumental study, *City and Region* (1964), Dickinson concluded that:

> It should be noted that the latter two interpretations [the sector theory and the multiple nuclei] theory do not refute, but rather modify, the concentric zone hypothesis. Residential areas, according to Hoyt, expand outwards concentrically by sectors. The same forces presumably operate in varying degree from the various lesser nuclei in the urban areas discussed by Harris as well as from a central point of origin [p. 130].

> ... refinement of the conception of the 'natural area' of the sociologists ... does not refute the concentric zone hypothesis of Burgess, which is the most comprehensive of these hypotheses and is the one that has received the most critical attention. Studies of European and American cities, from the standpoint of their historical development, the density of built-up land, and the movements of population, substantiate this general theory [p. 131].

What the Chicago school of urban ecology and its successors had produced was a simple descriptive model of metropolitan growth under American capitalism. Interestingly enough, the underlying structural relationships which they recognized as the fundamental causes of this physical expansion, the division of social labour and the market economy, were the same factors identified by Engels nearly a century before. But the valuation they gave to these factors was very different.

The ecologists' models of urban growth reinforced and legitimized the contentions of metropolitan planners, providing scientific 'proof' that metropolitan (physical) expansion was inevitable. When used as normative models for the development of human communities, social ecology was set in direct opposition to the equally 'ecological' precepts of Mumford and Odum. Both lines of theory embraced an organically-delineated territorial unit, but the metropolitan vision of Park and his disciples tended to justify the functional integration of national economic space, while the regional approaches of Odum and Mumford explicitly opposed it.

It was the enthusiastic celebration of 'The Rise of Metropolitan Communities', written by McKenzie in 1933 as part of the report of the President's Research Committee on Social Trends, that helped promote a metropolitan perspective within the newly formed National Planning Board. McKenzie's article made a thorough survey of the metropolitan transformation of American life, and presented the rise of the metropolis as a signal of progress. This authoritative assessment, along with the personal metropolitan planning experiences of NPB members Merriam and Delano, helped to create the confrontation between *functional* and *territorial* views of regionalism from which the first doctrine of regional planning would be forged.

The National Planning Board and its successors

Soon after the inception of the National Planning Board in July 1933, Roosevelt encouraged its three members to broaden their responsibilities from merely programming public works projects to the co-ordination of all government public works affecting natural resources (Graham, 1976, p. 52). Later this led to research and long-range planning in such varied fields as consumer incomes, job security and technological assessment. The NPB's suggestions for a comprehensive programme in the areas of education, health, old-age insurance, and unemployment were to become a primary source of ideas for the famous Beveridge Plan in the United Kingdom (Merriam, 1944, p. 1083).

It is our purpose here to review only those elements of the Board's work which directly affected the formulation of regional planning doctrine. Their most relevant fields of investigation were: (1) resource development, (2) regionalism, and (3) urbanism.

The Planning Board's several changes in name and organization[16] occurred primarily as a result of the manoeuvring between Roosevelt and the legislature, following a joint resolution by Congress in early 1934 which asked the President to prepare a comprehensive plan for the development of the country's rivers. Roosevelt responded enthusiastically to the Congressional mandate, replying that such a plan:

> would put the physical development of the country on a planned basis for the first time ... and would include ... flood control, soil erosion, the question of submarginal land, reforestation, agriculture and the use of the crops, decentralization of industry, and finally, transportation, and water power ... [Graham, 1976, p. 53].

This turn of events, along with the evolution of the Tennessee Valley Authority and the traditional federal responsibility for interstate navigation, created an almost fortuitous association between planning, resource development and river basin management which was to have a profound impact on regional planning throughout the world.

1. Resource development

After an initial abortive attempt to produce the required 'comprehensive plan for the development of the nation's rivers' through normal departmental channels, Roosevelt, almost instinctively, turned to the NPB for help. While the resulting document, known subsequently as 'A Plan for Planning' (NPB, *Final Report*, 1933–4), in fact failed to blueprint an approach to comprehensive development of the country's water resources, it did set out the framework for an ongoing process of national planning and revealed the ideological tenor of the Board's economic theorizing.[17]

The 'Plan for Planning' was an eclectic document, containing several important elements. First, the report surveyed the vast array of local, state and regional planning activities already underway in the United States, quite obviously trying to 'legitimize' planning in the American context. As part of this task, maps and listings were compiled which were intended to make a striking impression on the reader, and special attention was paid to the role of state and multi-state (regional) planning efforts in the development of natural resources.

In this connection, two important points were made. The first was an appeal for co-ordination of all sub-national planning activities by a national planning agency which could act as a clearing-house and provide help 'through circulars and bulletins ·on standards, procedure and experience. . . .' (p. 7). Second, the careful distinction, formerly maintained by theoreticians, between regional and metropolitan planning was permanently, if somewhat ambiguously, abandoned. Figure 3.3, taken from the Board's report, shows that metropolitan planning commissions, such as those in Los Angeles, Chicago and St Louis, were portrayed as equivalent to broader regional undertakings like the Tennessee Valley Authority. A desire to promote large-scale planning organizations quickly took precedence over critical evaluation of the probable substantive direction of their work.

Another major section of the report reviewed federal agencies involved in the planning and development of natural resources. After ten pages of confusing tables, the conclusion was reached that: 'There is an obvious need for co-ordination of these activities. None of the co-ordinating agencies described has either the powers or the resources for surveying the national scene as a whole and for discerning how it is shifting and what are the forces which may be harnessed to give it direction' (p. 84).

Next, turning to the private sector, and giving a clear portrayal of the NPB's collectivist and institutionalist leanings, the Board wrote:

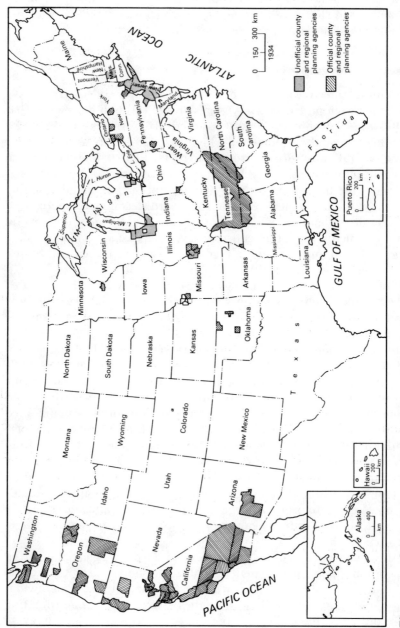

Figure 3.3 County and regional planning agencies in the United States, 1934 (source: National Planning Board, 1933–4, p. 6).

... practical experience has demonstrated that, great as are its contributions to social welfare, business planning has certain inherent limitations that are making it more and more necessary to improve planning in household management on the one side and planning in Government activities on the other.

(1) Business planning can secure effective coordination of effort only within the limits of each independent business enterprise; that is each group of business activities subject to a single financial control....

(2) The planning of business enterprises aims at making money. If the ultimate test of economic efficiency is that of satisfying the most important social needs in the most economical manner, then business planning must be warped by inequality in the distribution of income ... [and]

(3) From the viewpoint of business itself, planning to make money is a precarious undertaking that often ends in heavy losses or financial ruin.... However skillfully the internal affairs of a corporation are managed, the whole venture may be wrecked by circumstances beyond the control and even beyond the knowledge of the managers [pp. 21–2].

They went on to observe that, even given the efforts of the new National Recovery Administration (NRA) and Agricultural Adjustment Administration (AAA) to co-ordinate inter-industry production with intermediate and final demand, further co-ordination was sorely needed. Without getting into the complicated political histories of these two short-lived New Deal experiments in economic planning, it is safe to accept the Board's view that there was little co-ordination between federal planning for secondary industry and for agriculture. And in the case of agriculture, the status of the AAA, independent of the traditional United States Department of Agriculture made problems even worse.

In a grand finale, the Board exhorted that all the problems it had identified could, in fact, be overcome:

The weakness of our American planning in the past has been the failure to bring the various plans and planners, public and private, into some form of concert with one another, to develop public interest planning in concert with planning in the private interest. The plans of business, the plans of science and technology, the plans of social welfare, the plans of government, have not heretofore been alined [sic] in such manner as to promote the general welfare in the highest degree attainable. Much of the unbalance, insecurity, and suffering, which our country had experienced in the past might be avoided in future by a more perfect co-ordination of the knowledge which we already possess [p. 22].

Its recommendation was for the federal government to 'create a permanent National Planning Board, directly responsible to the country's Chief Executive' (p. 35). Such a planning board

> might facilitate the interchange of experience and information regarding a wide variety of planning devices in many lines and on many levels....
>
> Standing apart from political and administrative power and responsibility, but in close touch with the Chief Executive. and under the control of the political powers that be, such a group of men would have large opportunity for rumination and reflection upon national trends, emerging problems and possibilities, and might well contribute to those in responsible control, facts, interpretations, and suggestions of far-reaching significance [p. 38].[18]

The report then spent over twenty pages explaining how the sciences, and especially the social sciences, would contribute to the success of such a national planning agency. This may represent one of the first official calls for planning to be considered as an applied social science.

We need to make one further observation about the 'Plan for Planning', which is of crucial significance for the later evolution of regional doctrine. Of all the various planning and development mechanisms analysed by the Board – and the list was considerably longer than the topics included in this summary – the agency which seemed particularly to catch the NPB's attention was the Tennessee Valley Authority. One explanation may be that the TVA was operating in the functional area most closely related to the Board's assigned area of investigation. But the reasons seem to go deeper than that.

While Chapter 7 of the report, dealing with the TVA, was less than two pages long, it was singularly devoid of the glossy generalizations which typified so much of the rest of the document. The analysis of TVA's central organizational conflicts, between its specific tasks such as electric power generation and its more general aspirations as an agency for comprehensive river basin development, were clearly perceived. Yet, in fairly straightforward institutionalist language, the Valley Authority was presented as a valuable model for further experimentation in regional planning, a model which 'dealt with large social issues, some of which involve substantial modifications of the existing institutional structure of the country' (p. 93).

It is useful to quote a part of the Board's incisive evaluation:

> There is a broad technical integration of the specific tasks assigned to TVA, which have raised fundamental issues of social policy and have involved planning on a scale unusual in the United States. To begin with the effort to set up a well managed, low-cost, self-supporting system of power production necessitates the integrated development of the Tennessee River. The prevention of soil erosion is necessary to prevent the dams from silting up within a century.

But erosion is a problem in its own right. To prevent it, a programme of afforestation and public works must be undertaken, and large areas must be turned from plough crops to grass. This cannot be done without experimental work in the development of phosphate fertilizers. To further this transformation and to develop the agricultural potential of the region, provision has been made for encouraging the co-operative movement. To find a market for the potential power has involved lowering the selling price of power for domestic use and the lowering of the price of electric appliances through the Electric Home and Farm Authority [p. 93].

The NPB hardly visualized in 1934 that it would eventually be necessary to undertake a massive programme of urban-industrialization to find outlets for the TVA's ever-increasing hydro-electric output. But they undeniably saw the TVA model as the first practical example of regional development.

2. Regionalism

By 1935, the National Planning Board had become the National Resources Committee, and it was during this period (1935–9) that the Committee made its most important contributions to regional planning. Besides technical and financial support for numerous state, regional and metropolitan planning organizations, the Committee produced two publications which left an indelible imprint. The first of these was a single volume released in December 1935, entitled *The Regional Factors in National Planning*. The second was a series of ten volumes called *Regional Planning*, which consisted of individual regional studies supported by the NRC.

a. *Regional Factors in National Planning* was a separate research report, prepared by the NRC's Technical Committee on Regional Planning, under the chairmanship of John M. Gaus of the University of Wisconsin. Including contributions by many of the distinguished 'regional scientists' of the period, it came to represent the NRC's theoretical statement on regionalism and regional planning.

The report was made up of eight related studies, the majority of which focused on river basin development.[19] With the exception of two sections covering metropolitan planning and the regionalization of federal administrative programmes, the rest of the document clearly espoused concepts similar to those enunciated by the RPAA and Howard Odum. Odum's ideas were frequently referred to, with regional planning, in its ideal form, defined as the development of natural resources within the context of historically defined cultural areas. In the Committee's own words: 'It is patent ... that the whole meaning of regional planning is to devise a cultural pattern which will fit a large cultural areal unit, and that the qualities inherent in the area not only dictate in large part the features of the plan but also its territorial extent' (p. 20). They went on to admit, however, that, 'In the majority of instances ... water resource development in some form or another has provided the urge for large-scale programming,' although, 'when all factors are considered, river basins [as physically bounded regions] are in many instances but little better than states [as politically bounded regions] for the purposes of planning and development' (p. 21). The Committee recognized that the problems of planned land use, industrial location and electrical power distribution were not typically defined by such artificial territorial units.

As in many concrete situations, however, the NRC was obliged to compromise the purity of its theoretical ideal. In this case, it felt compelled to commit itself, *de facto*, to the doctrine of comprehensive river basin development. This happened for two reasons. First, in the American federal system if there was to be a nationally sponsored programme of regional resource development, it had to be justified constitutionally on accepted principles of federal intervention in 'state' affairs. An emphasis on river basin development provided the core of such a justification, with many historical precedents, related to interstate commerce, navigation, and flood control on the major rivers. Secondly, and perhaps most important in this particular instance, river basin developments of one type or another were already successfully underway in several parts of the country.

The bulk of *Regional Factors in National Planning* described four prominent examples of regional planning on the river basin model. These undertakings varied widely in scope, but all had a common focus on resource development within areas roughly defined on the basis of physical watersheds. The first was the Colorado River Basin Compact, which directly involved six states in the United States, and indirectly involved Mexico and several Indian tribes. The real impetus for the compact was competition over who would benefit from the waters of the Colorado River, and the most important outcome of the project was the building of Boulder Dam.

For its second, and most important example of river basin development, the NRC looked to the Tennessee Valley Authority. However, since the TVA is discussed in some detail later in this chapter, we will not treat it here. Federally sponsored regional planning commissions in New England and the Pacific Northwest were the other illustrations given in the report. Although the New England Regional Commission had a long independent history, starting with the New England Regional Planning League in 1929, and then the New England Council, the NRC report emphasized, rather naturally, the regional commission's contemporary interests in resource development and its report on the Connecticut River watershed.[20] The Pacific Northwest Regional Planning Commission will be dealt with below in the discussion of *Regional Planning*.

Publication of *Regional Factors in National Development* marked a crucial turning point in American regional planning; it played a key role in crystallizing planning doctrine. While encompassing many contradictory ideas, regional planning could no longer be considered a nebulous concept in official government circles. It had undeniably become associated with comprehensive river basin development.

b. In contrast to the preceding volume, the series of publications called *Regional Planning* was a group of actual planning studies. They were important chiefly for their publicity value, demonstrating the NRC's vision of planned regional development in a number of different American settings. A striking anomaly was an alternating concern for regional and metropolitan problems in the same series of publications. A brief discussion of Parts 1 and 2 of the ten-part study will suffice to demonstrate this pattern.

Part 1, released in May 1936, dealt with the Pacific Northwest.[21] It was primarily a regional resource survey, containing a summary of regional development potentials and an outline of the area's organization for planning. In the report's recommendations to the National Resources Committee it concentrated on raw materials and industrial development, forest and water resources, power generation, and future uses of electrical power. The last two topics were the real kernel of the report, for the main body of the document consisted of the regional commission's *Columbia Basin Study*, requested by the NRC in July 1935.

The true reason for the formation of the regional commission had been a federal decision to construct two great dams on the Columbia River, the Bonneville and the Grand Coulee, and Washington now wanted state governments in the area to prepare themselves to confront the new situation. Unlike the TVA, no separate basin-wide development corporation had been established, so it was left in large part to state and local governments in the region to cope with the undertaking themselves.

Washington's intentions had been to use the dams to provide work relief for the unemployed, water for irrigation, and 2.5 million kilowatts of electric power for rural electrification and industrial purposes. And that is exactly what the regional commission's report reflected. It defined the Pacific Northwest region as the Columbia Basin and went on to outline a scheme for electric power generation and industrialization. Regional planning, under an ever-strengthening federal government, was quickly eluding the somewhat anarchistic visions of Mumford and Odum. Territorialist worries about erosion control, an end to flooding, resource conservation, and rural electrification were there, to be sure, but the preservation of rural folkways and ecological settlement patterns was yielding to the imperatives of urban-industrialization. Nationally sponsored regional planning was reproducing the functional system of which it was a part. River basin development was not transforming metropolitan America; it was expanding it.

Part 2 of *Regional Planning* was concerned with the metropolitan region of St Louis. The NRC's interest in the area was the city's interstate setting on the Mississippi River and the need to identify appropriate locations for public works projects. Very little distinguishes the report itself. Prepared by Harland Bartholomew, after his internship on the *Regional Plan for New York and Its Environs*, it was a mini-version of that *magnum opus*. In summary form, its recommendations to the NRC were:

1. *Continuous Regional Planning*: A continuing regional or interstate advisory planning activity and planning organization for the St Louis Region should be provided through co-operation of planning agencies of the cities, counties, and two States, and with the assistance of Federal officials in the area.

2. *A Regional Agency*: In order that construction and development of appropriate facilities may be provided and in order that abuses of resources which affect the whole or more than one State in the region may be prevented, the advantages and utility of a regional agency established by the acts of Legislatures of Illinois and Missouri with Federal participation and Federal consent to an interstate compact, be called to the attention of the State and Federal authorities [p. viii].

One noteworthy point, whether of primarily empirical or theoretical origins, was that projections of growth for the St Louis area, in terms of population, land use and public facilities, tended to conform to Hoyt's sector theory of metropolitan growth, discussed earlier in this chapter.

The implications of *Regional Planning* for the evolution of planning doctrine were two-fold. First, river basin development had, indeed, become the primary focus of regional policy. And, second, the anti-metropolitan ideas of Howard Odum and the RPAA had been all but purged from the concept of regionalism. Urban-industrialization was a legitimate goal of comprehensive river basin development.

3. Urbanism

Our Cities: Their Role in the National Economy appeared in June 1937 as the report of the Urbanism Committee of the NRC. It was the National Resources Committee's principal statement on metropolitan growth and built largely on the earlier work of the Chicago school of urban ecology and the writings of Charles Merriam. In fact, the Urbanism Committee's debt to Chicago sources was so profound that it made a special acknowledgment 'to the Social Science Research Committee of the University of Chicago for financial contribution, technical assistance, and use of facilities in producing most of the studies dealing with the social and certain governmental aspects of urbanization and urban life ...' (p. 86).

The Committee's staff was made up largely of metropolitan planners and other urban specialists. The study group on urban government was headed by Albert Lepawsky, a student of Merriam, while the more 'ecological' elements of the report were prepared under the supervision of Louis Wirth. In many ways, *Our Cities* was an expansion of McKenzie's famous study four years earlier, 'The Rise of Metropolitan Communities'. Yet from another perspective, it contained several striking features, often discussing themes destined for much greater prominence in later decades.

As the report's title suggested, the emphasis of *Our Cities* was on the role of the urban system in the national economy. The first two-thirds of the report was a documentary on the growth of cities in the United States and the integration of the American urban system, anticipating the emphasis of a later regional planning doctrine by some twenty years (see chapter 4). After an enumeration of urban 'problems', the Committee turned to the four main themes of metropolitan planning, discussed earlier in this chapter, and transformed them by a rather unfashionable assumption.

Because of the marked slowing down of our population growth, the Committee recommends that all national and local policies, public and private, pertaining to cities, which have proceeded on the expectation of continuous and unlimited growth, be re-examined in the light of this approaching stabilization of our population [p. 74, italics in the original].

Given this novel steady-state interpretation, several of the Committee's central recommendations seem very contemporary and progressive:

The concentration of so large a proportion of the urban population in extremely limited areas is wasteful of resources, time, and energy. The same would be true of undue dispersion. The Committee believes that the most desirable environment for the urban dweller and for the effective use of human and material resources is more likely to be found somewhere between these two extremes [p. 84].

More radically, they went on to urge:

If private enterprise cannot or does not solve the problem of submarginal communities, then Government should supplement in appropriate cases the local resources or opportunities for employment, as it is doing in the case of depressed rural areas, in order to raise the standard of life in these urban communities to an acceptable minimum. Where, because of a disappearing economic base, the conditions seem to be chronic and appear to offer no promise of self-support at an acceptable minimum standard, the reorganization of the community or a programme of resettlement will have to be undertaken jointly by the several governmental units involved [p. 73, italics in the original].

This last idea, resettlement of the 'submarginal' urban population, was one of the report's most striking features, and leads us to consider another New Deal experiment, the Resettlement Administration.

The Resettlement Administration

Rexford Tugwell was the instigator and sole administrator of the Resettlement Administration, another of the separate 'alphabet' agencies, set up by special executive order in April 1935. In its short eighteen-month life span, the RA made two significant contributions to planning doctrine. First, its Greenbelt New Towns programme, which was in operation during the same period that the Urbanism Committee was writing its report, obviously helped mould the Committee's concept of urban resettlement and its utility in metropolitan planning. Second, by mixing purposeful metropolitan expansion with broader land use and rural conservation measures, the agency helped to give credence to a model of regionalism which endorsed both resource development and urban growth.

The Resettlement Administration, an amalgam of New Deal programmes which had been scattered throughout different governmental agencies, was made up of four main divisions: Suburban Resettlement, Rural Rehabilitation, Land Utilization and Rural Resettlement. These last three branches were concerned with technical assistance to poor farmers, retiring submarginal agricultural land, and, where appropriate, resettling rural families in new, more productive locations.

Rural resettlement, which occurred mainly in the South, often took the form of co-operative agricultural villages, and drew heavy criticism from conservatives for its collectivist tendencies.

Tugwell, following Veblen's technological interpretation of history, felt that the land utilization and suburban resettlement activities of the RA were the most important. As we saw in chapter 2, technological advances were driving farmers off the land. Tugwell believed that the only hope for the unemployed, in both rural and urban areas, was an orderly, planned expansion of the metropolis (Myhra, 1974; Sternsher, 1964; Conkin, 1959). In the cities, with proper planning, people could find decent housing and jobs.

The RA, through its Suburban Resettlement Division, set out to demonstrate how a co-ordinated programme of metropolitan, regional and economic planning could come to grips with the worst ravages of the Great Depression. Satellite towns, in the commuter zone of the Burgess model, were to provide an amenable living environment, from which workers could commute to industrial jobs in the central city.[22] Industrial recovery and growth were, of course, prerequisites for the viability of Tugwell's scheme, but, in fact, these were his very motives. In 1936, he wrote:

> In the strictest sense, the Resettlement Administration is not in the housing field at all. It is building houses, true, but its considerations go beyond the fact, important as that fact is, that millions of Americans need new homes if a minimum standard of decency is to be attained. What the Resettlement Administration is trying to do is to put houses and land and people together in such a way that props under our economic and social structure will be permanently strengthened [Tugwell, 1936, p. 28; quoted in Myhra, 1974, p. 177].

In the end, the RA built only three Greenbelt New Towns: Greenbelt, Maryland; Greenhills, Ohio; and Greendale, Wisconsin. (Subsequently these communities have become integral parts, respectively, of the Washington, Cincinnati, and Milwaukee SMSAs). Plans for another Greenbelt town near St Louis were dropped because of opposition from the St Louis Plans Commission. In a final legal controversy over construction of a fifth satellite community in New Brunswick Township, New Jersey, the entire Greenbelt programme was declared unconstitutional by the US District Court of Appeals. As with other New Deal experiments, like the National Recovery Administration, institutional economics and *laissez-faire* interpretations of the US Constitution found little common ground.

The Resettlement Administration experience clearly demonstrated the ambiguity among regional planners as to their proper role in rebuilding American society. Four members of the Regional Planning Association of America – Henry Wright, Clarence Stein, Tracy Augur and Catherine Bauer – advocates of ecological balance, biotechnics and regional communities, found themselves playing active roles in planning Tugwell's Greenbelt towns: purposive extensions of the metropolis. Even twenty years later, Clarence Stein declared that the Greenbelt Towns, along with the Tennessee Valley Authority, were the only two New Deal experiments which were not, in fact, 'boondoggles' (Stein, 1957, p. 119).[23]

The TVA and comprehensive river basin development

Finally we come to the most famous of the New Deal regional planning experiments, the project which brought comprehensive river basin development serious international attention. Like the river basin doctrine itself, formation of the Tennessee Valley Authority was almost a chance occurrence – the product of several disparate events and attitudes, unique to the American scene of the period.

1. From munitions plant to planning agency

During World War I the federal government had built two explosive plants at Muscle Shoals, Alabama. A large dam was constructed at the site, on the Tennessee River, to supply the necessary electricity for nitrate production. It was originally intended that after the war the facilities should be used to manufacture fertilizer. This proved to be a difficult ideological issue, however, because Congress found itself forced to decide who was to own and operate the dam and fertilizer plants. Should it be the government, which had built them and held title to the land, or should it be private industry, that had traditionally controlled all productive facilities in the country? During the 1920s, with Republican administrations in Washington and business in its 'Golden Age', the question was unsolvable.

For Progressives, Muscle Shoals, became a *cause célèbre*. Gathering behind Senator George Norris of Nebraska, Chairman of the Senate Committee on Agriculture and Forestry, which had jurisdiction over the facilities, they proposed formation of a public corporation to operate Muscle Shoals. There were really three popular issues at stake. Foremost was the idea of breaking the monopoly position of private utility companies in the field of electric power generation. At that time a group of powerful holding companies, led by the Insull Group, literally dominated the country's energy industry, fixing prices and quashing all competition. Liberals felt that government entry into this arena could change matters.

A related question dealt with rural electrification. Various reform groups, such as the Regional Planning Association of America, felt that wide distribution of electrical power in outlying areas would lead to a real transformation of rural life. Given the exhorbitant rates charged by private industry, and the immensity of the task itself, they argued that this was obviously a sphere for government intervention.

Finally there was the matter of fertilizer production. The overworked lands of the Tennessee Valley were badly in need of revitalization and more considerate management. As Howard Odum had argued, poor land makes poor people. Norris and others believed that a publicly sponsored programme of fertilizer production and agricultural experimentation could help change the plight of poverty stricken farmers, and that a 'Muscle Shoals Corporation of the United States' was the proper solution.

Twice, in 1928 and 1931, legislation found its way to the White House which would have re-initiated government operation of the Muscle Shoals facilities. But both times the bills were vetoed by business-oriented Republican presidents.

In 1932 everything changed. With Franklin Roosevelt in the executive seat and the depression deepening every day, some kind of positive resolution of the question was assured. Roosevelt's vision for the Tennessee Valley, however, was significantly broader than the earlier Norris proposals. Drawing on his enthusiasm for planning and rural reform, he expanded the Muscle Shoals project into a programme of comprehensive river basin development. He declared:

> It is clear that the Muscle Shoals development is but a small part of the potential public usefulness of the entire Tennessee River. Such use, if envisioned in its entirety, transcends mere power development; it enters the wide fields of flood control, soil erosion, afforestation, elimination from agricultural use of marginal lands, and distribution and diversification of industry. In short, this power development of war days leads logically to national planning for a complete river watershed involving many States and the future lives and welfare of millions [Roosevelt, 1938, p. 122; quoted in Derthick, 1974, p. 20].

The Tennessee Valley Authority Act, passed in May 1933, contained provisions which provided a legal basis for undertaking the broad tasks Roosevelt had outlined. Section 22 of the Act gave the president power to make 'general plans' for the entire river basin, and Section 23 instructed him to recommend legislation: 'to realize a wide range of public purposes in the valley, including flood control, navigation, generation of electric power, proper use of marginal lands, reforestation, and "the economic and social well-being of the people"' (Derthick, 1974, p. 20).

The remainder of the law created a public development corporation, the Tennessee Valley Authority, and a three-man Board to oversee its actual operations. Regional planners with viewpoints as different as Benton MacKaye and Rexford Tugwell saluted the TVA as the potential beginnings of a new civilization, but their hopes and expectations were quite unrealistic.

2. TVA: the realities

In 1933, the TVA seemed to symbolize all the regional ideals discussed in the last chapter. RPAA members Benton MacKaye and Tracy Augur came to help the Authority with conservation projects and new-town building. Thomas J. Woofter (1934), one of Howard Odum's colleagues, praised the Authority's plans in the pages of *Social Forces*. The National Resources Committee held out TVA as a model for further experimentation in 'regional development and planning'. Proposals were made for a number of river basin authorities that would blanket almost the entire country (see Figure 3.4). President Roosevelt himself promised 'seven more TVAs' in his re-election campaign of 1936. There could be little question that regional planning had been captured by the TVA idea.

But what were the realities of the TVA?[24] How did its actual historical course affect the doctrine of regional planning?

From the very outset, the TVA's task was shrouded in controversy. This sprang mainly from the diverse expectations the agency aroused, and the differing interpretations of its mission held by its three-man board of directors. Given the lack of historical precedents and the vagueness of the enabling legislation, TVA could have been anything from a regional government to a fertilizer plant. It took five years for a series of relationships to develop which would determine its long-term course.

During these years, the Authority built dams, sold electricity, and produced fertilizer. Navigation and flood control on the Tennessee River and its tributaries was greatly improved. It developed a 'grass-roots' agriculture programme which worked through traditional land grant colleges and state agricultural extension offices. Afforestation was started through a more centralized, collectivist approach. And new towns were built. According to the NRC:

> In the town of Norris the TVA has realized several of its objectives.
> The planning of the town from a practically uninhabited area to

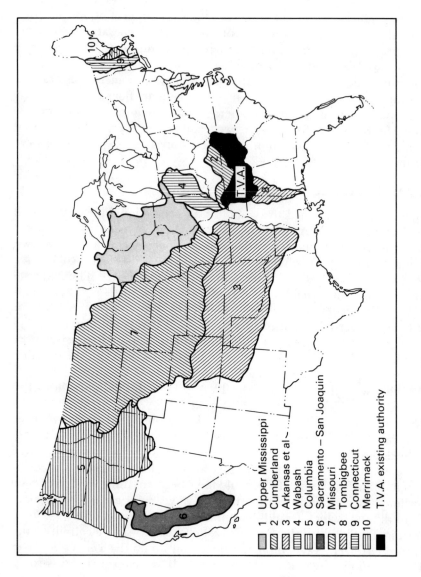

Figure 3.4 Proposed Valley Authorities, 1934 (source: National Resources Committee, 1935, p. 106).

the finished product has demonstrated the possibility of future developments in town planning, efficient government, electrical heating of homes and aesthetic municipal development [NRC, 1935, p. 97].

Significantly, though, the Regional Planning Division of TVA, under the direct control of board chairman Arthur Morgan, was never activated. To Morgan's chagrin, his fellow members of the board felt that the Authority should generate electricity and produce fertilizer. If it had to build dams to accomplish these aims, fine. If it had to support extension services and build power lines, well enough. But social planning on a regional scale, as envisioned by their colleague, was thought impractical and inappropriate.

Morgan was allowed some rein in building Norris and in the Forestry Division's purchase of submarginal land. But the two-man majority, which came to control all the board's administrative decisions, soon put an end to these kinds of commitments. In 1936, the US Supreme Court decided that it was constitutional for the TVA to sell electric power to local distributors, in competition with local utility companies. TVA's course was changing.

After the 1936 election Roosevelt actually submitted to Congress a request for the creation of further river basin authorities, but by that time the domestic New Deal was over and Congress was uninterested. Feuding increased within the TVA board and, by 1938, when Arthur Morgan's term had expired, a less enthusiastic Roosevelt would not reappoint him. The Board's only advocate of 'regional planning' was replaced, and the chairmanship was given to David Lilenthal, the co-ordinator of TVA's power operation. In a subsequent realignment of the Authority's internal organization, the regional planning unit was eliminated altogether, the radically-minded foresters were tucked away safely within the agricultural division, and a new, stronger emphasis on power generation and industrialization was begun. 'From 1936 on,' Tugwell wrote, 'the TVA should have been called the Tennessee Valley Power Production and Flood Control Corporation' [Tugwell and Banfield, 1950, p. 50].

In the late 1930s and early forties, the TVA began to demonstrate its potential for promoting urban-industrial expansion. In charging lower rates to bulk users than to domestic consumers, it soon provided the cheapest source of industrial power in the country. Large-scale industries began to be established in the Tennessee Valley. 'By 1950, every fifth worker in the region held a job in manufacturing, with a total of 355,000 in factory employment. This represented a gain of more than 160,000 workers since the days of the pre-war prosperity in 1929' (Friedmann, 1955, p. 21). Later analyses attributed 'one-third of the new industrial jobs and at least one-half of the increased value added by industry' in the Tennessee Valley to TVA (Robock, 1967, pp. 114–15; cited in Derthick, 1974, p. 42).

As a corollary to this rapid industrial growth, people moved to the Valley's metropolitan areas:

> Between 1930–50, metropolitan counties in the Tennessee Valley gained population at more than twice the rate for the region as a whole and, during the latter half of this period, gained at four times the regional rate of growth.... Nearly two-thirds of the population gain from 1930–50 occurred in metropolitan counties. And, during the 1940s, practically all of the 410,000 additional inhabitants of the region were to live in metropolitan counties [Friedmann, 1955, pp. 55–7].

Far from ushering in Mumford's biotechnical civilization, the TVA had proven itself to be a powerful instrument of urban-industrial expansion. If the TVA was to be a model for comprehensive river basin development, it would be a model which funnelled resources and people into the metropolis.[25]

3. River basin development as a planning model

In 1942 Alvin H. Hansen and Harvey S. Perloff used the Tennessee Valley experience as the basis for their widely distributed publication, *Regional Resource Development*. Their theme was that:

> Business opportunities can be created and the public welfare advanced by a comprehensive program of regional development. A long-range expansionary program would stimulate private enterprise and enable business to plan its investments on a more secure basis [p. 2].

This was a far cry from the goals which had inspired regional planning a decade earlier, but it accurately reflected the realities of TVA's historical evolution. While covering all the topics which had come to be associated with river basin planning during the 1930s, their real emphasis was on resource development as a means of economic expansion.

> The development of natural resources will be fruitful to the extent that it is directly related to the expansion of economic opportunity.... Growth in one region generally fosters growth all around.... It is in the interest of all to encourage the full and balanced utilization of resources in every region of the country, as a base for the expansion and diversification of agriculture and industry [*ibid.*, p. 19].

The hints of Howard Odum's influence had become very slight by this time; the idea of interregional balance was transposed into a self-fulfilling function of regional economic growth. Hansen and Perloff stressed the importance of electrical power for industrial expansion, and identified the river basin as an appropriate and manageable area for regional development. They introduced a whole series of considerations which would come to dominate industrial development policies in later years: transport links between resource centres and markets, vocational education, infrastructure location, tax incentives, etc. According to them, such concerns were essential if full employment and national income growth were to be maintained after the war.

In 1950 The President's Water Resources Policy Commission tried to re-emphasize some of the broader aspects of comprehensive river basin development, but by then the economic growth idea was quickly becoming the centrepiece of development planning. Focus was shifting from the local and regional levels to consideration of national and international development. Comprehensive river basin development was to reappear in Colombia, Ghana, India, and elsewhere, but like the reality of the TVA, these would be development corporations meant to encourage urban-industrial expansion.

The final, practical synthesis of regional planning doctrine, following the great debates of the 1920s and thirties, was anchored firmly to the notion of urban-industrial growth. Three decades were to pass before regional planning would rediscover the concept of territorial regionalism.

Notes

1. The incredible proliferation of executive agencies in modern government probably started with FDR's 'alphabet' agencies, so called because of their confusing acronyms. The ones we will be discussing here include the NPB (National Planning Board), NRB (National Resources Board), NRC (National Resources Committee), NRPB (National Resources Planning Board), NRA (National Recovery Administration), AAA (Agricultural Adjustment Administration), RA (Resettlement Administration), and the TVA (Tennessee Valley Authority).

2. 'Bull Moose' Republicans were a Progressive splinter group, the Progressive Party, formed around Theodore Roosevelt when he ran for an unprecedented third presidential term in 1912. Fragmentation of the Republican Party cost it the election, Democrat Woodrow Wilson winning a plurality of 42 per cent of the popular vote and 82 per cent of the ballots of the electoral college (Schlesinger, 1941, p. 331).

   Otis L. Graham Jr (1967) gives a detailed and absorbing explanation of why most of the old Progressives could not support the New Deal. Positive government involvement, rather than mere regulation, the resultant support of bigness in both government *and industry*, and Roosevelt's contradictory political manoeuvres were their main grievances.

3. The term 'pork barrelling' refers to conspicuous political favouritism in the allocation of public resources and jobs, similar to the British term 'jobbery'. It originated with the first great 'democratization' of government in the United States under Andrew Jackson.

4. The following section is not meant to present a history of metropolitan planning. Several detailed syntheses are available, including: Hall (1975), Clawson and Hall (1973), Cherry (1972, 1974), Scott (1969), Gallion and Eisner (1963) and Adams (1935). The intent here is only to identify the major emphases of metropolitanism, so that its impact on regional planning doctrine can be examined.

5. In the most famous of the New York housing commission reports, De Forest and Veiller (1903) wrote:

Although the housing problem is one of the leading political questions of the day in England, the conditions which exist there are ideal compared to the conditions in New York. The tall tenement house, accommodating as many as 100 to 150 persons in one building, extending up six or seven stories into the air, with dark, unventilated rooms, is unknown in London or in any other city of Great Britain [Reprinted in Pease, 1962, p. 104].

6. A good contemporary discussion of the housing question in New York at the turn of the last century is provided in De Forest and Veiller (1903), quoted above in Note 5. For the active but short-lived role of housing reformers in the early American city planning movement, see *Proceedings of the First National Conference on City Planning* (1910). There is a relatively critical appraisal of the relationship between housing reform and early US urban planning in Walker (1941), especially chapters 1 and 2. Hall (1975, chapters 2 and 3) covers much of the same material for the United Kingdom. Friedrich Engels (1887) presented a radical interpretation of early European approaches to housing reform. Concluding Part II of *The Housing Question*, Engels wrote:

> This [the 'migration' of the 'Little Ireland' district in Manchester*] is a striking example of how the bourgeoisie settles the housing question in practice. The breeding places of disease, the infamous holes and cellars in which the capitalist mode of production confines our workers night after night, are not abolished: they are merely *shifted elsewhere*. The same economic necessity which produced them in the first place produces them in the next place also. As long as the capitalist mode of production continues to exist it is folly to hope for an isolated settlement of the housing question or of any other social question affecting the lot of the workers [pp. 73–4].

7. The quote is taken from Engels (1887), p. 57. The German outline of solutions to the housing question he was criticizing was Emil Sax, *The Housing Conditions of the Working Classes and Their Reform* (1869). Engels chose this book to dissect because it made an attempt 'to summarize as far as possible the bourgeois literature on the subject'.
8. While accounts of Burnham's career are available from several sources, the most thorough coverage is given in Hines (1974).
9. The Chicago plan was an early example of planning by and for the upper middle class. Norton, Wacker and Delano were all wealthy entrepreneurs, and the plan was initiated and paid for by the Commercial Club of Chicago. This became a model. Mel Scott, in his history of American urban planning (1969), refers to metropolitan planning during the 1920s as, 'City Planning in the Age of Business'. Planning was conceived as a quasi-public activity, undertaken by leading citizens out of a sense of civic duty. Leading citizens meant, primarily, business leaders, industrialists and professional people; civic duty for such men was defined as promoting metropolitan growth.
10. The New York Plan had surprisingly little impact outside the planning profession, and few serious discussions of its substantive proposals were generated. The classical debate is found in Mumford's historical exchange with Adams in the pages of the *New Republic* (cf. Mumford, 1932; Adams, 1932). Probably the most thorough analysis of the plan is Johnson (1974).

One interesting outgrowth of the New York plan was a new-found interest in planning education. In 1928 a Conference on Research and Instruction in City and

* Little Ireland was one of the vilest workers' districts in Manchester during the mid-19th century. Engels' description of its flooded cottages and shabby inhabitants is found in Engels (1892), pp. 99–100. The 'sanitary police' closed down Little Ireland only for it to spring up on the other side of the river. It provided an early example of Harvey's (1973) argument that reformist urban planning cannot do away with the externalities of capitalist production; it can only move them around.

Regional Planning was held at Columbia University. It was presided over by Frederic Delano, and was attended by, among others, Thomas Adams and Charles Merriam. The next year saw the opening of the first formal American training programme in planning at Harvard University, twenty years after the founding of the School of Civic Design at the University of Liverpool.

11. 'Boss-rule' refers to the system of political machines, based on ethnic allegiances and patronage, which were run by minor tyrants in many American cities in the late nineteenth and early twentieth centuries. Boss Tweed of Tammany Hall in New York and Boss Pendergast in Kansas City were examples.

'Muckracker' was the term, originally applied by Theodore Roosevelt to Lincoln Steffens, for critical journalists and writers who attempted to expose the 'shame' of the cities around the turn of the twentieth century. Like most Progressives, their aims were to ameliorate the abuses of what they perceived as a basically sound social order. Pease (1962, p. 25) notes, 'when Lincoln Steffens exposed graft and corruption as the "shame" of the cities in 1903, his was a lover's quarrel, revealing only a little despair and a good deal of confidence in the political system....' It was not until later that Steffens' ideological position shifted decidely towards the left.

12. Whatever its other accomplishments, the trend towards technocracy in local government secured political power firmly in the hands of respectable representatives of the middle class. This effectively disenfranchised the immigrant tenement-dwellers who had formed the power base for boss government. Henceforth, decisions were to be made on the basis of economy and technical efficiency. (And, of course, there was nothing more economical or efficient than enhancing the municipal tax base through urban expansion and higher property values).

13. See Merriam (1933) for a complete review of the organizational changes suggested at different levels of government. This article was written as part of the report of the President's Research Committee on Social Trends (1933), the forerunner of the National Planning Board.

14. In this publication Merriam discussed at some length the role of planning in regional government. This discussion is elaborated in Walker (1941).

15. The neo-Darwinian origins of urban ecology are evident. From this view, the 'natural' course of metropolitan growth fits within a broader evolutionary framework, and the results of social competition during urbanization can only be perceived as just.

16. Roosevelt's evolving national planning advisory group went under four different names during its career. As an independent board it was known as the National Planning Board (NPB), 1933–4; the National Resources Board (NRB), 1934–5; and the National Resources Committee (NRC), 1935–9. From 1939 to 1943 it became an integral part of the new Executive Office of the President as the National Resources Planning Board (NRPB). Theoretical considerations aside, throughout its several name and membership changes this was essentially the same organization serving the same functions.

17. It was not until seventeen years later that a comprehensive plan of water resource development would be formulated. And by 1950 regional planning was beginning to define its tasks along entirely different lines, so the report's grand vision was belatedly stillborn. See, The President's Water Resources Policy Commission (1950).

18. For a more thorough examination of the NPB's predominant economic philosophy see Gruchy, 1939a and 1939b; also Rexford G. Tugwell, 1933 and 1935. The whole concept of a 'consort of interests' and scientific 'conjunctural' planning – to be adopted as 'indicative' planning two decades later in France – was the central theme of Tugwell's early writings. Tugwell's theory of conjunctural planning as a 'directive' fourth branch of government was seldom tested in practice, but, from the mid-1930s to the early 1950s it formed the core of what has come to be known as *planning theory*. For a fascinating introduction to Tugwell's ideas, see Padilla, ed. (1975).

19. Paraphrasing the Technical Committee's own statement (pp. v–vi), they made special studies of:

(A) interstate compacts and interstate co-operation;

(B) interstate metropolitan planning, illustrating the growth of the city-planning idea into areas involving more than one state;

(C) the Colorado River Basin as an example of the Interstate Compact device supplemented by Federal action (including a discussion of Boulder Dam);

(D) organization of the New England Regional Planning Commission;

(E) the Pacific Northwest Regional Planning Commission, supplemented by a special investigation of the Columbia River Basin and the Bonneville and Grand Coulee Dams;

(F) the Tennessee Valley Developments and Authority as an example of the federal co-operation method of procedure in attacking interstate problems;

(G) Federal administrative and planning regions and the methods used by Federal bureaus for decentralization of their activities; and

(H) the nature and significance of regionalism in the United States as it affects national development policies.

With exception of Sections B, G and H, *the entire report focused on regional planning as resource development, centred on water resources and river basins.*

Section H, Part IV of the Report, deserves special mention. It was written by several leading geographers, including Richard Hartshorne and Preston E. James, as well as two noted regional sociologists, Roderick D. McKenzie and Thomas J. Woofter. The problem of defining the nature of regions was probed in detail, and various criteria for regionalization were discussed, from 'single factor homogeneous regions' to 'metropolitan spheres of influence'. To our knowledge, this is the most sophisticated treatment of the regional concept available in an official government planning document, even today.

20. The New England Regional Planning Commission consisted of the states of Maine, Massachusetts, New Hampshire, Rhode Island, Vermont and Connecticut.

21. The Pacific Northwest Regional Planning Commission's jurisdiction included the states of Idaho, Montana, Oregon and Washington.

22. Myhra (p. 187) quotes Tugwell to the effect that: 'The conception of suburban resettlement came less from the garden city of England than from studies of our own population movements which showed steady growth in the periphery of the cities. . . . In other words, [Greenbelt] accepted a trend instead of trying to reverse it' (Tugwell, 1937, p. 43).

23. Stein (1957, pp. 118–87) provides a detailed description of the Greenbelt New Towns, especially the first one: Greenbelt, Maryland.

24. The TVA has been one of the most studied public institutions in the United States; for varying interpretations of its career, see, Lilienthal (1944); Selznick (1949); Tugwell and Banfield (1950): McKinley (1950); Martin, ed. (1956); Moore, ed. (1967); and Owen (1973).

25. The TVA has grown to be the largest electric power producer and coal consumer in the United States. It is a fearless advocate of economic growth and has been one of the country's strongest supporters of building nuclear generating stations. Deborah Shapley wrote in 1976:

> Today, TVA continues to live by this same philosophy [i.e. using cheap power to promote economic growth]. It is expanding at the electric utilities' time-honoured, historic rate, doubling every 10 years; it wants to preserve its rate structure, which, as in the past, charges higher prices to home-owners than to bulk users, such as industry and government. It argues that its conservation programs, which consist of study and demonstration efforts instead of mass promotion campaigns, are adequate. However, in the view of TVA's would-be reformers, in the valley, in Washington, and in New York, there is a serious question as to whether these policies are adequate in the post-1973 energy era [p. 814].

She goes on to conclude:

TVA's situation is almost the reverse of what it was four decades ago, when amid cries of 'Socialist' and 'Yankee' it began trying to help the poor people there build more prosperous lives. TVA's friends today are the establishment: business, labor, state government. Its newest foes are the 'socially handicapped': the poor people, the anti-establishment advocates of public interests, and environmentalists [p. 818].

Bibliography

Adams, T. 1935: *Outline of town and city planning.* New York: Russell Sage Foundation.

　1932: A communication: in defense of the regional plan. *New Republic* **71**, 207–10. Reprinted in Sussman, C., editor 1976, 260–7.

Burgess, E. W. 1923: The growth of the city. *Proceedings of the American Sociological Society* **18**, 85–9. Reprinted in Park, R. E., *et al.*, 1925, 47–62.

　1926: *The urban community.* University of Chicago Press.

Burnham, D. H. and Bennett, E. H. 1909: *Plan of Chicago*, Moore, C., editor. Chicago: The Commercial Club.

Cherry, G. 1972: *Urban change and planning.* London: Foulis.

　1974: *The evolution of British town planning.* Heath & Reach (England): Leonard Hill Books.

Clawson, M. and Hall, P. 1973: *Planning and urban growth: an Anglo-American comparison.* Baltimore: Johns Hopkins University Press.

Committee on Plan of New York, 1929–31: *The regional plan for New York and its environs*, 10 volumes. New York: Russell Sage Foundation.

Conkin, P. 1959: *Tomorrow a new world: the New Deal in the suburbs.* Ithaca: Cornell University Press.

De Forest, R. W. and Veiller, L. 1903: *The tenement house problem.* New York: Macmillan.

Derthick, M. 1974: *Between state and nation: regional organization in the United States.* Washington, DC: Brookings Institution.

Dickinson, R. E. 1964: *City and Region: a geographical interpretation.* London: Routledge & Kegan Paul.

Engels, F. 1887: *The housing question.* London. Current edition published in 1975 by Progress Publishers, Moscow.

　1892: *The condition of the working-class in England.* London. Originally published in German in 1845 at Leipzig; current edition published in 1973 by Progress Publishers, Moscow.

Friedmann, J. 1955: *The spatial structure of economic development in the Tennessee Valley: a study in regional planning.* Chicago: University of Chicago, Program of Education and Research in Planning, Research Paper No. 1.

Friedmann, J. and Alonso, W., editors 1964: *Regional development and planning.* Cambridge, Mass.: The MIT Press.

Gallion, A. B. and Eisner, S. 1963: *The urban pattern: city planning and design*. New York: Van Nostrand Reinhold.

Graham, O. L. 1967: *An encore for reform: the old progressives and the New Deal*. New York: Oxford University Press.

1976: *Toward a planned society: from Roosevelt to Nixon*. New York: Oxford University Press.

Gruchy, A. G. 1939a: Economics of the National Resources Committee. *American Economics Review* **29**, 60–73.

1939b: The concept of national planning in institutional economics. *Southern Economic Journal* **6**, 121–44.

Hall, P. 1975: *Urban and regional planning*. New York: Halstead Press.

Hansen, A. H. and Perloff, H. S. 1942: *Regional resource development*. Washington, DC: National Planning Association.

Harris, C. D. and Ullman, E. L. 1945: The nature of cities. *Annals of the Academy of Political and Social Science* **242**, 7–17. Reprinted in Mayer, H. M. and Kohn, C. F., editors 1959, 277–86.

Harvey, D. 1973: *Social justice and the city*. Baltimore: Johns Hopkins University Press.

Hines, T. S. 1974: *Burnham of Chicago: architect and planner*. New York: Oxford University Press.

Hoyt, H. 1939: *The structure and growth of residential neighborhoods in American cities*. Washington, DC: Government Printing Office.

Jensen, M., editor 1951: *Regionalism in America*. Madison: University of Wisconsin Press.

Johnson, D. A. 1974: *The emergence of metropolitan regionalism: an analysis of the 1929 regional plan of New York and its environs*. Ph.D. dissertation. Columbia University.

Kellogg, P. U., editor 1914: *The Pittsburgh survey*. New York: Survey Associates, Inc. Published for the Russell Sage Foundation.

Lilienthal, D. E. 1944: *TVA: democracy on the march*. New York: Harpers.

McKenzie, R. D. 1924: The ecological approach to the study of the human community. *American Journal of Sociology* **30**, 287–301.

1926: The scope of human ecology. *Journal of Applied Sociology* **10**, 316–23.

1933: The rise of metropolitan communities. In the report of the President's Research Committee on Social Trends, 1933, 443–96.

McKinley, C. 1950: The valley authority and its alternatives. *American Political Science Review* **44**, 607–31. Reprinted in Friedmann, J. and Alonso, W., editors 1964, 554–78.

Martin, R. C., editor 1956: *TVA: the first twenty years*. Knoxville: University of Tennessee Press.

Mayer, H. M. and Kohn, C. F., editors 1959: *Readings in urban geography*. University of Chicago Press.

Merriam, C. E. 1933: Government and society. In the President's Research Committee on Social Trends, 1933, 1489–1541.

1944: The National Resources Planning Board; a chapter in American Planning Experience. *The American Political Science Review* **38**, 1075–88.

Merriam, C. E., Parratt, S. D. and Lepawsky, P. 1933: *The government of the metropolitan region of Chicago.* University of Chicago Press.

Moore, J. R., editor 1967: *The economic impact of TVA.* Knoxville: University of Tennessee Press.

Mumford, L. 1932: The plan of New York. *New Republic* **71**, 121–6, 146–54. Reprinted in Sussman, C., editor 1976, 224–59.

1938: *The culture of cities.* New York: Harcourt Brace.

Myhra, D. 1974: Rexford Guy Tugwell: initiator of America's greenbelt new towns. *Journal of the American Institute of Planners* **40**, 176–88.

Owen, M. 1973: *The Tennessee Valley Authority.* New York: Praeger.

Padilla, S. M., editor 1975: *Tugwell's thoughts on planning.* San Juan: University of Puerto Rico Press.

Park, R. E., Burgess, E. W. and McKenzie, R. D. 1925: *The city.* University of Chicago Press.

Pease, O., editor 1962: *The progressive years: the spirit and achievement of American reform.* New York: George Braziller.

The President's Research Committee on Social Trends 1933: *Recent social trends in the United States.* New York: McGraw-Hill.

The President's Water Resources Policy Commission 1950: *A water policy for the American people,* 3 volumes. Washington, DC: Government Printing Office.

Proceedings of the first national conference on city planning, Washington, DC, 21–2 May 1909. Washington, DC: Government Printing Office, 1910. Reprinted in 1967 by the American Society of Planning Officials, Chicago.

Robock, S. N. 1967: An unfinished task: a socio-economic evaluation of the TVA experiment. In Moore, J. R., editor: *The economic impact of the TVA.* Knoxville: University of Tennessee Press.

Roosevelt, F. D. 1938: *The public papers and addresses of Franklin D. Roosevelt,* Vol. 1. New York: Random House.

Sax, E. 1869: *The housing conditions of the working classes and their reform.* Vienna.

Schlesinger, A. M. 1941: *Political and social growth of the American people, 1865–1940.* New York: Macmillan.

Scott, M. 1969: *American urban planning since 1890.* Berkeley: University of California Press.

Selznick, P. 1949: *TVA and the grass roots.* Berkeley: University of California Press.

Shapley, D. 1976: TVA today: former reformers in an era of expensive electricity. *Science* **194**, 814–18.

Stein, C. 1925: The road to good houses. *Survey Graphic* **54**, 165–8, 189.

1957: *Toward new towns in America.* Cambridge, Mass.: The MIT Press.

Sternsher, B. 1964: *Rexford Tugwell and the New Deal.* New Brunswick, NJ: Rutgers University Press.

Sussman, C., editor 1976: *Planning the fourth migration: the neglected vision of the Regional Planning Association of America.* Cambridge, Mass.: The MIT Press.

Tugwell, R. G. 1933: *The industrial discipline and the governmental arts.* New York: Columbia University Press.

    1935: *The battle for democracy.* New York: Columbia University Press.

    1936: Housing activities and plans of the Resettlement Administration. *Housing Officials Yearbook* 28–34. Washington, DC: National Association of Housing.

    1937: The meaning of the greenbelt towns. *New Republic* **90**, 42–3.

Tugwell, R. G. and Banfield, E. 1950: Grass roots democracy – myth or reality? *Public Administration Review* **10**, 47–59.

United States National Planning Board 1934: *Final report, 1933–34.* Washington, DC: Government Printing Office.

United States National Resources Committee, 1935: *The regional factors in national planning.* Washington, DC: Government Printing Office.

    1936–43: *Regional planning,* 10 volumes. Washington, DC: Government Printing Office.

    1937: *Our cities: their role in the national economy.* Washington, DC: Government Printing Office. Reprinted in 1974 by Arno Press, New York.

Walker, R. A. 1941: *The planning function in urban government.* University of Chicago Press.

Weber, A. 1899: *The growth of cities in the nineteenth century.* New York: Macmillan.

Wirth, L. 1942: The metropolitan district as a planning unit. *American Society of Planning Officials Newsletter* **8**, 49–50.

    1951: The limitations of regionalism. In Jensen, M., editor 1951, 381–93.

Woofter, T. J. 1934: Tennessee Valley regional plan. *Social Forces* **12**, 329–38.

Part II: A spatial framework for capitalist planning

Chapter 4

A spatial framework for unequal development: the formative years

With the coming of World War II, regional planning was laid aside. More important tasks were at hand. The national economy had to be mobilized. And, when the war ended, it was difficult to arouse interest in the issues which had moved a generation of planners and social scientists a bare ten years before. To understand why this was so, we shall have to distinguish among three theatres of action: the United States, Western Europe, and the newly developing countries.

America had emerged from the war with a new sense of national unity. The federal government had been immensely strengthened at the expense of the states, and though its war powers were quickly dismantled, the government continued to play a key role both in domestic affairs and in the world. Almost against its will, the country had been projected into a major international role. More than ever, Americans saw themselves as a single nation.

The economy became unabashedly growth-oriented. On one hand, new regions had been opened up to rapid, sustained growth, especially California and the southwest and Gulf Coast states (Alexander, 1952). They had benefited from war production and were now busy converting their productive plant to peacetime uses. Pent-up consumer demand engendered a growth cycle that seemed to banish, once and for all, the unhappy story of boom and bust to which the economy had become accustomed. Counter-cyclical Keynesian policies would ensure stability. If only growth could be sustained, distributive measures might be rendered all but superfluous. Growth would become a substitute for distribution.

The logic of this thought was simple enough. With economic growth, the labour force would be fully employed. This would exert pressure on wages and level up workers' income even as profits increased. In a growth economy everyone was bound to share in the general prosperity. The politically thorny subject of redistribution could then be either avoided altogether or more easily resolved than under conditions of stagnation.

This held for the regional redistribution of incomes as well. The country's major 'backward' region, the South, was rapidly industrializing as older industries 'migrated' from the North, particularly from the high-cost region of New England (McLaughlin and Robock, 1949). In return, the South was sending its rural population, both white and black, to northern cities such as Chicago and Detroit. Some southern cities also grew precipitously during this period. A heady feeling of change was in the air. Editorial writers exulted over the New South.

These shifts, which showed the national economy to be a single integrated market area for capital, labour, and commodities, gave rise to a small number of regional economic studies for the traditional problem regions: New England (Council of Economic Advisors, 1951; Harris, 1952) and the South (Hoover and Ratchford, 1951). But valuable as these studies were in calling attention to continuing economic problems in these historical areas, they did little to advance planning doctrine, and their influence on national policy was slight. The country was in no mood to worry about regional problems; it was caught up in the euphoria of an expanding consumer society. The first comprehensive programme to promote economic development in lagging regions did not get launched till 1961 (Cumberland, 1971).

The regionalism of the 1930s seemed to have vanished from the earth. Its planning philosophy produced only few works of interest. The first was a modest attempt to apply the tools of physical planning on a regional scale. Guided by Maurice Rotival, a French expatriate planner, it introduced French notions of *aménagement du territoire* to the United States (Yale University, 1947). The other was a book that tried to rekindle a philosophy of organic regionalism in the tradition of Howard Odum (Jensen, ed., 1951). Although containing a number of well-argued essays, it caused scarcely a ripple in academic circles and found no audible echo in public policy.

Western Europe, meanwhile, was wrestling with problems of post-war reconstruction. The machinery of national planning which had grown up in response to war-time needs was now being refurbished for another overriding national purpose. Reconstruction and economic growth required some form of national guidance. Power which had accumulated at the national centre during the war remained centralized when the shooting stopped. Europe's recovery was spectacular, and as historically unprecedented rates of economic growth were achieved, it seemed as though the traditional regional questions could be by-passed.[1]

The major questions were not, at least immediately, sub-national but European: first, the forming of supra-national functional linkages that would culminate in the European Coal and Steel Community and the European Economic Commission and, second, the recognition that Western Europe had a common industrial heartland or *core area*, dynamic and prosperous, and, attached to it, a set of disjointed rural *peripheries* on the extremities of the subcontinent that were traditional in culture, technologically backward, and poor (United Nations, Department of Economic and Social Affairs, 1955). The United Nations Economic Commission for Europe which thus focused on what was to become the classic issue of regional policy – i.e. the imbalanced relations between core and periphery – was then headed by Gunnar Myrdal whose theory of cumulative causation was to be one of the leading contributions to the emerging doctrine of regional planning (see chapter 5). But that was later. For the moment, Europe, no less than America, showed little inclination to worry about regional inequities. To be sure, Britain, Italy, and France made tentative gestures towards a strategy for industrial dispersion; but, except for Britain, the multi-national management of resources and market areas were the matters of primary concern. Everywhere, central governments were strengthened at the expense of local powers. Governments and private cartels formed a corporate unity (Cohen, 1969).

Finally, the early post-war period saw the decolonization of formerly colonial territories and the establishment of the United Nations. Over the next two decades, these 'new' countries would be known variously as backward, underdeveloped, emerging, developing, Third World, and less developed. On the whole, they could be characterized by the lack of a deep national tradition, the low productivity of their agriculture, the absence of indigenous industry above the handicraft stage, a rickety and thinly spread social and economic infrastructure, low indices of urbanization, and a legacy of colonialist thinking.

It would evidently be necessary to reconstruct relations between the 'newly developing world' and the industrialized economies of the West which until recently had dominated most of them not only economically but politically as well. Towards this end, the United Nations appointed a Committee of Experts to study the situation and to recommend appropriate action (United Nations, 1951). The Committee suggested that the problem of 'underdevelopment' must be understood in the context of some vision of 'development'. On this point, they took it for granted that western industrialized countries were already *developed*, and that the cure for 'underdevelopment' was, accordingly, to become as much as possible like them. This seemed to suggest that the royal road to 'catching up' was through an accelerated process of industrialization. To guide this process and, indeed, to make it possible in the first place, national planning would be required. Regional planning was not mentioned (see Appendix).

The first explicit reference to a regional planning perspective for 'underdeveloped' countries came only four years later in a critical review of one of the first of the United Nations-sponsored missions to report on national development (Friedmann, 1955b). The country in question was tiny Haiti. For all its size, a spatial dimension had to be considered. The following quotation foreshadows what was to become the major thrust of regional planning doctrine during the 1960s, or the national planning of regional development (pp. 52–3):

> Spatial structure concerns those aspects of economic development which have geographic or locational significance. It deals with the persisting interrelations and interdependencies of spatially segregated activities. A study of spatial structure in relation to economic develop-

ment would probe the economic and social implications of alternative patterns of industry location and transport routes; explore the complex interrelations between town and country and their respective contributions to total development; analyse internal population movements in their effect upon the ability of different regions to sustain economic progress; and delimit geographic boundaries of development projects....

Instead of focusing development efforts successively on a limited number of individual projects, a sound approach would be based on the principle of 'structural interdependency'. In fact, the process of economic development itself may be looked upon as a process leading to increasing specialization and to greater interdependency, not only functionally, but also in terms of space. Such an approach would require the planner to examine the multiple spatial inter-relations of any undertaking, the existing and potential flows of commodities and people, and the expected local impact of any given project. Eventually, it would lead him in the direction of 'balanced' regional development conceived in the sense of a continuous adjust-ment of growth in one region to changes in all other regions.

This quotation also illustrates how the emerging doctrine of regional planning took its major cues from the doctrine of economic growth and development, accepting as its starting point the broad policy directions around which professional consensus was building up (United Nations, 1951). It restricted itself to the *locational aspects* of these policies; other facets of development policy were left untouched.

The doctrine of unequal development

In the first post-war decade, then, regional planning did not figure prominently on the public agenda. The concern of policy-makers and politicians had shifted from measures dealing with economic depression and under-used productive capacity, which had plagued the 1930s, to policies for promoting reconstruction and rapid economic growth.

Received regional planning doctrine was mute on questions of economic growth. Before the war, regional planners had been concerned with either philosophical approaches (Lewis Mumford, Benton McKaye) or broad questions of social policy (Howard Odum). The one substantial example of regional planning in practice, the TVA, was largely the handiwork of engineers, and the small number of working professional planners were preoccupied with urban design. The conceptual apparatus for linking regional planning with the new ideology of economic growth was still missing.

Some facets of this ideology are worth looking at. They would be decisive for thinking about regional planning as it evolved during the latter part of the fifties and sixties.[2]

It most fundamental aspect, perhaps, was the *doctrine of unequal development*, which determined the conceptual approach to economic policy. According to this doctrine, whose origins lay deeply buried in the philosophy of neoclassical economics (Robinson, 1962), questions of efficiency in production were to be radically distinguished from questions of equity in distribution. Economics claimed to be a value-free science, and equity was thought to be an ethical/political matter and thus an improper subject for economists. In actual fact, however, the doctrine of unequal development, posing as an objective doctrine, maintained a very definite position on income distribution: *it argued for inequality on grounds of economic motivation.* It was self-evident, the reasoning went, that the rich saved more out of their incomes than the poor and that high profit levels were essential as an incentive to private (corporate?) saving. Arthur Lewis, the famous theoretician of economic development, put it this way:

> ...economic growth may be deplored in so far as it depends on inequality of income. That this dependence exists cannot be denied since growth would be small or negative if differential awards were not available for hard work, for conscientious work, for skill, for responsibility and for initiative. It is arguable in any given situation whether the existing differentials are too great or too small, in the restricted sense of being greater or less than is required to achieve the desired rate of economic growth. But it is not arguable ... that significant economic growth could be achieved even if there were no differentials at all.... The economic test in such matters is that of supply and demand: 'reasonable' differentials are those salaries and profits which are objectively necessary ... to secure the required skill or initiative. But what is 'reasonable' on this test may well be 'unreasonable' by some other standard or merit or social justice [Lewis, 1955, pp. 428–9].

The argument boiled down to this: inequality was efficient for growth, equality was inefficient. Moreover, it was widely believed that distributional questions would not become politically salient so long as the economy continued to grow at a rapid pace. This doctrine was called 'trickle down', but the only sure thing about it was the growing concentration of income and wealth at the top.[3]

Given these assumptions about economic growth, the expansion of manufacturing was regarded as the major propulsive force (League of Nations, 1945; Mandelbaum, 1945; Clark, 1951). Moreover, because it was regarded as typically an urban enterprise, the expansion of manufacturing would occasion a massive exodus of population from agriculture into the growing centres of production. As the countryside became depopulated, rural entrepreneurs would be enabled to reorganize the farm economy along more efficient and commercial lines. In the long run, the use of 'factors' in the agricultural sector would be rendered as productive as in industry (Schultz, 1953). Economists envisioned a condition of system-wide equilibrium in which labour and capital would be equally compensated 'at the margin'. Translated into spatial terms, this suggested an economy in which no further locational shifts would be required, because all economic activities had found their 'optimum' location (Lefeber, 1958).

As a result of urban-industrial expansion and the reorganization of agriculture along commercial lines, old territorial unities would be dissolved at sub-national levels, giving rise to an integrated space-economy at the level of the nation whose structure would no longer be made up of bounded territories (regions) but of *nodes* and *linkages* (i.e. cities and inter-city flows of capital, workers, information, and commodities).

Emerging studies in the economics of location

This reinterpretation of regionalism in functional, non-territorial terms was accomplished around 1955. But to explain how this came about some preliminary work has to be done. The link between economic growth and regional planning turned out to be the economics of location and, in particular, industrial location. Location studies received tremendous impetus during the 1950s and 1960s. Despite the fact that the classic in the field, Alfred Weber's theory of industrial location, had been available in English since 1929 (Friedrich, ed., 1929), the analysis of location represented a fairly new interest in the United States.[1] Important theoretical work had been done before the war in Germany by Christaller (Baskin, 1957) and Lösch (English edition 1954), and in Sweden by Palander and Ohlin (Isard, 1956, chapter 2). But until Edgar Hoover introduced them to an English-speaking audience (1937 and, especially, 1948), their work was practically unknown in the United States.

Official interest in the problem may be dated to 1943, the year which marked publication of the monumental study on *Industrial Location and National Resources* by the National Resources Planning Board.[5] This report established the basis for subsequent efforts to promote industrialization in specific localities and so, by inference, to guide the processes of economic growth in lagging areas. In exemplary fashion, the report concentrated on major policy variables that could affect the process of selecting industrial locations by private firms, such as taxes and tariffs. From the standpoint of methodology, the NRPB study remains a landmark for contemporary planning practice. Nothing has been written since that would invalidate its findings, and practical efforts at industrial promotion are still following a framework laid down more than a generation ago.

Industrial location studies 'took off' soon after the conclusion of the war.[6] Since our purpose here is not to assess them critically, we shall confine ourselves to showing their considerable variety. Five types of study may be identified:

- empirical-statistical: Florence, 1948; Alexander, 1952; Harris, 1954;
- empirical-behavioural: McLaughlin and Robock, 1949;
- agricultural location: Dunn, 1954;
- industrial complex analysis: Isard and Vietorisz, 1955;
- inductively-rational: Greenhut, 1956.

Grand syntheses were made both at the beginning of this creative period (Hoover, 1948) and at its end (Isard, 1956). But Isard's work also marked the transition from traditional location economics to the new and more eclectic discipline of regional science.[7] Before proceeding to a critical appreciation of the latter, however, we need a brief assessment of the four main ways in which industrial location studies influenced the formation of regional planning doctrine:

(1) Emphasis on mobility, particularly of financial capital, and on the conditions of influencing the location of investment in national 'space' marked a major shift in emphasis from territorial to functional regional planning. Under the emerging doctrine, one no longer developed places or regions but *locations*. By guiding industries towards their optimal locations (assuming no difference between the private and social calculus of optimality), planners would be able to increase remuneration to all factors of production, including labour. Hence, labour would, or rather *should*, 'flow' towards the principal centres of industrial expansion. In general, it was considered uneconomic to move industry to where a potential labour force resided, merely because it was already there.

(2) Emphasis on individual plants (and systems of plants, or industrial complexes) together with their efficient location made it possible to integrate the economics of location with the new economics of growth. Efficient plant location would contribute to system-wide efficiency and hence, under the given constraints, to maximum economic growth. The difference in the measure of private and public optimality would be the size of the required subsidy. This criterion suggested the appropriate approach to public policy, which was to encourage private industrial operations to move to their socially most efficient locations. For a long time, planning was committed to a strict incrementalism in regional development.

(3) Because least-cost solutions were generally thought to be urban locations (external economies of scale were assumed), location studies helped to focus academic interest on cities and more specifically on urbanization processes and the 'role' of cities in

economic growth and development (Hoselitz, 1953; 1955; Lampard, 1955).

(4) Industrial location studies drew attention away from agriculture. At the time, Edgar S. Dunn's work (1954) was practically the sole exception to this overwhelming bias. From the standpoint of urban-industrial development, agriculture appeared as an essentially passive sector that might receive the impact of the former but could not be expected to generate its own dynamic growth (Schultz, 1953; Ruttan, 1955).

Social physics

One set of studies related to, but different from, the work on industrial location was essentially statistical in nature. It looked for significant *empirical regularities,* tendencies or 'laws', that would remain invariant over a wide spectrum of possible observations. Scholars in this tradition worked primarily with distributional phenomena, urban populations being one of their favourite subjects.

One of the pioneers of this tradition was Rutledge Vining of the University of Virginia whose stochastic models of population systems (1949; 1953; 1955) suggested a policy approach to regional development that went beyond the incrementalism of guided industrial location to the resetting of major policy 'parameters' (e.g. transportation costs).

Vining's sometime associate, Carl Madden, made contributions in another direction (1956a, b). Madden studied historical trends in city size distribution and growth rates for the United States. His findings suggested a long-term movement of size distributions in relation to economic growth. Perhaps his most important conclusion, however, was that individual cities do not grow independently of other cities but as a function of their relative location *within the system of all cities.* Madden found that these systems displayed considerable *stability* in their growth patterns over time. This work was subsequently evolved by Brian J. L. Berry (1961, 1964) into a major policy doctrine which held that 'log-normal'[8] city-size distributions were also the most efficient in the management of the space economy.

Finally, we must mention the work of certain statisticians who noted striking, if somewhat puzzling regularities in their data and attempted to model these phenomena according to a principle of 'least effort' (Stewart, 1947; Zipf, 1949). Marching under the banner of 'social physics' (James Q. Stewart had actually started his professional life as a physicist), these scholars evolved the important analytical tool of 'gravity models' which was to come into widespread use, especially in transportation analysis (Carrothers, 1956). Generally speaking, these models established (1) that human interaction tends to decline as a function of distance from a given centre and (2) that the volume of interaction between any two places can be predicted according to the formula $\dfrac{P_1 . P_2}{d^n} . k,$

where P is the population (or some other pertinent measure of volume or size, such as employment or income) at a given place, d is equal to distance (usually expressed as a measure of physical distance), with n an empirically determined parameter and k an empirical constant.

Together, these statistical approaches to the study of distributional phenomena involving large numbers helped to inaugurate the field of *analytical (quantitative) geography* that would come into full flower during the 1960s (Schaefer, 1953; James and Jones, 1954; Bunge, 1962). What appealed to geographers was the empirical (inductive) approach of social physics which held out hopes of discovering invariant patterns. Economists were more committed to theoretical (deductive) studies. Regional science tried to combine both approaches.

Isard's location and space economy

In an extraordinary feat of synthesis, Walter Isard (1956) brought many of these strands of research – economic location theory, geographic location theory, social physics – into a single, integrated theory of what he called – following German practice – the space economy (*Raumwirtschaft*). He subtitled his book ambitiously: 'A General Theory Relating to Industrial Location, Market Areas, Land Use, Trade, and Urban Structure.' Within the framework of neoclassical economics, then at the height of its vogue in the United States and Great Britain, Isard's theory represented a major amendment. Economics had always used differential calculus to determine rates of change, allowing for a temporal dimension of events, but it had remained completely ignorant of spatial relationships. The major clue to Isard's work was the observed empirical regularity that distance influenced the intensity of interaction and especially the flow in the physical volume of trade. Translated into economic terminology, the principal ordering variable in location was the cost of 'overcoming the friction of distance' or, as Isard chose to call it, 'transport-inputs' (i.e. the movement of a unit of weight over a unit of distance). Isard's claim was that transport-inputs were as fundamental to production as any other factor, such as capital or labour. In short, he decided to treat transportation as a major element in the costs of production.

Our intent here is not to summarize this seminal and complex work. The following general observations are pertinent, however. To begin with, the theory was cast in a form familiar to neoclassical economists, including the assumption of a self-generated and self-maintaining 'spatial' equilibrium. It was, therefore, a static framework for the study of location. Very differently from August Lösch, who grew up in the tradition of German political economy, Isard had little to say about either policy or planning. On the other hand, he contributed significantly to the theory of location and regional development. His graphic representations of the topography of a space economy were particularly suggestive (see Figure 4.1). For the first time, planners could actually 'see' a regional landscape that had a 'structure' but no boundaries.

Figure 4.1   An agricultural land-use pattern (from Isard, 1956, p. 277).

Among other things, Walter Isard was an incredibly effective organizer. His major achievement in this direction was the founding of the Regional Science Association in 1954 (Regional Science Association, 1955). Initially, this brought together economists interested in location theory and analytical geographers who were just beginning to find their own identity. Eventually, the RSA became internationalized and even initiated its own academic programmes, offering graduate studies in a number of American universities, notably at the University of Pennsylvania and Cornell.

Location theory and economic growth

Isard had achieved a general theory of spatial equilibrium in a capitalist economy. What remained to be done was to link location theory to the theory of economic growth. This was done in quite different ways by Douglass C. North and Charles Tiebout, on the one hand, and John Friedmann, on the other.

Douglass North was an economic historian whose researches on the Pacific Northwest had led him to formulate an *export-base* model of regional economic growth (North, 1955, 1956). Offered as a substitute for a so-called stage theory of economic growth (Hoover and Fisher, 1949), for which he could find no evidence in American history, North devised a two-region model in which the first region traded with the second, receiving capital and consumer goods from the latter in return for its own exports of primary (and subsequently also of processed and manufactured) products.[9] Economic growth in Region I was thus *induced* by an existing demand in the economically more powerful Region II. Production for export, which at least initially would be financed with capital from Region II, was then translated, via a series of multiplier effects, into the growth of a residentiary sector (i.e. a sector producing for an expanding internal demand within Region I).[10] Given this relationship, said North, regional 'interests' would strive as mightily as they could to expand the region's export base. And significantly, he added: 'The extent of such activity is too obvious in the contemporary American political scene to require extended discussion' (1955, p. 251). Export-base theory was a genuine American product! As North had said, it was 'self-evident'.

Although export-base theory did not play a significant role in American regional planning, it came to have an extraordinary appeal for those who were spinning economic growth doctrines for Third World countries. There, the successive policies of import- and export-substitution became one of the mainstays of foreign advice on how to 'develop' an 'under-developed' economy (Paauw and Fei, 1973). Region II, in this case, was represented by the core countries of the emerging world economy (Western Europe, the United States, Japan), and Region I was a given 'developing' country. With this redefinition of regions, North's export-base doctrine could be applied without modification. But what had appeared to be relatively free of ideological bias in a culturally homogeneous national economy, such as the United States, assumed a much more sinister aspect in the context of an international economy in which power is very unequally divided among nations.

North's major critic was Charles Tiebout (1956a, b), a colleague at the University of Washington in Seattle. Tiebout's argument was as technical as it was pointed. He showed that the division between export and residentiary sectors was, in fact, an arbitrary one which depended entirely on how the region was defined. Small regions would have large export sectors, large regions would have predominantly residentiary industries. The translation of growth in one sector into growth of another sector could therefore scarcely be said to reflect a 'basic' relationship. Growth was a more complex phenomenon than North's analysis suggested.[11]

A point not raised by Tiebout was that North's model was, in any event, of limited usefulness where the dominant imagery was that of *spatial systems* that had internal structure but no boundaries. As Madden had demonstrated (1956a, b), whether one talked of regions or of cities, growth was positional. The lack of clearly defined boundaries, and the rather elliptical criterion suggested by North for delineating regions (the area controlled by export industries), rendered the whole export-base doctrine of questionable value.

Friedmann's analysis of a region – the Tennessee Valley – was more in line with the currently fashionable systems perspective (Friedmann, 1955a, 1956a). His proposal was simple enough: to shift both analysis and planning from natural regions, such as river basins, to city-dominated, functional regions.

This concept of a city region was certainly not new. It had been used extensively by Robert E. Dickinson (1947) in his important work on urban regionalism and, several years earlier, in an address to professional planners by Louis Wirth (1942). But Wirth had in mind enlarging the scope of city planning to the size of the existing functional economic area. What was new in Friedmann's proposal was the linking of urbanism with regionalism, or rather the extension of urbanism from the single city to a regional system of cities. This involved a change in the meaning of regional planning from a concern with the development of bounded regions to the management of open city systems.

> Linkages among city regions extend into all directions, joining dominant city to dominant city, sub-center to sub-center. The economic relationships which are expressed by these linkages in an advanced stage of economic development make up the central subject matter of regional economic planning *beyond* the immediate boundaries of the city region itself.
>
> These interrelationships are characteristic of any economy which is organized on a modular pattern with functional differentiation among its parts.... This system is the structural framework within which economic development takes place and which, at any time, places the maximum limits on the extent of possible development in any particular segment of the system. The main purpose of metropolitan planning is to realize the economic potentials of just one segment (the city region) within the over-all limits imposed by the entire system.
>
> Beyond metropolitan planning, therefore, lies no longer regional planning in the traditional sense of the term, but planning that is

oriented along specific functional lines.... Functional planning will
dictate its own area of operation ... [Friedmann, 1955a, p. 143].

The idea of comprehensive planning which had been advocated by
Mumford, McKaye, Odum, and the other regionalists, not least by
Rexford Tugwell, was thus to be replaced by functional-spatial planning. Later, it turned out, integration in space could only be achieved
at the appropriate unit of territorial closure which, in this case, was the
nation. Cultural regionalism was no longer a vital force in national
development. It was, in fact, regarded as a rather old-fashioned idea, and
attempts to resurrect it were roundly ignored by the younger generation of
planners (Friedmann, 1956b). The reality they understood was of another
sort.

Friedmann's formulation opened the way for linking up regional plan-
ning with economic growth theory via the theory of location and the
budding field of regional science. It presaged a more general theory of
polarized development that would facilitate a convergence with the emerging
French tradition of regional economics based on the seminal work of
François Perroux (1955). Perroux himself had lectured at Harvard in 1949
(Perroux, 1950), but his talk had no visible repercussions. Only Walter
Isard, then at Harvard, would have been able to grasp the significance
of Perroux's discussion of 'abstract economic space'. But Isard's own
magnum opus (1956) failed to include any reference to his work.

Summary

The first post-war decade was one of conceptual retooling to bring regional
planning doctrine in line with the new doctrines of economic growth and
unequal development. However, it was too early yet for a specific regional
doctrine to emerge. Nor was there much pressure for such a doctrine.
Except in a few countries of Western Europe, there was precious little
interest in regional planning, as countries faced problems of national
reconstruction and supra-national economic integration. And where
regional planning did figure somewhat more prominently, it was seen
primarily as an answer to economic backwardness in poor, declining
regions on the periphery of major core areas. Core regions (or 'poles')
grew by themselves, in response to market conditions and without much
outside help except for the guidance of macro-economic variables by
central planners. Formulating an appropriate regional planning doctrine
did not seem an urgent task.

The mid-1950s marked the critical breakthrough of theoretical studies
contributing to regional planning. This was accomplished by changing
the old paradigm of regional resource development to one of economic
growth in a spatial dimension. Terms such as 'spatial structure' and
'functional integration' came to dominate the literature. The findings of
urban geography and urban economics would be used to underwrite the

more doctrinal assertions of regional planners. Another decade was to pass, however, before the full policy implications of the new paradigm would become known.

Notes

1. On early post-war European planning, see Wellisz, 1960; Hackett and Hackett, 1963; Tinbergen, 1955; 1958; 1964; United Nations Department of Economic Affairs, 1965; and Hagen and White, 1966.
2. A somewhat longer critical appreciation of the new doctrine will be found in the Appendix to this chapter.
3. The clearest formulation of this doctrine is found in Schultz, 1949, p. 9:

> 1. The basic analytical core of political economy is based upon the *maximization* of the gains to be had from production and trade by achieving (a) an efficient allocation of resources (with the main stress on long-run relationships) and, (b) sufficient stability of the main economic magnitudes to permit the economy to perform efficiently in (a) above and,
> 2. the *minimization* of the adverse economic effects of public measures intended to reduce the inequality in the personal distribution of income on the capacity of the economy to perform its task of keeping resources fully and efficiently employed.

This formulation implies that efficiency (under existing economic organization) leads to inequality in the distribution of income (the distribution of wealth is not mentioned at all!) and claims that (a) efficiency and equity are in conflict and (b) the duty of economists is to minimize the *adverse* effects of social policies for redistribution on efficiency in production! The argument is carried further in the following quotation:

> This dualism within agriculture rests on a functional dichotomy of *resources for production and income for welfare*. It is very important to make this separation.... From the point of view of society in terms of political economy, the objective in production should be put as follows: to achieve economy in the use of resources. The test for this achievement is allocative efficiency. In welfare, the objective should be stated along these lines: a level of income, a distribution of income among persons, and a utilization of income to achieve the highest attainable level of welfare. Here, the test of achievement is in terms of social efficiency [*ibid.*, p. 12].

What Schultz does *not* say is that allocative efficiency (as interpreted by economists) implied policies that were socially inefficient. Within the doctrine of unequal development, efficiency and equity were fundamentally in conflict. Social justice had to be postponed. It is telling that Schultz was one of the authors of the United Nations Report of 1951 which laid out the basic framework for development policy. Economic development would be unequal development.

This bald assertion is no longer fashionable (cf. Chenery *et al.*, 1974). Nor is the view that unlimited growth is bound to improve human welfare in the long run (Hirsch, 1976). Nevertheless, most western-trained economists still hold that efficiency and equity are contradictory in principle, requiring 'trade-offs' to be made.

4. Early location theory concerned itself entirely with the economics of the firm, specifically the industrial firm which had a problem of choosing an 'optimal' location in terms of a principle of either profit maximization or cost minimization. (Much of the early controversy in location studies revolved around the question of appropriate criterion.) The way to the study of agricultural location was pioneered by Johann Heinrich von Thünen, but his work, originally published in 1826, was not translated

into English until a generation after Weber's work had become known in the English-speaking world. Cf. Hall, ed., 1966.

5. The study was directed by Glenn E. McLaughlin, and among its staff could be found such luminaries as P. Sargant Florence, Edgar Hoover, Gardner Ackley and Lincoln Gordon.

6. Typically, in the area of location studies, the United States was still lagging behind Germany. Already by 1950 Heinz Dörpmund had published a text evaluating the various known methods for 'guiding' industrial location through public policies. For a *prewar* British example, comparable to the NRPB study but more sharply focused on the relation between industrial location and economically depressed areas, see Dennison, 1939, and *Report of the Royal Commission on the Distribution of the Industrial Population,* 1940.

7. Of course, location theory continued to produce 'refinements'. By 1968, however, an elegant textbook managed to summarize the essence of the subject in 125 pages (Beckmann, 1968). (Agricultural location theory was restated by Chisholm, 1962.)

8. A log-normal size distribution is one in which the second ranking city (arranged by a convenient measure of size) is one-half the size of the largest city, the third-ranking city is one-third its size, and so forth.

9. For practical reasons, Region I was defined in terms of its export sector and the economic activities clustered about it, while Region II was set equal to the 'rest of the nation'. This regionalization, of course, predetermined the outcome of empirical studies testing the export-base proposition.

10. For the concept of a regional employment multiplier, see Hildebrand and Mace Jr, 1950. Much of the recent criticism of export-led economic growth is that the benefits from multiplier effects of expanded production in Region I in fact accrue primarily in Region II.

11. Tiebout's argument was not entirely fair. Given a region of a certain size, was the historical relationship such that residentiary industries increased more rapidly than export industries? That was the empirical question to be decided. On the other hand, this line of inquiry would not explore the alternative process of an internally-generated, self-reliant development.

Bibliography

Alexander, J. W. 1952: Industrial expansion in the United States, 1939–47. *Economic Geography* **28**, 128–42.

Baskin, C. W. 1957: *A critique and translation of Walter Christaller's 'Die zentralen Orte in Süddeutschland'.* Ph.D. dissertation. University of Virginia.

Beckmann, M. 1968: *Location theory.* New York: Random House.

Berry, B. J. L. 1961: City size distribution and economic development. *Economic Development and Cultural Change* **9**, 573–87. Reprinted in Friedmann, J. and Alonso, W., editors 1964, 138–52.

—— 1964: Cities as systems within systems of cities. *Papers Regional Science Association* **13**, 147–64. Reprinted in Friedmann, J. and Alonso, W., editors 1964, 166–37.

Bunge, W. 1962: *Theoretical geography.* Lund Studies in Geography, Series C. General and Mathematical Geography, No. 1. Lund: C. W. K. Gleerup.

Carrothers, G. A. P. 1956: An historical review of the gravity and potential concepts of human interaction. *Journal of the American Institute of Planners* **22**, 94–102.

Chenery, H., *et al.* 1974: *Redistribution with growth*. Oxford University Press.

Chisholm, M. 1962: *Rural settlement and land use*. London: Hutchinson University Library.

Clark, C. 1938: *National income and outlay*. London: Macmillan.

  1951: *The conditions of economic progress*. London: Macmillan.

Cohen, S. 1969: *Modern capitalist planning: the French model*. Cambridge, Mass.: Harvard University Press.

Council of Economic Advisors 1951: *The New England economy: a report to the President*. Washington, DC: Government Printing Office.

Cumberland, J. H. 1971: *Regional Development experiences and prospects in the United States of America*. The Hague and Paris: Mouton.

Dennison, R. 1939: *The location of industry and the depressed areas*. Oxford University Press.

Dickinson, R. E. 1947: *City region and regionalism*. London: Kegan Paul, Trench, Trubner & Co.

Dörpmund, H. 1950: *Die Mittel der Standortlenkung und die Grenzen Ihrer Anwendbarkeit*. Bremen-Horn: Walter Dorn Verlag.

Dunn, E. S. 1954: *The location of agricultural production*. Gainesville, Florida: University of Florida Press.

Florence, P. S. 1948: *Investment, location, and size of plant*. Cambridge University Press.

Friedmann, J. 1955a: *The spatial structure of economic development in the Tennessee Valley. A study in regional planning*. Department of Geography, Research Paper 39. Chicago: University of Chicago.

  1955b: Development planning in Haiti: a critique of the UN report. *Economic Development and Cultural Change* **4**, 39–54.

  1956a: Locational aspects of economic development. *Land Economics* **32**, 213–27.

  1956b: The concept of a planning region. *Land Economics* **32**, 1–13. Reprinted in Friedmann, J. and Alonso, W., editors 1964, 497–518.

Friedmann, J. and Alonso, W., editors 1964: *Regional development and planning. A reader*. Cambridge, Mass.: The MIT Press.

  editors 1975: *Regional policy. Readings in theory and application*. Cambridge, Mass.: The MIT Press.

Friedrich, C. J., editor 1929: *Alfred Weber's theory of the location of industries*. The University of Chicago Press.

Friedrich, C. J. and Harris, S. R., editors 1963: *Public policy. Yearbook of the Harvard University Graduate School of Public Administration* **12**. Cambridge, Mass.: Harvard University Press.

Greenhut, M. L. 1956: *Plant location in theory and in practice: the economics of space*. Chapel Hill, NC: University of North Carolina Press.

Hackett, J. and Hackett, A.-M. 1963: *Economic planning in France*. London: Allen and Unwin.

Hagen, E. E. and White, S. F. T. 1966: *Great Britain: quiet revolution in planning*. New York: Syracuse University Press.

Hall, P., editor 1966: *Von Thünen's isolated state*. Oxford: Pergamon Press.

Harris, C. D. 1954: The market as a factor in the localization of industry in the United States. *Annals of the Association of American Geographers* **44**, 315–48.

Harris, S. E. 1952: *The economics of New England: case study of an older area*. Cambridge, Mass.: Harvard University Press.

Hildebrand, G. H. and Mace, A., Jr 1950: The employment multiplier in an expanding industrial market: Los Angeles County, 1940–1947. *Review of Economic Statistics* **32**, 241–9.

Hirsch, F. 1976: *Social limits to growth*. A Twentieth Century Fund study. Cambridge, Mass.: Harvard University Press.

Hoover, C. B. and Ratchford, B. U. 1951: *Economic resources and policies of the South*. New York: Macmillan.

Hoover, E. M. 1937: *Location theory and the shoe and leather industries*. Cambridge, Mass.: Harvard University Press.

1948: *The location of economic activity*. New York: McGraw-Hill.

Hoover, E. M. and Fisher, J. 1949: Research in regional economic growth. Reprinted in Universities-National Bureau Committee for Economic Research, *Problems in the study of economic growth*. New York: NBER.

Hoselitz, B. F. 1953: The role of cities in the economic growth of undeveloped countries. *The Journal of Political Economy* **61**, 195–208.

1955: Generative and parasitic cities. *Economic Development and Cultural Change* **3**, 278–94.

International Labour Office 1972: *Employment, incomes and equality: a strategy for increasing productive employment in Kenya*. Geneva: ILO.

Isard, W. 1956: *Location and space economy*. New York: The Technology Press of MIT and John Wiley & Sons.

Isard, W. and Vietorisz, T. 1955: Industrial complex analysis and regional development, with particular reference to Puerto Rico. *Paper and Proceedings Regional Science Association* **1**, U1–U17.

James, P. E. and Jones, C. F., editors 1954: *American geography: inventory and prospect*. New York: Syracuse University Press.

Jensen, M., editor 1951: *Regionalism in America*. Madison: University of Wisconsin Press.

Kuznets, S. 1941: *National income and its composition 1919–1938*. New York: National Bureau of Economic Research.

Lampard, E. E. 1955: The history of cities in economically advanced areas. *Economic Development and Cultural Change* **3**, 81–136. Reprinted in Friedmann, J. and Alonso, W., editors 1964, 321–42.

League of Nations, 1945: *Industrialization and foreign trade*. Series of League of Nations Publications II, Economic and Financial.

Lefeber, L. 1958: *Allocation in space: production, transport, and industrial location*. Amsterdam: North Holland Publishing Co.

Lewis, W. A. 1955: *The theory of economic growth*. London: Allen and Unwin.

Lösch, A. 1954: *The economics of location* (translation of *Die räumliche Ordnung der Wirtschaft*, 2nd edition 1944). New Haven: Yale University Press.

McKee, D. L., Dean, R. D. and Leahy, W. H., editors 1970: *Regional economics: theory and practice*. New York: The Free Press.

McLaughlin, G. E. and Robock, S. 1949: *Why industry moves south*. Washington, DC: National Planning Association.

Madden, C. H. 1956a: On some indicators of stability in the growth of cities in the United States. *Economic Development and Cultural Change* **4**, 236–52.

 1956b: Some spatial aspects of urban growth in the United States. *Economic Development and Cultural Change* **4**, 371–87.

Mandelbaum, K. 1945: *The industrialization of backward areas*. Oxford Institute of Statistics, Monograph No. 2. New York: Kelley and Millman.

National Resources Planning Board 1943: *Industrial location and national resources*. Washington, DC: Government Printing Office.

North, D. C. 1955: Location theory and regional economic growth. *Journal of Political Economy* **63**, 243–58. Reprinted in Friedmann, J. and Alonso, W., editors 1964, 240–55; and in Friedmann, J. and Alonso, W., editors 1975, 332–47.

 1956: The spatial and interregional framework of the United States economy: an historical perspective. *Papers and Proceedings Regional Science Association* **2**, 201–9.

Paauw, D. S. and Fei, J. C. H. 1973: *The transition in open dualistic economies. Theory and Southeast Asian experience*. New Haven: Yale University Press.

Perroux, F. 1950: Economic space: theory and applications. *Quarterly Journal of Economics* **64**, 89–104.

 1955: Note sur la notion de 'pôle de croissance'. *Cahiers de l'Institut de Science Economique Appliquée*, Série D, No. 8. English version 1970: Note on the concept of 'growth poles'. In McKee, D. L., Dean, R. D. and Leahy, W. H., editors 1970, 93–103.

Regional Science Association, 1955: *Papers and Proceedings* 1. First Annual Meeting of the Regional Science Association, Detroit, Michigan, 27–9 December 1954.

Robinson, J. 1962: *Economic philosophy*. Chicago: Aldine.

Ruttan, V. W. 1955: The impact of urban-industrial development on agriculture in the Tennessee Valley and the Southeast. *Journal of Farm Economics* **37**, 38–56.

Schaefer, F. K. 1953: Exceptionalism in geography. *Annals of the Association of American Geographers* **43**, 226–9.

Schultz, T. W. 1949: *Production and welfare of agriculture*. New York: Macmillan.

 1953: *The economic organization of agriculture*. New York: McGraw-Hill.

Stewart, J. Q. 1947: Empirical mathematical rules concerning the distribution and equilibrium of population. *Geographical Review* **37**, 461–85.

Tiebout, C. M. 1956a: Exports and regional economic growth. *Journal of Political Economy* **64**, 160–9. Reprinted in Friedmann, J. and Alonso, W., editors 1964, 256–60; and in Friedmann, J. and Alonso, W., editors 1975, 348–52.

   1956b: The urban economic base reconsidered. *Land Economics* **32**, 95–9.

Tinbergen, J. 1955: *On the theory of economic policy.* Amsterdam: North Holland Publishing Co.

   1958: *The design of development.* Baltimore: Johns Hopkins University Press.

   1964: *Central planning.* New Haven: Yale University Press.

United Nations. Department of Economic Affairs 1951: *Measures of the economic development of underdeveloped countries.* New York.

   1965: *Planning for economic development.* Vol. II: *Studies of national planning experience.* Part 1, Private and mixed economies. New York.

United Nations. Department of Economic and Social Affairs 1955: Problems of regional development and industrial location in Europe. In United Nations. Economic Commission for Europe, Research and Planning Division, 1955, 136–71.

United Nations. Economic Commission for Europe, Research and Planning Division 1955: *Economic Survey of Europe, 1954.* Geneva.

Universities-National Bureau Committee for Economic Research 1967: *Problems in the study of economic growth.* New York: National Bureau of Economic Research.

Vining, R. 1949: The region as an economic entity and certain variations to be observed in the study of a system of regions. *American Economic Review* **39**, 89–104.

   1953: Delimitation of economic areas: statistical conceptions in the study of the spatial structure of an American economic system. *Journal of the American Statistical Association* **48**, 44–64.

   1955: A description of certain spatial aspects of an economic system. *Economic Development and Cultural Change* **3**, 147–95.

Wellisz, S. 1960: Economic planning in the Netherlands, France, and Italy. *The Journal of Political Economy* **68**, 252–83.

Wirth, L. 1942: The metropolitan region as a planning unit. *National Conference on Planning*, **141–51**. Chicago: American Society of Planning Officials.

Yale University. Directive Committee on Regional Planning 1947: *The case for regional planning. With special reference to New England.* New Haven: Yale University Press.

Zipf, G. K. 1949: *Human behavior and the principle of least effort.* Cambridge, Mass.: Addison-Wesley.

Appendix:

Concerning the origins of the modern paradigm of economic development

The modern paradigm of economic development made its first appearance in the late 1940s. Circumstances leading up to it and helping to shape its form and substance included the beginnings of massive decolonization, post-war reconstruction, the discovery of Keynesian macro-economics in the 1930s, and the related invention of national income accounts, principally by Colin Clark (1938) and Simon Kuznets (1941). The new theoretical thinking was formulated for a wider audience of policy-makers in a famous 'Expert Report' prepared for the United Nations in 1951. Entitled *Measures for the Economic Development of Underdeveloped Countries* (United Nations, 1951), the report represented the first comprehensive, non-technical account of the paradigm that would reign virtually un-challenged down to the end of the 1960s. Even today it is still widely used as a framework for discussions of development policy.

In reading contemporary works on economic growth or in studying national development plans, one quickly identifies their intellectual kin-ship to this early ancestor. This is true for even the most recent policy thrusts of the World Bank (Chenery *et al.*, 1974) and the International Labour Office (1972), with their emphasis on employment generation and a more equal distribution of income. Although regarded as 'innovative', these newer approaches are little more than variants of the basic paradigm that emerged more than a quarter century ago. The funda-mental challenge of its assumptions in the form of a rival doctrine of *equal development* remains a minority view (see chapter 7).

The United Nations experts had been given the task 'to prepare, in light of the current world economic situation and of the requirements of economic development, a report on unemployment and underemploy-ment in underdeveloped countries and the national and international measures required to reduce such unemployment and under-employment'. The experts who had been called to speak upon these matters came from Chile, India, Lebanon, Jamaica, and the United States. Although from different national backgrounds, they had all been schooled in the same science of economics. This common professional background and a general orientation towards things western made agreement on questions of ideology and substance natural and easy. At the same time, it may be taken as an indicator of the experts' own alienation from the national societies of their origin.

There remains much in this report that makes for fascinating reading. For the moment, however, we should like to call attention only to those aspects that will show how economic development came to be discussed originally as a *success model*.

The report firmly established the now well-worn dichotomy of *developed* and *underdeveloped* countries. Two things about this distinction are especially noteworthy. First, reference is specifically to *countries* rather than economies, as if the two terms were wholly interchangeable.

A national economy may be viewed as that system whose performance can be *measured* by national product accounts. As a consequence, it comprises only those economic sectors that are monetized and so, to some extent, 'integrated' into the world economy, where they form part of the international division of labour. (This is true even where the market value of subsistence consumption is estimated.) But in poor agrarian countries these sectors form little more than enclaves of the world economy. By treating country and economy as virtually identical, the enclave comes to represent the whole of the economy and, by implication, the territorial system of social relations that includes it. Economists' values thus become the only relevant values in national affairs.

By using country and economy as substitutes for one another, the claim is sustained that economic structure and performance are decisive for wider country characteristics. This curious logic gives rise to such notions as 'backward societies', 'modernization', and 'social development', all of which are treated more or less as adjuncts and/or concurrent conditions of gains in production. This primary stress on economic relations tends to enhance the economists' *obiter dicta* on national policy. Accordingly, few distinctions have come to be made between such terms as development, national development, and economic development: they are all thought to converge upon the same socio-economic process of change and transformation.

Second, and most important, the report left no doubt that development occurred along only a *single dimension* of valued change, that of the market value of production. Development could therefore be measured by using national economic accounts and was said to occur where these accounts showed a sustained and secular rise in the value of production per head of population.*

Although the United Nations experts had been assigned the task of formulating basic policies for combating unemployment and underemployment in poor, agrarian countries, they chose to depart from the

* In national accounts, physical production is measured either in accordance with the concept of value added or at factor prices. In both cases given market prices are assumed to be substantially 'correct' indicators of economic scarcity or value. At least they are treated as such, despite misgivings that market values need not coincide with social valuations.

fashionable Keynesian approach of deficit spending by substituting an *economic growth approach*. In the case of the core countries of the world capitalist economy, unemployment of labour power went hand in hand with an under-utilization of already existing capacity for production. According to Keynes, demand could here be stimulated through government spending or other fiscal and monetary measures. But in the case of poor and essentially still pre-industrial societies, the problem was seen to be a very different one; namely, of how an adequate supply of productive plant and equipment might be created to generate employment at a scale sufficient to absorb the growing bulk of 'surplus' (i.e. low-productivity and unemployed) labour. Economists might have gone back to Adam Smith to study the early theories of political economy. Instead, they drastically simplified the problem: economic growth and development came to be viewed as primarily a problem in the rate of capital accumulation.

Having established a single dimension of 'development', it was natural to see the rich countries as more *advanced* and poor countries as relatively *backward*. Being backward (in the sense of both primitive and retarded), the problem of poor countries was said to be how to *catch up* with and become rich, modern, and powerful like the West.

The choice of a single dimension for the measure of economic development represented an enormous simplification of policy problems (few variables, an historical precedent, identical growth paths); it also gave the so-called theory of economic development an aura of scientific objectivity. National economic accounts 'revealed' the economic superiority of the West and did so in seemingly objective terms. But, of course, they also implied a more general superiority of culture without which – it was believed – their economic superiority could not have been achieved. This held especially true for technology – another measurable, objective entity – which clearly involved a whole cluster of new and presumably desirable traits, such as science, research, rationality, practicality, achievement criteria, innovation, belief in progress, geographical mobility, and so forth, *without which* economic development and modernization could not conceivably be obtained. This seemingly objective and historical character of development lent the paradigm its extraordinary powers of persuasion. (See Figure A.1.)

The acceptance of a single dimension for the measurement of economic development had yet another consequence, still largely implicit in the approach, but soon to be turned into a major article of faith. In accordance with the basic separation of efficiency in allocation from equity in distribution, which underlies the doctrine of unequal development, questions of fair distribution were almost completely ignored. Attention came to be focused instead on *growth efficiency* and hence on questions of efficient resource allocation, rapid capital accumulation, and technological change.

Given this conceptualization, development theory could be reduced to

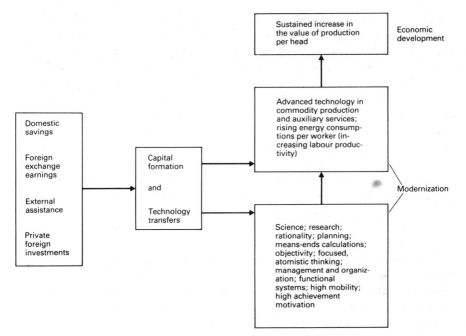

Figure A.1 A simple model of economic development, *circa* 1951.

the technical question of how poor countries might someday become rich. To lay out such a theory, however, meant to devise a *success model* of economic development.

The Report identified four basic conditions for success:

a. *An interdependent ('open') development with the already developed core countries of the world economy.* In practice, this meant: continuing to supply 'developed' countries with raw materials and specialized food-stuffs; accepting foreign capital, both public and private, in its various forms as direct investments, loans, and grants-in-aid; accepting and using technical foreign assistance as a means for accelerating progress towards 'modernization'; accepting repeated interference with and even continuing guidance in such domestic matters as budgetary allocations, fiscal and monetary policy, and political behaviour as a condition of continued foreign assistance; reducing tariff barriers to imports from the developed countries, especially for manufactured commodities; and taking part through trade in an international division of labour that was claimed to be beneficial for everyone.

b. *An urban-based process of accelerated industrialization.* Little hope was held out for activating agriculture as a leading economic sector. Economic development was virtually identified with industrial-ization and, more specifically, with the expansion of large-scale, technically modern enterprise. Although agricultural productivity had to be raised as well, it was thought that this would occur only if 'excess labour' were withdrawn from agriculture to be employed in cities. Reducing population pressure in rural areas would, in due course, lead to needed adjustments in agriculture, including its technical modernization. Or, as the report put it: '... a programme of agricultural improvement has to *start* by developing manufacturing industries which will absorb the surplus population of agriculture ... the development of manufacturing industry is ... of the highest priority' (United Nations, 1951, p. 59, italics added).*

c. *A high rate of capital formation* through both domestic savings and foreign exchange earnings retained for the importation of capital equipment and producer goods. As one of the authors of the report later put it, countries had to change from being 5 per cent to being 12 per cent savers (Lewis, 1955). They had to learn how to 'shape up'. In effect, this requirement was interpreted to mean that incomes should be concentrated in the hands of those with the highest *propensity* to save and invest, i.e. a small group of private 'entrepreneurs' and, of course, the State. Furthermore, it was clearly understood from the outset that poor countries, like poor people, had only a restricted capacity for mobilizing savings and would have to be 'assisted' to achieve the desired rates of growth.

d. *National economic planning* for central resource allocation and the maintenance of the basic macro-economic balances was regarded as an essential tool of successful economic development. So powerful, in fact, was the belief in the efficacy of planning, that planning and development came to be used as virtually synonymous terms, and the preparation of formal planning documents was required as a precondition for receiving foreign aid.

On all these points, the report was quite emphatic and declared them to be conditions necessary for 'development'. In addition, it announced that '... rapid economic progress is impossible without painful readjustments. Ancient philosophies have to be scrapped; old social institutions have to disintegrate; bonds of cast, creed, and race have to be burst; and large numbers of persons who cannot keep up with progress have to have their expectations of a comfortable life frustrated. Very few communities are willing to pay the full price of economic progress' (p. 15).

To properly understand this Schumpeterian rhetoric ('galestorms of creative distruction'), one has to read between the lines. It is fair to say that the authors of the report had in mind the emergence of *a universal, cosmopolitan civilization in which autonomous individuals would freely enter into*

---

* The assumption that agriculture is typically conducted in the countryside, while non-agricultural pursuits and especially manufacturing are distinctly urban activities simplified the picture but was clearly wrong. In many, and especially in small, cities, agriculture is one of the mainstays of the local economy, whereas industries are often located among the wheatfields. In a city such as Los Angeles, or in Southern Germany, country and city intermingle and, except in their physical form, such as density, land use, architecture, and other *derived* characteristics are often indistinguishable from one another.

contractual relationships with one another on the basis of an enlightened self-interest. No doubt, they saw themselves as standing in the vanguard of a 'modernizing elite' that would help to bring about this transformation. And they implied that countries unprepared to pay this price, would be condemned to remain forever 'backward'.

This call for a universal economic culture foreshadowed the spectacular rise of the transnational corporation during the last decade as the principal agent and bearer of capitalist development. The focus on *national* economic development was temporarily convenient, because territorial governments were still required for the 'successful' capitalist exploitation of resources. But it had never been an essential element of economic growth; and mystified more than it revealed.

Chapter 5
Polarized development

Following the breakthrough into the new paradigm which occured in the mid-fifties, regional planning studies experienced a great upsurge which lasted for more than two decades and propelled the field to its present state of development. The logic of unequal development, in its specific form of urban-based industrial growth, led to certain conclusions for regional planning: an emphasis on the growth of large cities, the pursuit of unequal development as a matter of policy, a view of regional planning that regarded it primarily as a way of influencing the location of manufacturing, and a belief that 'growth impulses' would eventually spread from major centres of innovation to the remainder of the economy. This focus on *polarized development* suggested that rural areas would take part in the general process of growth diffusion only to the extent that they were subject to the impact of the metropolitan economy. Access to large and rapidly growing cities was seen as a major, and possibly even as the principal, variable in rural development.

The Basic Paradigm

Towards the end of the fifties, two studies appeared which set the course of regional planning for the next two decades. The first was by Gunnar Myrdal (1957) who had acquired fame as Director of the United Nations Commission for Europe as well as for his early work on American race relations. In his new book, *Economic Theory and Underdeveloped Regions*, Myrdal introduced the notion of *circular, cumulative causation*, arguing that the course of capitalist development would be marked by deepening interregional inequalities. His analysis introduced the concepts of *backwash* and *spread* effects which he used to denote, respectively, the negative and positive spatial consequences of concentrated economic growth. Albert Hirschman's *The Strategy of Economic Development* (1958) was the second epoch-making work. Covering much of the same intellectual terrain, Hirschman explicitly employed the imagery of polarized development. But, contrary to Myrdal, he sidestepped the political issue of inequality. The language he used reflected his ideological position. Instead of backwash, he spoke of *polarization* and, instead of spread, of *trickle-down* effects.

Both writers described the impacts of a capitalist process of economic growth on spatially distributed population groups. The difference between them was chiefly one of values and political tradition. As a European, Myrdal examined the process of economic growth from a perspective in which questions of distribution could not be meaningfully separated from questions of efficiency. Hirschman, on the other hand, though born in Europe, revealed an attitude much more in tune with American thinking. Accepting polarization as inevitable during the beginning phases of economic growth, he was sanguine about the longer term in which trickle-down effects would begin to equalize regional differences.

This contrast is a classic one. Myrdal's perspective leads to the advocacy of strong government intervention to counteract the normal tendency of the capitalist system to create inequalities. Hirschman, by contrast, believed in what he regarded as the more or less spontaneous processes of capitalist development, in which the search for increased profits would eventually spin off growth-inducing industries to the more backward, peripheral regions of a national economy. In this process, the role of government would be limited to offering inducements that would hasten a recovery of spatial equilibrium.

The empirical evidence could be read in several ways but, on the whole, scholars who engaged in related research tended to side with Hirschman on this question (Borts and Stein, 1962; Williamson, 1965; Mera, 1965, 1973, 1975; Alonso, 1968b, 1971b). The gist of their argument, most clearly expressed by Williamson, was this: after an initial increase in regional income inequality, continued and efficiently directed economic growth would bring about a decrease in the relevant indices. Data for the United States and for Japan supported this conclusion. The question was whether it was also valid for the currently underdeveloped areas of the world.[1] The actual record was one of growing inequality, but perhaps a turning point was in the offing. For those who believed in the virtues of capitalism, it was convenient to place their bets on the 'hidden dynamics' of behaviour that were supposed to re-establish equilibrium. Only three conditions, it was thought, needed to be satisfied to make the theory come true: high labour mobility, a path of agricultural transformation from subsistence to corporate farming, and the absence of 'artificial' barriers to the transnational movement of capital. The object of development policy would be to ensure the presence of these conditions.

The paradigm of polarized development – of unequal development in its spatial dimension – had been elaborated somewhat earlier in France than in the United States (Perroux, 1964; Paelinck, 1965). The difference was partly one of language and intellectual style. In Perroux's vocabulary, polarization originally referred to leading industries that were highly interconnected with other sectors of the economy. In time, and largely through the efforts of Jacques Boudeville (1961), the term acquired a predominantly spatial connotation. In this usage, however, it contravened

certain conventions of the English language. Partly for this reason, Friedmann (1966) coined the term *core region* to replace it. In doing so, however,
the original meaning of polarized, together with its wider implications,
was lost.

For more than a decade, French and American schools of regional
economics and planning evolved along independent paths. Attempts to
bridge the cultural gap between them were not particularly successful
(Boudeville, 1966). Hirschman (1958) had referred to some of Perroux's
earlier work, and a volume of conference proceedings edited by Walter
Isard and John Cumberland (1961) further helped to spread the word.
But it was not until Niles M. Hansen's detailed account of regional planning in France (1968) that the theoretical background of this experience
came to be better known in the United States. The first full-length comparative treatment of French and American concepts came only the
following year (Darwent, 1969).

This time lag made it possible to develop an independent American
approach to the same problem. What was involved was the synthesis of
a large and diverse body of empirical work in a number of social sciences
that would account for the observed phenomena of geographic concentration (Ullman, 1958; Perloff and Wingo, 1961). Paelinck had tried to do
so in 1965, but Paelinck wrote in French, and his essay was not widely
distributed abroad. In the Anglo-American tradition of social science, a
first serious attempt at a synthesis was made by Friedmann (1972, original
version 1967, revised 1969). In this model, Hirschman's distinction
between a 'developed' north and an 'underdeveloped' south was transformed into a *core* and a *periphery* respectively. The latter was defined as
a region that stood in a relation of external dependency to powerful core
region interests. This unequal relationship could as easily produce increasing tension, conflict, repression (Myrdal) as it could result in gradual
reform and adjustment (Hirschman). At heart, it was not so much an
economic as a political relationship which concerned the organization and
distribution of territorial power (Hilhorst, 1971; de Britto, 1972; Friedmann, 1972, 1973a).

All told, the theory of polarized development had a rather unwieldy
structure. Although some small empirical research was started (e.g.
Schmidt, 1973), theoretical discussions lost themselves in vague generali-
ties (Brookfield, 1975). An incisive critical perspective was still needed.

A special place must be assigned to a monumental study of regional
economic growth, *Regions, Resources, and Economic Growth*, which appeared
at the beginning of the sixties (Perloff *et al.*, 1960). A milestone in
empirical research, it provided a sweeping view of over seventy years of
American economic history. To accomplish this feat, Harvey Perloff had
brought together some of America's leading scholars of the 'space
economy', including Edgar S. Dunn, who had completed his doctorate
on agricultural location under Walter Isard; Eric E. Lampard, an
economic historian with a special interest in the role of cities in generating

and mediating economic growth; and Richard F. Muth, an economist concerned with regional and urban problems.

The book was innovative in a number of ways. As a common framework for their analysis, the authors adopted economic location theory. In their empirical analysis, they focused on population, income, and employment. Most importantly, they decided to look at the economic fate of particular regions (specifically, of states and aggregations of states) exclusively in terms of their interrelationships with the larger national economy. They were thus concerned with relative, rather than absolute, regional performance; and the method of analysis which they evolved, known as shift-and-share, is still widely in use. According to this perspective, getting and holding on to the right kind of economic activity appeared as the best way to ensure high economic performance. Survival required regions no less than industrial firms to edge up their advantage over possible competitors. With changing technology and shifts in consumer demand, older regions might not be able to maintain their position. Sooner or later, economic decline was inevitable. In choosing between 'rich places' and 'rich people', the authors of *Regions, Resources, and Economic Growth* opted for the latter (p. 607):

> Economic decline in an area is an extremely difficult thing to face, particularly in our growth-minded culture, and yet the relative decline of certain areas in the *volume* of economic activities is an inevitable feature of a rapidly changing economy. It seems important that we learn to face up to problems involved in declines in volume if we are to achieve the important objective of rapid increases in *family* levels of living, particularly for those currently in the lower income groups.

This paragraph is revealing in a number of ways. To begin with, it shows how thoroughly the authors disregarded the possibility that some places might have a sufficiently integrated history and culture to deserve to exist in prosperity within a prosperous nation, even if this should come into conflict with measures of profit maximization at the level of the individual enterprise. That such places existed was the major assumption underlying the regionalist doctrine of the 1930s. It is also interesting that the decline of regions was regarded as inevitably a part of economic progress. Even though differences in inter-regional per capita incomes or other measures of development might decline over time, substantial differences would always remain and the theoretical ideal of spatial equilibrium would never be attained.[2] The United States was thus treated as virtually an open economy, with nothing but 'artificial' and 'harmful' barriers to the movement of people, capital, and goods. By its self-regarding actions, each optimizing atom would miraculously bring benefits to the aggregation of all the atoms. The economic problem was to maintain high rates of national growth in productive activity and to match people with jobs. All other problems were merely transitional, dealing with some of the 'inevitable' and 'difficult' social costs of this process.

In many ways, *Regions, Resources, and Economic Growth* was an unusual book. An intensely empirical work, it stood outside the prevailing paradigm of polarized development. Yet it was also no stranger to that model. In 1961 Perloff and Wingo published a paper which, to all intents and purposes, stated a core-periphery theory of regional economic growth. The empirical part of their study drew heavily on the earlier compendium. *Regions, Resources, and Economic Growth* was clearly not an easy book to pigeonhole.

The paradigm of polarized development served not only as a basis for understanding the historical process of industrial transformation, but also as a framework for policy. Two publications provided the appropriate imagery: Rodwin (1963) and Friedmann (1966). Both were attempts at translating French concepts of polarized development for an English-speaking audience. Lloyd Rodwin, for instance, not unlike Perroux, spoke of a strategy of 'concentrated decentralization', while Friedmann evolved a strategy for creating subsidiary 'core regions' in the peripheral areas of a national space economy. In line with the new paradigm, both authors regarded regional planning as primarily a national responsibility, and consequently as a dimension of *national* planning. They followed what might be called a systems approach, similar to that of Perloff *et al.*, but more 'nodalized', more spatially focused. Friedmann defined a set of interdependent development regions whose boundaries would shift in the course of economic growth. To this extent, he treated place values with the same disregard expressed by the authors of *Regions, Resources, and Economic Growth*. His ultimate concept was of a nationally integrated space economy that would facilitate the efficient attainment of further increments of economic growth. The elimination of a 'periphery' through the careful implantation of new core regions became the principal intermediate objective.[3]

Regional planning as a field of study

In 1961 Friedmann was appointed to teach regional planning in the Department of City and Regional Planning at MIT. This was something of a challenge. As a subject for professional study, regional planning scarcely existed. There were no textbooks and no clearly defined doctrine. The only thing resembling a doctrine was comprehensive river basin development (President's Water Resources Policy Commission, 1950). But this was clearly not in favour with students who had come to learn about the economic development of urban-based regions.

Leaning on prior work by Harvey Perloff (1957, Pt II), Friedmann believed that regional planning might be presented as an applied field of regional science. Launched only a few years earlier, regional science already offered an impressive array of analytical methods (Isard *et al.*, 1960; Isard and Cumberland, 1961; Bendavid, 1974). They included economic base analysis, input–output analysis, cost-benefit analysis, factor analysis, spatial interaction models, industrial complex analysis, social accounting, and locational analysis. In fact, Isard staked out his claim for a regional science on the strength of these methods of 'scientific' study. Regional accounting turned out to be one of the more abiding concerns, as witness the large number of studies which were generated over the decade (Stone, 1961; Hoover and Chinitz, 1961; Perloff and Leven, 1964; Leven, Legler and Shapiro, 1970). Unfortunately, implementation often lagged behind theory and hampered its further development, which could be significantly advanced only through practice.[4]

By linking regional planning with regional science, the intellectual traditions and ideological biases of that field would, of course, be inherited. This heritage was clearly reflected in Friedmann's terse definition (1963, p. 171):

> Regional planning is concerned with the process of formulating and clarifying social objectives in the ordering of activities in supra-urban space. The basic question is: how are activities to be distributed in space so as to meet social objectives? Alternatively, what are the proper social objectives in accordance with which activities are to be allocated in space?

And he concluded with a sibylline comment: 'This formulation links regional planning to its basis in the pure theory of location without, however, achieving an identity.'

In retrospect, this attempt to define regional planning was important only in so far as it gave notice that an effort was underway to establish a new academic subject. The following year, the *Journal of the American Institute of Planners* published a special issue on regional development and planning (Friedmann, ed., 1964). Here the link to the 'pure theory of location' was made even more explicit with a contribution by Edwin von Böventer (1964) entitled 'Spatial Organization Theory as a Basis of Regional Planning.'[5]

That same year, Friedmann and Alonso (1964) published a volume of readings which assembled examples from the three areas of knowledge which, the editors believed, comprised the intellectual foundations of the new discipline: spatial organization, urbanization, and regional growth theory.[6] These fields were themselves rather new at the time and gained a sharp identity only during the subsequent decade. As a result, when the second edition was published in 1975, only a handful of 'classics' was retained. Most of the articles included in the later edition were based on very recent research. To facilitate comprehension, however, we shall discuss the pertinent contributions without respect to the time when they were made.[7]

1. Spatial organization

This broad topic may be divided into four subfields:

a. *Urban systems*. Brian Berry (1961, 1963, 1971) was the leading scholar of the population-size arrangements of cities. The question was, to what extent did systems of cities arrange themselves according to the statistical rule of log-normality, if population size was taken as the appropriate measure.[8] The form of the distribution and, as a special case of this form, the degree of city primacy, was taken to be significantly related to economic growth. Most students of the subject and most politicians agreed that a large (or growing) primacy index was perhaps inevitable, but there was more heat than reason in their argument. In any event, discussions of urban primacy (which had to do with spatial organization) were closely related to the question of optimum city size and efficient location, which will be discussed more fully later on. Despite a great deal of ingenuity in analysing urban population size distributions, however, little of genuine value emerged, except for the belief that a good and even mix of city sizes might be favourable to national development. But this notion was extremely vague, posing intricate problems of measurement. Its usefulness for policy proved to be quite limited.

b. *Modernization surfaces*. These were essentially a mapping exercise, using factorial or component analysis as their principal method. Geographers found that they could isolate clusters of related variables, giving each cluster an analytically significant name or label based on the most important variables it contained. The resulting values could be mapped, and the product came to be called a 'modernization' surface (Soja, 1968, 1974; Gould, 1970).[9]

Such surfaces were visually evocative. Ostensibly, their purpose was to depict the spatial extent of socio-economic development. In fact, they merely succeeded in mapping the penetration of neo-colonial capitalism. Whatever their meaning, the maps did little to clarify the processes by which the actual configurations were produced.

In the late sixties, Brian Berry devised an interesting traverse measure by which he could produce graphs that showed appropriate variations in index values for given sections of a line connecting two cities (Berry and Neils, 1969; Berry, 1970). The index numbers stood for variables that were thought to be significant for economic growth and for which location-coded data, such as migration, income, population density, agricultural production, etc., were available. Berry's graphs purported to show the impact of cities on their surroundings, as well as the ecological dominance of larger metropolitan centres (Lamb, 1975). The traverse diagrams appeared to validate the more theoretical notions of polarized development. Accordingly, one might also say that the theory confirmed the past. But was it correct to project it, willy-nilly, into the future as well? Would the future be determined by the same forces? Furthermore, had the correct forces been identified? Obviously, no one knew for sure. Still, it was more comfortable to believe that the future would be roughly like the past than to invent a future *a priori*.

c. *Corridor development.* A special case of 'modernization surfaces' is the geography of corridor development. Although the French geographer A. Pottier (1963) had written an important article on the subject several years earlier, the principal work (in English) was done by Whebell (1969). Basically, corridor development took place along transportation 'axes' that attracted modern industry and other activities of high productivity. Corridor development fitted with the assumptions of 'gravity models' as well as with related studies on spatial innovation diffusion which, as Allan Pred (1971) had pointed out, were heavily dependent on patterns of communication. Whebell had applied himself to a study of Canadian linear developments, and the generalized forms of economic landscape which he constructed from his empirical results were highly suggestive and useful as a rough and ready way for predicting the probable shape of spatial development effects of improvements in transportation.

d. *Spatial diffusion processes.* If economic growth was 'polarized' in primate cities (or core areas), what were the chances that it might spread to other parts of the country? Work on modernization surfaces suggested that a regular diffusion process was at work that might be detected through statistical analysis. Geographers, and especially Swedish geographers, had done extensive work on the theory of spatial innovation diffusion; but it was left to Poul Ove Pedersen, a Danish planner, to relate this research to processes of spatial (regional) development (1970). Innovation, information flows, contact systems, locational choice, and diffusion were suddenly merged in a heuristically fruitful framework. Related studies by Törnqvist (1970), Berry (1972) and Pred (1973) did a good deal to round out the picture. In his usually bold fashion, Berry (1972) formulated what has since become the basic proposition in spatial diffusion research: that innovations diffuse outward from core to periphery via a process of hierarchical diffusion, down the urban hierarchy, and from given urban centres to their surrounding hinterlands in 'wave-like' fashion. In any event, urban growth and the spatial diffusion of innovations seemed to be closely linked. But whether the process of spatial diffusion was also capable of being guided via public policy remained in doubt.

2. Urbanization

The person most responsible for showing how urbanization as a social process (and the city as a social artifact) were related to economic growth was Bert Hoselitz, a professor of economic history at the University of Chicago and editor of *Economic Development and Cultural Change*. His first statement (1953) posed the general question of the role of cities in economic growth, especially in developing countries. This question stood in sharp contrast to the prevailing view which either failed to acknowledge that economic growth might have a partially or independent social dimension or refused to see the city as a generator of economic growth, seeing urbanization as merely a problem, one of the unavoidable costs of economic progress.[10]

In 1953, Hoselitz convened a conference on the role of cities in which a number of germinal papers were presented, notably a broad-ranging cultural-historical appraisal by Redfield and Singer (1954), Hoselitz's own contribution to the proceedings on 'generative and parasitic cities' (1955), and Eric Lampard's initial attempt to write a prolegomenon to a history of cities and urbanization in advanced industrial societies (1955). All three of these papers have since become classics in the continuing attempt to comprehend the socio-economic and spatial forces shaping our lives.

Unfortunately, this brave attempt to link social (and inherently spatial) phenomena to what was still conceived as an essentially economic process did not generate much new research. Hoselitz's theme was eventually taken up by John Friedmann (1961), who emphasized the spatially integrative role of cities and thus related the multi-disciplinary literature on urbanization to regional planning.

But the subject did not go away. In particular, a series of volumes resulted from UNESCO-sponsored international conferences that explored the relationships between urbanization and industrialization on three continents: Africa (International African Institute, 1956), Asia (Hauser, ed., 1957) and Latin America (Hauser, ed., 1961).[11] These studies formed part of a more comprehensive effort to find a role for sociology in the booming field of development studies (Hauser and Schnore, eds, 1965). In what must be considered the classical tradition of urban sociology in the United States, the primary focus had always been on urban *pathologies* – on the slums, rootlessness, poverty, and anomie engendered in cities by the processes of economic growth. This was the *negative* side of Hoselitz's urban generation of economic growth, though even Hoselitz had countenanced the possibility that cities might be 'parasitic' on the national economy. This tradition of urban pathology has continued till the present day, at least as a motivation for research, even though nearly all the more recent studies have arrived at reasonably hopeful assessments of the urbanization experience (Nelson, 1969; Perlman, 1976).

In 1964, the Indian economist N. V. Sovani published a well-known paper in which he asked whether the rapid influx of migrants into cities, which took place despite the fact that these cities were not industrializing at anywhere near the rate which had come to be expected as 'normal' in Western Europe and the United States, was not an instance of 'over-urbanization' and thus dysfunctional for economic growth. His answer was inconclusive and suggested that further research needed to be done to clarify the issue.

The Hoselitz–Hauser–Sovani theme was taken up again by Friedmann (1969) in a paper for a conference on the contribution of the social sciences to the study of urbanization (Miller and Gakenheimer, 1971). Friedmann's arguments were generally positive. Like Hoselitz, he attributed all manner of 'generative' forces to urbanization, partly to counteract what he felt to be the excessively pathogenic view of sociologists. Friedmann's upbeat interpretation came under scathing criticism. Richard Morse, a distinguished urban historian, frankly doubted the possibilities of a general theory of urbanization (1971). Urbanization could be studied only as an historical process.

Nevertheless, several attempts were made to sketch some elements of a comprehensive theory of urbanization (Friedmann *et al.*, 1971; McGee, 1971; Friedmann, 1973b, Part I). They were essentially frameworks for the study of urbanization, and their general form cast serious doubt on the emerging doctrine of growth centres. This was especially so in the case of McGee who elaborated Hoselitz's earlier notion of 'parasitic' cities.

But urbanization studies, conducted at an increasing tempo in all of the social sciences, were not easily squeezed into a theoretical mould. Each science preferred to work its own pastures, and a major review essay by Friedmann and Wulff (1976) found little reason to rejoice. In spite of literally hundreds of studies, overall knowledge of urbanization had advanced very little. Indeed, it might be questioned whether the urbanization paradigm as such was as useful as had been thought. Marxist critics, for instance, suggested that one had to look to relations of production rather than to urbanization as the fundamental explanation of changes in the space economy and of the social processes which had come to be subsumed under the study of urbanization (Harvey, 1973).

3. Regional growth theory

At the time when Friedmann and Alonso published their first book of readings (1964), the only fully articulated regional growth theory was the economic base theory of Douglass North (1955, 1956). As we have shown in chapter 4, North used a two-region construct to develop his model; and he applied the model to problems that were, essentially, territorial. Although his regions were open to the extent that they traded with the outside world, receiving flows of capital in return, they were essentially bounded by virtue of their common history and the common nature of their problems, such as the Pacific Northwest (Pfister, 1963) or the Mezzogiorno in Italy (Chenery, 1962; Allen and MacLennan, 1970).

This model contrasted sharply with the model of a *dynamic spatial system* which was territorially linked only at the level of the *national economy*. Spatial systems did not have boundaries but nodes, linkages, and areas of influence that could be portrayed as a continuous surface (for example, as a 'geography of health', a 'modernization surface'). Within spatial systems analysis, properly speaking, regions did not exist. Bounded regions could be superimposed only uneasily on spatial systems (Friedmann and Stuckey, 1973).

Spatial systems theory envisaged the following development process: a set of dynamic nodal areas (urban economies) would attract migrants from less dynamic agricultural areas (Hathaway, 1960; Okun and Richardson, 1961). Following an absolute decline in rural population densities, *agricultural adjustments* would follow, raising the productivity of labour in agriculture and integrating rural with urban corporate structures (Schultz, 1953; Ruttan, 1955; Nicholls, 1961). The final outcome of this process would be an *interregional equilibrium* (Borts and Stein, 1962; Lefeber, 1958).

Harvey Perloff and his colleagues tried to reconcile conflicting regional growth theories (Perloff *et al.*, 1960; Perloff, 1963) by constructing a model which consisted of a national system of territorial regions, so that economic growth in one would be partially dependent on growth in every other region. At the same time, Perloff adopted an 'input–output access' approach, which allowed him to think of an overlay of spatial (nodal) systems. Despite this effort at integrating fundamentally different approaches to regional study, it cannot really be said that he succeeded. The final result was a separate treatment: regional-territorial in Perloff *et al.* (1960), and spatial-functional in Duncan *et al.* (1960).[12]

More recent work in regional growth theory has struggled with much the same problem. Siebert (1969), for example, was aware of the existence of the problem; but in the end he came down on the side of territorial (regional) theory and, like North, used a two-region model of growth. Perhaps the most sustained effort at modelling regional economic growth was Harry Richardson's. His first major book (1969) ignored the spatial systems approach. His most recent treatment, on the other hand, constitutes a relatively successful attempt to integrate the two approaches (Richardson, 1973b, 1978). It may be regarded as the most viable of regional growth theories to date.

Summary

In review, it is apparent that 'as a field study' regional planning was an extraordinarily ambitious subject which hoped to achieve a unification of economics and geography and, in addition, to introduce new sociological perspectives. When we turn to the doctrine of regional planning, which was more explicitly normative, political and public administration perspectives were added. Clearly, so vast a synthesis of nearly all the social sciences would be difficult to negotiate. Not unexpectedly, the literature in the field remains disconcertedly eclectic. The spatial systems perspective promised to be a grand solution to the problem of integrating the bases of social science knowledge; but only geographers, it turned out, were persuaded of its utility. With a few notable exceptions, economists, sociologists and political scientists shunned the spatial systems approach. This left geographers and economists somewhat uneasily allied in their attempt to fashion a field of regional studies and planning.

Regional planning doctrine: growth centres and growth poles

The preceding theories were funnelled and made operationally tractable in a policy doctrine that was to dominate the entire decade of the 1960s and beyond. The doctrine of growth centres became the normative counterpart to the positive theory of polarized development with its strong commitment to systems analysis. This doctrine came to have a singular fascination for regional planners. Its attractiveness stemmed from its commonsense appeal ('you can't be everywhere at the same time'), empirical observation (urban-industrial development under capitalism was, in fact, 'polarized'), and the desire for technocratic authority (the doctrine was rooted in several social science disciplines, and especially in economics, the most prestigious of the lot). It was, moreover, easy to conceptualize and to communicate. And it had, as we shall see, a strong political appeal: growth centre designations could be awarded like medals.

The idea of growth centres originated with François Perroux (1950, 1971 [1955]), whose original notion of 'growth pole' was intended to convey a non-spatial polarization of the economy which had a great deal in common with problems of inter-industry linkages and multiplier effects. These same questions were being examined in the United States by Walter Isard and his colleagues (Isard, 1951; Isard and Vietorisz, 1955; Isard, Schooler and Vietorisz, 1959; Isard, Langford and Romanoff, 1966) and by Roland Artle in Sweden (1965). But input–output and industrial complex studies were highly technical, whereas concepts such as 'economic polarization' and 'growth pole' held an intuitive appeal that fired the imagination and ensured their quick acceptance.

In any event, if it was to serve as the basis for a regional doctrine, the Perrouvian theory of the polarized economy had to be brought to the ground. For Europe, this task was accomplished by Boudeville (1961, 1966), Pottier (1963), Davin (1964), Perroux (1964), and Paelinck (1965). Now it was no longer just an economic space that was being polarized, but the entire space-economy ('räumliche Wirtschaft'). This inversion proved to be decisive.

Perroux's idea of polarization came to inspire Hirschman who in his principal work on economic development (1958) had explicitly (if fleetingly) referred to 'growth poles'. At least in the Anglo-American context, however, the specific application of the growth pole idea to regional planning can be traced to Lloyd Rodwin's 1963 article which bore the pointed title 'Choosing Regions for Development'. Rodwin enunciated a doctrine of 'concentrated decentralization' which was simply a growth centre doctrine by another name. The basic idea was that urban-industrial growth could be diffused to the backward regions of a developing country by concentrating infrastructure and directly productive investments at selected points (or subregions) which had a potential for economic expansion. In this way, growth might be decentralized from primate city areas and yet benefit from the presumed advantages of external economies and the division of labour which large cities made possible. In a study of Venezuela, Friedmann (1966) generalized this doctrine, extending it to a multiple system of growth centres or core regions.

Growth centre doctrine now evolved rather rapidly, with critical assessments of the French experience by Niles M. Hansen (1967, 1968) and a sweeping review by D. F. Darwent (1969). A key paper by the Spanish economist, José Ramon Lasuén (1969), succeeded in linking the evolving doctrine to organization theory and the first Anglo-American applications to problems of regional planning were made by Brian Berry (1969) and Gordon Cameron (1970).

By this time, geographers had begun to enter the picture and to appropriate the concept of growth centres to emerging geographic theory (Thoman, eds, 1974; Helleiner and Stöhr, eds, 1974). Geographers found in it a method for negotiating the difficult transition from economic growth theory to the theory of spatial organization, as well as a way to 'crash' the somewhat fluid and applied field of regional planning. The resulting interaction with economists, regional scientists and regional planners led to the identification of two major problems that pre-empted much of the discussion: optimum city size and the spatial diffusion of growth.

a. *Optimum city size.* The debate revolved around the questions whether large cities were growth-efficient or, alternatively, whether smaller cities were equally as capable of generating self-sustaining growth and filtering this growth into the less-developed periphery. The argument was largely carried on among economists, though geographers chimed in with their concepts of urban primacy and city-size distributions, a literature which we have already reviewed. One of the earliest contributions was by G. M. Neutze (1965), an Australian economist, who concluded that cities of less than a million population were quite as efficient as larger, metropolitan cities and might therefore be helped to decentralize production and population. He also suggested that, instead of looking for a single 'optimum' city size, it might be more reasonable to think of optimum size *distributions*. This suggestion, of course, brought his discussion back into the realm of the geographer's 'spatial organization'.

Neutze's advocacy of middle-sized cities was challenged by William Alonso (1968b, 1971a, 1972b) who argued strongly that the presumed inefficiency of large cities lacked concrete evidence. At the same time, the obvious preference of industrialists for location in or near metropolitan cities suggested that it might, indeed, be very difficult to reverse this preference by the kinds of incentives that regional planners normally offered. Alonso held that market signals were probably better indicators of efficient allocations in space and that, as his student Koichi Mera had shown, relative prices of factors of production would favour the periphery once the centre had become too crowded.

This see-saw debate swung back again to a consideration of the advantages of medium-sized cities with the important work by E. A. J. Johnson (1970) who, for the first time, considered the problem of rural development in a context of regional planning, arguing persuasively that smaller cities were necessary to integrate the rural with the larger urban economy. His thinking was heavily influenced by many years of work as a consultant in India and by his critical reading of central place studies. Although he recognized the importance of large cities for industrial growth, he emphasized the tail-end of city-size distributions as essential to developing a space-economy that included – as indeed it had to include – the rural 'sector'. In a sense, Johnson supported Neutze's position that what had to be considered were city-size distributions, or entire systems of cities.[13]

Whereas Johnson advocated quite local growth centres – thinking perhaps of John P. Lewis's admonition which had, as early as 1962, called for a town-centring policy that would promote industrial development in cities of around 50,000 population (Lewis, 1962) – Niles Hansen (1970) emphasized cities four or five times as large. But Hansen was writing in an American context and had in mind the application of Federal policy to depressed areas, such as Appalachia.

Very little may be concluded from this survey: the question of city size appeared to be a very emotional issue, even to politicians, but the existing evidence could be turned in a variety of ways to suit one's predilections. In a masterful summary, Harry Richardson (1973a) pulled the rug from underneath the growth-size theorists by arguing that none of the models so far introduced brought down decisive evidence favouring any one optimum size or distribution of city sizes. This conclusion freed the planners to formulate urban-regional policies for a variety of urban settlement patterns.

b. *The spatial diffusion of growth.* Diffusion problems were of special interest to geographers, some of whom set out to measure the 'spread' and 'backwash' effects of accelerated urban-industrial growth at some convenient growth centre. Among the better-known studies of this sort are those by Nichols (1969), Moseley (1972) and Lamb (1975). The results of their measures were inconclusive. In the immediate vicinity (and along major transport routes), the predicted positive balance of spread over backwash could be observed, but at even moderate distances effects became barely noticeable and, for certain layers or bands, backwash rather than spread effects appeared to dominate. However, a problem with all of these studies was that they merely looked for spatial indicators (the so-called 'effect') and did not concern themselves with the supposed mechanisms that led to the observed results. T. W. Schultz (1953) had suggested that the market functioned most efficiently near cities, but what if the rural economy was of the plantation or subsistence type? Then market forces might have very little influence on rural areas even in the vicinity of very large cities (Baldwin, 1956). In short, there was no assurance that economic growth effects would everywhere be 'filtered' via so-called wave-like actions into the hinterlands of growth centres.

These were scientific niceties, however, that did not prevent the march of the growth centres doctrine across the globe. Antoni Kuklinski, a Polish geographer who was heading a research programme concerned with regional development planning at the UNRISD, Geneva, had much to do with the world-wide spread of the evolving growth centres doctrine (Kuklinski, eds, 1972; Kuklinski and Petrella, eds, 1972). Despite their superficial appeal, there was little evidence that growth centres actually helped to diffuse economic growth. Indeed, there was mounting evidence to the contrary.[14]

For one thing, it had become politically popular to identify hierarchies of growth poles, centres, and points (ODEPLAN, 1968). Not only this; there was a good deal of competition among cities that vied with each other for nomination as a growth centre. As governments responded first to this, then to that, regional pressure, there were frequent re-orderings of spatial priorities (Richardson, 1971). So long as a 'growth centre' designation was merely honorific and did not, as in Venezuela, actually involve a major policy commitment, this practice could continue with impunity.

Both Rodwin and Friedmann had argued for limiting policy intervention to only a few major growth centres, as opposed to reaching down the urban hierarchy (Rodwin and Associates, 1969; Friedmann, 1973b, chapter 14). Their argument, however, concerned implementation. And questions of implementation were rarely touched upon in the growth centre literature.

Rodwin and Associates (1969) had documented what it would take to carry out the construction of a major urban-industrial complex. William Alonso, on the other hand, had pointed out that an economy, such as the United States, might have many 'spontaneous' growth centres which would flourish at various points and for varied periods in its history (Alonso and Medrich, 1972). Continuing in this vein, he then suggested that most national policies had differential spatial (urban) effects. If one wanted to be truly effective in guiding the spatial growth of the economy, one had to gain a better understanding of these 'implicit' policies, a task that was surely stupendous (Alonso, 1972a).

Finally, there were suggestions that the solution to the problems of regional growth lay in the decentralization of effective political power

(Miller, 1971; Weiker, 1972). These suggestions, however, were not followed up by research and merely added fuel to the eternal controversy between centralizers and their opponents.

In 1974 Malcolm Moseley published what until now is by far the most complete, well-balanced, and theoretically adequate account of the growth centre doctrine (Moseley, 1974). Although its conclusions were on the whole pessimistic, Moseley kept the doctrine alive by advocating an 'intermediate-size city' strategy for Great Britain and proposing an agenda for research.

In all of this, it is surely surprising that regional planning almost succeeded in making a fetish of growth centres to the neglect of other dimensions of regional policy.[15] Area or territorially specific policies receded into the background of academic discussions. As a result, insufficient attention was paid to questions of natural resources, political implementation, administrative organization, and above all, to rural development. Growth centres had become the universal solution to every regional problem. But no one was really sure what this implied.

Notes

1. This was not the only question, but it was the only issue which appeared to be relevant at the time. Among the questions which might have been raised, but were not, were these: why should regional equality be measured only in terms of income flows, rather than stocks of wealth, or access to the means of production? Would unemployment data show the same distribution as income? What were the human costs of income equalization in terms of social disruption, and the abandonment of past investments? How were income and wealth socially distributed within each region? How did the economic structures of each region evolve over time and with what consequences for the long-term welfare of regional populations? By making Williamson's income analysis into a fetish, the whole issue of regional imbalance and inequality was reduced to banality. (There were, in addition, significant technical questions of measurement that were ignored. Examples include the definition of regions – the larger the regions, *cet. par.*, the less the income differential – or the compilation of income estimates – i.e. whether they were calculated on an income or expenditure basis.)

2. This conclusion flatly contradicted the later studies of Borts and Stein (1962) who were quite forthright in stating the income equalization hypothesis: 'We therefore conclude that the United States interregional and interindustrial growth pattern seems to be tending towards an interregional competitive equilibrium and hence towards intertemporal efficiency' (p. 214).

3. Both Rodwin and Friedmann had evolved their policy doctrines in the course of consulting practice abroad: Rodwin in Turkey and Venezuela, and Friedmann in Brazil, the Republic of Korea, and Venezuela as well. In retrospect, it is curious to see how decisive Latin American experience proved to be for the development of regional planning doctrine. Both Perroux and Boudeville had done work there; so had Paelinck. Hirschman's book of 1958 was partly based on his experiences as a consultant to the government of Colombia. Hilhorst has worked for years in Argentina and Peru. And it was in Chile, roughly from 1964 to 1970, that the new doctrine was first put to work under the sponsorship of the Ford Foundation.

Some years later, timid attempts were made – on the whole unsuccessfully – to introduce systems thinking to urban growth policies in the United States (Thompson, 1972; Wingo, 1972; Cameron and Wingo, eds, 1973). The attempt did not succeed, in the sense that there was never any serious experiment with the approach. An explanation might be that the United States did not have an established system of national planning; that, in contrast to Turkey, Venezuela, and Korea, it was a federated nation with a very different regional politics; that urban growth in America could probably be managed successfully only through local initiative, with only a minimum of central direction; and that federal controls on urban growth were, in the nature of the case, quite limited.

4. See, for instance, the excellent theoretical paper by Leontiev and Strout (1963) on interregional input–output analysis. To our knowledge, a full-scale input–output study for a national system of regions has never been carried out.

5. Böventer had absorbed the tradition of Christaller and Lösch and could properly be regarded as Lösch's successor in Germany. He is currently teaching at the University of Munich.

6. William Alonso was the first Ph.D. from Walter Isard's Department of Regional Science at the University of Pennsylvania. At the time, he was teaching in the Department of City and Regional Planning at Harvard University. Like Friedmann, he was a frequent visitor to the Joint Centre for Urban Studies in Cambridge.

7. The scientistic character of the emerging regional planning doctrine is no accident. It is the result of an effort to give academic recognition to an activity that is nothing if not practical. Given the institutional arrangements for regional planning, it is indeed questionable whether professionals with a degree in regional planning should be automatically entrusted with the work. Nearly all regional planning throughout the world is being done by non-professional planners! During the early 1960s in the United States, there was little hope that regional planners might actually find employment in their 'profession'. The market for regional planners was primarily overseas. Meanwhile, however, there was an amusing game to be played by trying to tease out the implications for policy of ongoing theoretical work in the social sciences. Little of that would turn out to be useful in practice (Friedmann and Stöhr, 1966).

8. This was indeed the question which appeared to be of some policy relevance. But its answer rested on a vast literature which had grown up around so-called central place theory (Berry and Pred, 1965; Berry, 1967). Central place theory might be defined as a theory of the location of trade and service activities. In reality, however, it came to absorb a much wider field of studies, involving among other topics urban size hierarchies, areal functional organization, internal business structure of cities, town–country relations, and innovation diffusion. Central place theory was the only deductive theory in geography, and so its influence on quantitative-analytical work was enormous. It was the ruling paradigm of the 1960s.

9. An earlier effort, using American data, was called a 'geography of economic health' (Thompson *et al.*, 1962).

10. A third view – introduced considerably later – was that cities were important because they allowed the efficient localization of industries via external (agglomeration) economies (Chinitz, 1961; Thompson, 1968; Alonso, 1968a, 1971a). This third view attempted, on the one hand, to account for the fact of spatial polarization and, on the other hand, to construct a theory of urban growth via the related concepts of backward and forward linkages and the theory of the employment multiplier. The theory of urban growth would be completed by incorporating appropriate aspects of migration theory (Shaw, 1975).

11. Hauser was a sociologist and professor at the University of Chicago, a colleague of Hoselitz, and had also been Director of the United States Bureau of the Census.

12. Subsequent studies, but with more historical perspective, include Pred, 1966 and 1973; Duncan and Lieberson, 1970.

13. Johnson gave rise to a new terminology in regional planning circles, according to which

large centres came conventionally to be called 'growth poles', medium-sized cities, 'growth centres', and localities that were strategically located with respect to rural areas, 'growth points'. With this, the entire city hierarchy became eligible for 'growth centre' designation.
14. For a critical assessment of growth centre doctrine, see chapter 7.
15. For a listing of these dimensions, see Friedmann, ed., 1970, and 1973b, chapter 12.

Bibliography

Alonso, W. 1968a: Industrial location and regional policy in developing countries. University of California, Institute of Urban and Regional Development, Working Paper No. 74. Berkeley: University of California. Reprinted in Friedmann, J. and Alonso, W., editors, 1975, 64–96.

  1968b: Urban and regional imbalances in economic development. *Economic Development and Cultural Change* **17**, 1–14. Reprinted in Friedmann, J. and Alonso, W., editors, 1975, 622–35.

  1971a: The economics of urban size. *Papers of the Regional Science Association* **26**, 67–83. Reprinted in Friedmann, J. and Alonso, W., editors, 1975, 434–50.

  1971b: Equity and its relation to efficiency in urbanization. In Kain, J. F. and Meyer, J. R., editors, 1971, 40–57.

  1972a: Problems, purposes and implicit policies for a national strategy of urbanization. In Mazie, S. M., editor, 1972, 635–47. Reprinted in Friedmann, J. and Alonso, W., editors, 1975, 639–49.

  1972b: The question of city size and national policy. In Funck, R., editor, 1972, 111–18.

Alonso, W. and Medrich, E. 1972: Spontaneous growth centres in twentieth century American urbanization. In Hansen, N., editor, 1972, 229–65.

Artle, R. 1965: *Studies in the structure of the Stockholm economy: towards a framework for projecting metropolitan community development.* Ithaca, N.Y.: Cornell University.

Allen, K. and MacLennan, M. C. 1970: *Regional problems and policies in Italy and France.* Beverly Hills, Ca.: Sage Publications.

Baldwin, R. E. 1956: Patterns of development in newly settled regions. *Manchester School of Economics and Social Studies* **24**, 161–79. Reprinted in Friedmann, J. and Alonso, W., editors, 1964, 266–84.

Barna, T., editor 1963: *Structural independence and economic development.* New York: Macmillan.

Bendavid, A. 1974: *Regional economic analysis for practitioners.* New York: Praeger.

Berry, B. J. L. 1961: City size distributions and economic development. *Economic Development and Cultural Change* **9**, Part I: 573–87. Reprinted in Friedmann, J. and Alonso, W., editors, 1964, 138–52.

1963: Cities as systems within systems of cities. *Papers and proceedings of the Regional Science Association* **13**, 147–64. Reprinted in Friedmann, J. and Alonso, W., editors, 1964, 116–37.

1967: *Geography of market centers and retail distribution.* Englewood Cliffs, New Jersey: Prentice-Hall.

1969: *Growth centers and their potentials in the Upper Great Lakes region.* Washington, DC: Upper Great Lakes Commission.

1970: The geography of the United States in the year 2000. *Transactions of the Institute of British Geographers* No. 51. (November), 21–53. Reprinted in Friedmann, J. and Alonso, W., editors, 1975, 106–36.

1971: City size and economic development: conceptual synthesis and policy problems, with special reference to South and Southeast Asia. In Jakobson, L. and Prakash, V., editors 1971, 111–56.

1972: Hierarchical diffusion: the basis of developmental filtering and spread in a system of growth centres. In Hansen, N. M., editor, 1972, 108–38.

Berry, B. J. L. and Neils, E. 1969: Location, size, and shape of cities as influenced by environmental factors: the urban environment writ large. In Perloff, H. S., editor, 1969, 257–304.

Berry, B. J. L. and Pred, A. 1965: *Central place studies: a bibliography of theory and applications. Including supplement through 1964.* Bibliography Series No. 1. Philadelphia: Regional Science Association.

Borts, G. H. and Stein, J. L. 1962: *Economic growth in a free economy.* New York: Columbia University Press.

Boudeville, J.-R. 1961: *Les espaces économiques.* Paris: Presses Universitaires de France.

1966: *Problems of regional economic planning.* Edinburgh University Press.

Brookfield, H. 1975: *Interdependent development.* London: Methuen.

Bruner, R. and Brewer, G., editors 1974: *A policy approach to the study of political development and change.* New York: The Free Press.

Cameron, G. 1970: Growth areas, growth centres, and regional conversion. *Scottish Journal of Political Economy* **17**, 19–38.

Cameron, G. C. and Wingo, L., editors 1973: *Cities, regions and public policy.* Edinburgh: Oliver & Boyd.

Chenery, H. B. 1962: Development policies for southern Italy. *Quarterly Journal of Economics* **77**, 26–39.

Chinitz, B. 1961: Contrasts in agglomeration: New York and Pittsburgh. *American Economic Review* **51**, 279–89.

Darwent, D. F. 1969: Growth poles and growth centres in regional planning: a review. *Environment and Planning* **1**, 5–31. Reprinted in Friedmann, J. and Alonso, W., editors, 1975, 539–65.

Davin, L. 1964: *Économie régionale et croissance.* Paris: Genin.

de Britto, L. N. 1972: La région et le phénomène du pouvoir. *Revue Tiers-Monde* **13**, 309–29.

De Salvo, J. S., editor 1973: *Perspectives on regional transportation planning.* Lexington, Mass.: Lexington Books.

Duncan, B. and Lieberson, S. 1970: *Metropolis and region in transition.* Beverly Hills, Ca.: Sage Publications.

Duncan, O. D., *et al.* 1960: *Metropolis and region.* Baltimore: Johns Hopkins University Press.

Friedmann, J. 1961: Cities in social transformation. *Comparative Studies in Society and History* **4**, 86–103. Reprinted in Friedmann, J. and Alonso, W., editors, 1964, 343–60.

1963: Regional planning as a field of study. *Journal of the American Institute of Planners* **29**, 168–74.

editor 1964: *Regional development and planning.* Special issue of the *Journal of the American Institute of Planners* **30**.

1966: *Regional development policy: a case study of Venezuela.* Cambridge, Mass.: The MIT Press.

1969: The role of cities in economic development. *American Behavioral Scientist* **12**, 13–21. Reprinted in Miller, J. and Gakenheimer, R. A., editors, 1971, 167–204. Including comments by R. M. Morse and rejoinder by J. Friedmann.

editor 1970: *Chile: contribuciones a las políticas urbana, regional y habitacional.* Santiago: Universidad Católica de Chile.

1972: A general theory of polarized development. In Hansen, N. M., editor, 1972, 82–107.

1973a: The spatial organization of power in the development of urban systems. *Development and Change* **4**, 12–50. Reprinted in Friedmann, J. and Alonso, W., editors, 1975, 266–304.

1973b: *Urbanization, Planning and national development.* Beverly Hills, Ca.: Sage Publications.

Friedmann, J. and Alonso, W., editors 1964: *Regional development and planning. A reader.* Cambridge, Mass.: The MIT Press.

editors 1975: *Regional policy. Readings in theory and application.* Cambridge, Mass.: The MIT Press.

Friedmann, J. and Stöhr, W. 1966: The uses of regional science in Chile. *Papers of the Regional Science Association* **18**, 207–22. Revised in Friedmann, 1973b, 255–72.

Friedmann, J. and Stuckey, B. 1973: The territorial basis of national transportation planning. In De Salvo, J. S., editor, 1973, 141–175.

Friedmann, J. and Wulff, R. 1976: *The urban transition: comparative studies of newly industrializing societies.* London: Edward Arnold.

Friedmann, J., *et al.* 1971: Urbanisation and développement national: une étude comparative. *Revue Tiers-Monde* **12**, 13–44. English version in Friedmann, J., 1973b, 65–90.

Friedrich, C. J. and Harris, S. E., editors 1963: *Public policy: Yearbook of the Harvard University Graduate School of Public Administration* **12**. Cambridge, Mass.: Harvard University Press.

Funck, R., editor 1972: *Recent developments in regional science.* London: Pion Ltd.

Gould, P. R. 1970: Tanzania 1920–63: the spatial impress of the modernization process. *World Politics* **22**, 149–70. Reprinted in Friedmann, J. and Alonso, W., editors, 1975, 244–65.

Hansen, N. M., 1967: Development of pole theory in a regional context. *Kyklos* **20**, 709–25.

— 1968: *French regional planning*. Bloomington and London: Indiana University Press.

— 1970: *Rural poverty and the urban crisis*. Bloomington: Indiana University Press.

— editor 1972: *Growth centers in regional economic development*. New York: The Free Press.

Harvey, D. 1973: *Social justice and the city*. London: Edward Arnold.

Hathaway, D. E. 1960: Migration from agriculture: the historical record and its meaning. *American Economic Review* **49**, 379–91.

Hauser, P. M., editor 1957: *Urbanization in Asia and the Far East*. Calcutta: UNESCO Research Centre on the Social Implications of Industrialization in Southern Asia.

— editor 1961: *Urbanization in Latin America*. New York: International Documents Service.

Hauser, P. M. and Schnore, L. F., editors 1965: *The study of urbanization*. New York: John Wiley & Sons.

Helleiner, F. and Stöhr, W., editors 1974: *Spatial aspects of the development process*. Vol. II, Proceedings of the Commission on Regional Aspects of Development of the International Geographical Union. (No publisher given.)

Hilhorst, J. G. M. 1971: *Regional planning: a systems approach*. Rotterdam: Rotterdam University.

Hirsch, W. Z., editor 1964: *Elements of regional accounts*. Baltimore: Johns Hopkins University Press.

Hirschman, A. O. 1958: *The strategy of economic development*. New Haven: Yale University Press. Pages 183–201 reprinted in Friedmann, J. and Alonso, W., editors, 1975, 139–57.

Hochwald, W., editor 1961: *Design of regional accounts*. Baltimore: Johns Hopkins University Press.

Hoover, E. M. and Chinitz, B. 1961: The role of accounts in the economic study of the Pittsburgh Metropolitan Region. In Hochwald, W., editor, 1961, 253–70.

Hoselitz, B. F. 1953: The role of cities in the economic growth of underdeveloped countries. *The Journal of Political Economy* **61**, 195–208.

— 1955: Generative and parasitic cities. *Economic Development and Cultural Change* **3**, 278–94.

International African Institute (London) 1956: *Social implications of industrialization and urbanization of Africa south of the Sahara*. Paris: UNESCO.

Isard, W. 1951: Regional and interregional input–output analysis: a model of a space economy. *Review of Economics and Statistics* **33**, 318–28.

Isard, W. and Cumberland, J. H., editors 1961: *Regional economic planning: techniques of analysis for less developed areas*. Paris: Organization for European Economic Co-operation.

Isard, W., Langford, T. W. and Romanoff, E. 1966: *Philadelphia region input–output study*. 2 vols. Philadelphia: Regional Science Association. Mimeo.

Isard, W., Schooler, E. G. and Vietorisz, T. 1959: *Industrial complex analysis and regional development*. New York: John Wiley & Sons.

Isard, W. and Vietorisz, T. 1955: Industrial complex analysis and regional development, with particular reference to Puerto Rico. *Papers and proceedings of the Regional Science Association* **1**, U1–U7.

Isard, W., *et al.* 1960: *Methods of regional analysis: an introduction to regional science*. London: John Wiley & Sons.

Jakobson, L. and Prakash, V., editors 1971: *Urbanization and national development*. Beverly Hills, Ca.: Sage Publications.

Johnson, E. A. J. 1970: *The organization of space in developing countries*. Cambridge, Mass.: Harvard University Press.

Kain, J. F. and Meyer, J. R., editors 1971: *Essays in regional economics*. Cambridge, Mass.: Harvard University Press.

Kuklinski, A., editor 1972: *Growth poles and growth centres in regional planning*. The Hague: Mouton.

Kuklinski, A. and Petrella, R., editors 1972: *Growth poles and regional policies. A seminar*. The Hague: Mouton.

Lamb, R. 1975: *Metropolitan impacts on rural America*. Department of Geography, Research Paper No. 162. Chicago: The University of Chicago.

Lampard, E. E. 1955: The history of cities in the economically advanced areas. *Economic Development and Cultural Change* **3**, 81–102. Partially reprinted in Friedmann, J. and Alonso, W., editors, 1964, 321–42.

Lasuén, J. R. 1969: On growth poles. *Urban Studies* **6**, 137–61.

Lefeber, L. 1958: *Allocation in space: production, transport, and industrial location*. Amsterdam: North Holland.

Leontiev, W. W. and Strout, A. A. 1963: Multiregional input–output analysis. In Barna, T., editor, 1963, 119–49.

Leven, C. L., Legler, J. B. and Shapiro, P. 1970: *An analytical framework for regional development policy*. Cambridge, Mass.: The MIT Press.

Lewis, J. P. 1962: *Quiet crisis in India: economic development and American policy*. Washington, DC: Brookings Institution.

McGee, T. G. 1971: Catalysts or cancers? The role of cities in Asian society. In Jakobson, L. and Prakash, V., editors, 1971, 157–81.

Mazie, S. M., editor 1972: *Population distribution and policy*. Commission on Population Growth and the American Future, Research Reports, Vol. 5. Washington, DC: Government Printing Office.

Mera, K. 1965: *Efficiency and equalization in interregional economic development*. Ph.D. dissertation. Harvard University.

1973: On the urban agglomeration and economic efficiency. *Economic Development and Cultural Change* **21**, 309–24.

1975: *Income distribution and regional development*. Tokyo: University of Tokyo Press.

Miller, J. 1971: The distribution of political and government power in the context of urbanization. In Miller, J. and Gakenheimer, R. A., editors, 1971, 211–33.

Miller, J. and Gakenheimer, R. A. 1971: *Latin American urban policies and the social sciences*. Beverly Hills, Ca.: Sage Publications.

Morse, R. M. 1971: Planning, history, politics: reflections on John Friedman's 'The role of cities in national development', with a rejoinder by John Friedmann. In Miller, J. and Gakenheimer, R. A., editors, 1971, 167–204.

Moseley, M. J. 1972: *The spatial impact of growth centres: case studies in Brittany and East Anglia*. Ph.D. dissertation. University of Reading.

1974: *Growth centres in spatial planning*. Oxford: Pergamon Press.

Myrdal, G. 1957: *Economic theory and underdeveloped regions*. London: Duckworth.

Nelson, J. M. 1969: *Migrants, urban poverty, and instability in developing countries*. Center for International Affairs, Occasional Papers in International Affairs 22. Cambridge, Mass.: Harvard University.

Neutze, G. M. 1965: *Economic policy and the size of cities*. Canberra: Australia National University Press.

Nicholls, W. H. 1961: Industrialization, factor markets, and agricultural development. *Journal of Political Economy* **69**, 319–40.

Nichols, V. 1969: Growth poles: an evaluation of their propulsive effects. *Environment and Planning* **1**, 193–208.

North, D. C. 1955: Location theory and regional economic growth. *Journal of political economy* **63**, 243–58. Reprinted in Friedmann, J. and Alonso, W., editors, 1964, 240–55.

1956: A Reply. *Journal of political economy* **64**, 160–9. Reprinted in Friedmann, J. and Alonso, W., editors, 1964, 261–4.

ODEPLAN (Oficinade Planificacion Nacional) 1968: *Política de desarrollo nacional: directivas nacionales y regionales*. Santiago, Chile.

Okun, B. and Richardson, R. W. 1961: Regional income inequality and internal population migration. *Economic Development and Cultural Change* **9**, 128–43.

Paelinck, J. 1965: La théorie de développement régional polarisé. *Cahiers de l'Institut de Science Économie Appliquée* serie L., No. 15, 5–48.

Pedersen, P. O. 1970: Innovation diffusion within and between national urban systems. *Geographical Analysis* **2**, 203–54.

Perlman, J. E. 1976: *The myth of marginality: urban poverty and politics in Rio de Janeiro*. Berkeley: University of California Press.

Perloff, H. S. 1957: *Educational for planning: city, state, and regional*. Baltimore: Johns Hopkins University Press.

1963: *How a region grows: area development in the U.S. economy.* Baltimore: Johns Hopkins University Press.

    editor 1969: *The quality of the urban environment.* Baltimore: Johns Hopkins University Press.

Perloff, H. S., Dunn, E. S., Jr, Lampard, E. E. and Muth, R. F. 1960: *Regions, resources, and economic growth.* Baltimore: Johns Hopkins University Press.

Perloff, H. S. and Leven, C. L. 1964: Toward an integrated system of regional accounts: stocks, flows, and the analysis of the public sector. In Hirsch, W. Z., editor, 1964, 175–209.

Perloff, H. S. and Wingo, L., Jr 1961: Natural resource endowment and regional economic growth. In Spengler, J. L., editor, 1961, 191–212. Reprinted in Friedmann, J. and Alonso, W., editors, 1964, 215–39; and Friedmann, J. and Alonso, W., editors, 1975, 307–31.

    editors 1968: *Issues in urban economics.* Baltimore: Johns Hopkins University Press.

Perroux, F. 1950: Economic space: theory and applications. *Quarterly journal of economic* **64**, 89–104. Reprinted in Friedmann, J. and Alonso, W., editors, 1964, 21–36.

    1964: *L'économie du XXe siecle.* Paris: Presses Universitaires.

    1971: Note on the concept of growth poles. In Livingstone, T., editor, *Economic policy for development: selected readings.* London: Harmondsworth. Original French version 1955.

Pfister, R. L. 1963: External trade and regional growth: a case study of the Pacific Northwest. *Economic Development and Cultural Change* **11**, 134–51.

Pottier, A. 1963: Axes de communication et développement économique. *Revue Économique* **14**, 58–132.

Pred, A. R. 1966: *The spatial dynamics of U.S. urban-industrial growth 1800–1914: interpretive and theoretical essays.* Cambridge, Mass.: The MIT Press.

    1971: Large-city interdependence and the preelectronic diffusion of innovations in the US. *Geographical Analysis* **3**, 165–81.

    1973: An urban system interpretation of the growth of large cities. In Pred, A. R., editor, 1973.

    editor 1973: *Urban growth and the circulation of information: the United States system of cities, 1790–1840.* Cambridge, Mass.: Harvard University Press.

The President's Water Resources Policy Commission, 1950: *A water policy for the American people* 3 vols. Washington, DC: Government Printing Office.

Redfield, R. and Singer, M. B. 1954: The cultural role of cities. *Economic Development and Cultural Change* **3**, 53–73. Reprinted in Friedmann, J. and Alonso, W., editors, 1975, 385–405.

Richardson, H. W. 1969: *Regional economics: location theory, urban structure, and regional change.* New York: Praeger.

1971: Regional development policy in Spain. *Urban Studies* **8**, 39–54. Reprinted in Friedmann, J. and Alonso, W., editors, 1975, 712–26.

1973a: *The economics of urban size.* Westmead (England): Saxon House.

1973b: *Regional growth theory.* New York: John Wiley & Sons.

1978: *Regional and urban economics.* Harmondsworth (England): Penguin.

Rodwin, L. 1963: Choosing regions for development. In Friedrich, C. J. and Harris, S. E., editors, 1963, 132–46. Reprinted in Friedmann, J. and Alonso, W., editors, 1964, 37–58.

Rodwin, L. and Associates 1969: *Planning urban growth and regional development: the experience of the guayana program of Venezuela.* Cambridge, Mass.: The MIT Press.

Ruttan, V. W. 1955: The impact of urban-industrial development on agriculture in the Tennessee Valley and the Southeast. *Journal of Farm Economics* **37**, 38–56.

Schmidt, C. F. 1973: *The South African regional system: political interdependence in an interacting space economy.* Ph.D. dissertation. University of South Africa.

Schultz, T. W. 1953: *The economic organization of agriculture.* New York: McGraw-Hill.

Shaw, R. P. 1975: *Migration theory and fact: a review and bibliography of current literature.* Bibliography Series Number 5. Philadelphia: Regional Science Institute.

Siebert, H. 1969: *Regional economic growth: theory and policy.* Scranton, Pa.: International Textbook Co.

Soja, E. W. 1968: *The geography of modernization in Kenya.* New York: Syracuse University Press.

1974: The geography of modernization: paths, patterns, and processes of spatial change in developing countries. In Bruner, R. and Brewer, G., editors, 1974, 197–243.

Sovani, N. V. 1964: The analysis of 'over-urbanization'. *Economic Development and Cultural Change* **12**, 113–22. Reprinted in Friedmann, J. and Alonso, W., editors, 1975, 421–33.

Spengler, J. L., editor 1961: *Natural resources and economic growth.* Washington, DC: Resources for the Future.

Stone, R. 1961: Social accounting at the regional level. In Isard, W. and Cumberland, J. H., editors, 1961, 263–96.

Thoman, R. S., editor, 1974: *Methodology and case studies.* Vol. I, Proceedings of the Commission on Regional Aspects of Development of the International Geographical Union. (No publisher given.)

Thompson, J. H., *et al.* 1962: Toward a geography of economic health: the case of New York State. *Annals of the Association of American Geographers* **52**, 1–20. Reprinted in Friedmann, J. and Alonso, W., editors, 1964, 187–206.

Thompson, W. H. 1968: Internal and external factors in the development of urban economies. In Perloff, H. S. and Wingo, L., editors, 1968,

43–62. Reprinted in Friedmann, J. and Alonso, W., editors, 1975, 201–20.

— 1972: The national system of cities as an object of public policy. *Urban Studies* **9**, 99–116. Reprinted in Friedmann, J. and Alonso, W., editors, 1975, 516–33.

Törnqvist, G. 1970: *Contact systems and regional development.* Lund Studies in Geography, Series B. Human Geography No. 35. Lund: C. W. K. Gleerup.

Ullman, E. L. 1958: Regional development and the geography of concentration. *Papers and Proceedings of the Regional Science Association* **4**, 179–98.

von Böventer, E. 1964: Spatial organization theory as a basis for regional planning. In Friedmann, J., editor, 1964, 90–9.

Weiker, W. F. 1972: *Decentralizing government in modernizing nations: growth center potential of Turkish provincial cities.* A Sage Professional Paper. International Studies Series, Vol. 1, No. 02–007. Beverly Hills, Ca.: Sage Publications.

Whebell, C. F. J. 1969: Corridors: a theory of urban systems. *Annals of the Association of American Geographers* **59**, 1–26.

Williamson, J. G. 1965: Regional inequality and the process of national development: a description of the patterns. *Economic Development and Cultural Change* **13**, 3–45. Reprinted in Friedmann, J. and Alonso, W., editors, 1975, 158–200.

Wingo, L., Jr 1972: Issues in a national urbanization policy for the United States. *Urban Studies* **9**, 3–28.

Chapter 6
The problem of residual areas

The meaning of economic backwardness

Economic backwardness sounded the minor chord to the major theme of polarized development. The problem was a universal one. In the introduction to the proceedings of an international forum held in 1967, E. A. G. Robinson wrote:

> There was no country represented in our conference and none known to any of us which could claim that it had no backward area. The Appalachian region of the United States, the Uzbek Republic of the USSR, the Mezzogiorno of Italy, the Slovak region of Czechoslovakia, the Montenegran region of Yugoslavia, the south-west of France present problems as difficult and recalcitrant as those of the Scottish Highlands, of Northern Ireland or Wales and that are so familiar to all my own countrymen. These problem areas exist in every type of country from the richest to the poorest, from the most perfectly socialist to the most *laissez-faire*. There are naturally differences of opinion as to what type of economy is most likely to help best to solve these problems and as to the best policies for doing it. But many of the basic problems transcend economic systems [Robinson, ed., 1969, pp. ix–x].

What Robinson called backward, others might label poor, distressed, depressed, or declining regions. In one embarrassing instance, they were even called 'little economies' (Gilmore, 1960). Each term conveyed a slightly different shade of meaning. *Backwardness* hinted at cultural and technological causes. *Poverty* had vague overtones of spirituality and suggested a moral obligation of the rich to give to those less fortunate than they. *Distress* conjured up images of dire need and crisis. And if *depression* seemed to refer to cyclical phenomena, *decline* suggested a gradual downward movement of economic indicators.

Still, nuances are important. They point to problem emphases as well as to solutions. The Dutch economist, Leo Klaassen provided one of the best conceptual discussions (1965, chapter 1). He wrote:

A distressed area is usually defined as an area that, at a given moment in time and in one respect or more, is economically at a disadvantage in comparison with other regions or, especially, with the country as a whole.... We may note that, in practice, two main variables enter into the definition of a distressed area: the level of unemployment and the level of income. Although, in many cases, these two factors are closely related, some attention might be given at this point to the conditions that would tend to make the use of one or the other preferable. It is a well-known fact that unemployment in agriculture is very hard to measure.... In such areas, income is usually a much better measure of the economic situation than the rate of unemployment. In industrial areas the two usually go together' [pp. 28–9].

But this customary definition, observed Klaassen, was deficient in one important way. Economic distress appeared as an unalterable condition when, in fact, it should describe both the condition and an evolving situation. In support of this contention, he quoted Solomon Barkin whose observations on areas of recent economic decline in the United States were to the point:

The fate which has befallen these communities might well become the destiny of many other areas now enjoying the peak of their economic growth. Economic and technical changes are continuing: they will, in the future, alter the position of many areas. No group is protected from the ravages of this highly turbulent and dynamic economy. The prosperous ones of today, tomorrow might be flat on their backs' [p. 29].

The wheel of fortune can bring disaster any day.

Proceeding from these general considerations, Klaassen devised a two-by-two matrix, as follows (p. 30):

	Income level compared to the national level	
Rate of increase in income compared to the national rate of increase	High ($\geqslant 1$)	Low ($\leqslant 1$)
High ($\geqslant 1$)	I Prosperity area	II Distressed area in process of development
Low ($\leqslant 1$)	III Declining Prosperity area (potential distress)	IV Distressed area

This was a useful scheme. Type-II areas were already caught up in a positive development cycle that would only require acceleration and consolidation. Type-III areas, on the other hand, needed some shoring up of their economies to prevent further decline and even, perhaps, to increase the relative growth in income and employment. The really intractible areas were those of Type IV. No one quite knew what to do with them.

In addition to its dynamic quality, Klaassen's definition emphasized the sharp contrast between his and the earlier regional concept associated with comprehensive river basin development. One of the most concise formulations of the latter is found in Volume I of The President's Water Resources Policy Commission Report of 1950. With great economy of words, the authors of that report propose, at one and the same time, an explanation of the regional *problematique*, a cultural objective, and a solution. How differently this reads compared to the ascetic, reductionist language of Leo Klaassen and those other economists who would help to shape regional doctrine during the subsequent two decades.

> These changes paralleled the ending of the free land, pioneer stage which opened up the continent. With its ending, a new regionalism began to develop as an economic revolt against the centralization of industrial and commercial wealth in the older Northern States. It was directed at the tendency to restrict the new regions to a semi-colonial, low per capita income, raw-material producing status. The revolt struck at all the institutional arrangements which tended to perpetuate this centralization. Particularly it found in the river basin programmes a means of developing better balanced rural-industrial economies which would increase opportunity, hold population, and raise general income levels.
>
> This new regionalism had other important objectives besides the mere correcting of economic maladjustments. Each region had its peculiar climate – products of its geography, its pioneer traditions, observances, customs, and spiritual tradition, and its indigenous economic activities. The people of these regions became increasingly conscious of their regional cultures as the pressure of economic centralization began, through a score of ingenious devices, to impose the cultural pattern of the metropolis, tending to obliterate regional identities. They saw a broad regional economic development which would restore a proper balance of regional opportunity and sustain the regional identity as their only hope of preserving rich regional values [p. 4].

The explicitly territorialist perspective of The President's Water Resources Policy Commission did not prevail, however. A functional approach which managed to avoid the language of colonial dependency and cultural regionalism was gaining favour. It was now fashionable to treat as 'backward' all those areas which had fallen behind in the competitive struggle for modern industry.

Such areas were typically found on the outer perimeter of core regions.

The fact that more and more industries came to be located near their markets implied the growing spatial concentration of industries and a reinforcement of the basic trend (Harris, 1954). At the same time, both agriculture and mining were becoming increasingly capitalized, rendering a major part of the rural labour force superfluous. These were the successful regions. Regions in economic distress were those whose agriculture and/or mining industries had failed to keep pace, whose cities were distant from major markets, whose economy was technologically backward. Perhaps their physical conditions were unfavourable, or the economy remained locked up within a quasi-feudal order that resisted absorption into the global structures of modern capitalism (Nicholls, 1960). For whatever reason, corporate capital was disinclined to exploit their economic potential. They were typed as 'low-productivity' regions that failed to return the profits on investments which were possible elsewhere.

Finally, there were the older urban centres with their aging physical plant, entrenched financial interests, and unionized working force. They appeared to have difficulty in making a conversion to the new technologies which provided the drive to economic expansion and sought out areas favourable to their needs. One should not wonder, then, that economic backwardness came to be seen as a characteristic inherent in certain areas, a consequence of 'natural' conditions that were ill-suited to nurture modern economic growth.

It was essentially this interpretation which led regional planners, such as William Alonso and Koichi Mera, to argue that any deviations in the pattern of economic location from the dominant polarization pattern to one of greater emphasis on regions of distress would mean significant losses for the efficiency of the economic system as a whole.

In terms of policy implications, regional decline and economic backwardness were typically considered problems of advanced industrial societies. Although newly industrializing countries might also have poor regions, as Professor Robinson had pointed out, the major policy issue there was not their economic backwardness, but overall expansion of the national economy. Under these conditions, polarization was widely regarded as inevitable. According to the reigning paradigm, economic growth would at first lead to an intensification of regional differences. Eventually, however, continuing growth would succeed in returning the economy to a spatial equilibrium. There was not much that could be done about the natural unfolding of this process. A huge country, such as Brazil, might show political concern over the integration of its national territory and take some measures to combat extreme regional disparaties (Hirschman, 1963, chapter 1; Robock, 1965). On the whole, however, regional planning doctrine had little to say about poor regions in poor countries (Friedmann, 1966b).

The context of policy

The earliest official recognition of regional economic backwardness is found in Britain in the *Report of the Royal Commission on the Distribution of the Industrial Population* (1940), better known as the Barlow Report. According to Peter Hall (1975, pp. 91–3), the Barlow Report was directly responsible 'for the events that led up to the creation of the whole complex post-war planning machinery during the years 1945–52.... The particular contribution of the Barlow Commission ... was this: it united the national regional problem with another problem, the physical growth of the great conurbations, and presented them as two faces of the same problem.'

The Barlow Report foreshadowed the more functional approaches of the fifties and sixties. Its declared objective was to divert industrial jobs from London to the periphery.[1] It was not until the end of World War II, however, that the newly elected Labour Government was able to forge the instruments that would translate its farsighted recommendations into political practice. Britain led the way with industrial dispersion policies. Italy followed in 1950 by creating the Cassa per il Mezzogiorno, to begin its long struggle with economic backwardness in the south (Chenery, 1962), and the first French efforts to redirect the centripetal flows of people, skills, and money from Paris to the less prosperous regions were initiated with a series of government decrees in 1954–5 (Sundquist, 1975). In the United States, on the other hand, little concern for depressed areas was evident until 1960 when President Kennedy created the Area Redevelopment Authority (Levitan, 1964; Cameron, 1970; Hansen, 1970; Rodwin, 1970; Cumberland, 1971).[2]

One may speculate why the United States lagged behind Europe in the formulation of policies for depressed areas. The American South, for instance, not unlike the Mezzogiorno, was an agrarian region. Even since the onset of the industrial revolution it had been economically retarded. After the Second World War, however, the South's economic problems seemed to resolve themselves without much outside help. Labour-intensive industries were moving South, abandoning traditional production areas in New England and the mid-Atlantic States (McLaughlin and Robock, 1949). Rapidly growing electrochemical complexes chose southern sites, taking advantage of low-cost power and spacious rural sites. At the same time, millions of southern workers, mostly from rural areas, went North in search of urban jobs. (Even southern metropoli, such as Atlanta, Memphis and New Orleans, showed huge population gains). But more than anything, it was the overpowering sense of rising national affluence which prevented poverty from becoming politically visible. After more than fifteen years of depression and wartime austerity, the most dramatic story of the day was the expansion of the national market.[3]

The jolt came in the early 1960s, when Michael Harrington's book, *The other America* (1962), suddenly catapulted poverty into the political arena and helped initiate a brief flirtation with regional planning. Even then, however, a prevalent view was that poverty remained only in 'pockets' where it could be quickly 'mopped up' (1961). The Committee for Economic Development (1961, p. 8) gave expression to the dominant ideology:

> In a free society, individuals are at liberty to live where they please and industries to locate where they please, subject to some necessary local controls. Each person and firm is free to seek out his own best interest, within the rules of the game laid down by the law. Movement to improve one's condition is a normal activity in such an economy.

Clearly, Americans were not prepared to tolerate 'guided' location to the same extent as Europeans. According to Marth Derthick (1974, p. 108):

> Title V of the Public Works and Economic Development Act of 1965 was a result of logrolling in the Senate at the time the Appalachian Regional Development Act (ARDA) was passed. Members from outside of Appalachia sought comparable benefits for their own states. To protect the Appalachian act from amendments yet assure its passage, the Johnson administration promised to introduce legislation to create regional commissions for other parts of the country. This legislation passed in August 1965 as one part of a comprehensive revision of laws for the aid of depressed areas.
>
> In the next seven years seven commissions were created with twenty-nine states as members, yet none of them really duplicated the Appalachian Regional Commission (ARC). Whereas in Appalachia's case the regional organization resulted from a major spending programme, in the Title V case the organizations came first – and then the spending programmes failed to follow. Lacking presidential support, the commissions have lacked funds, and they may have no future. The Nixon administration had proposed to end federal participation in them altogether.

They have indeed ceased to exist. Given this record, and the ARC's emphasis on highway construction,[5] it is scarcely surprising that American regional planners have either championed the view that the free market would in due course resolve all regional problems or turned their attention to Third World countries where their not inconsiderable talents were absorbed by growth centre and related policies.[6]

The 'free market' was helping to bring about the spatial integration of the national economy in the US in the sense that most of the country's population came to live in metropolitan regions. This, of course, left many rural areas in a fairly depressed state, increasingly devoid of population (see Figure 6.1). Poverty had migrated to the city where it would explode into the blind violence of the late sixties.

Eventually, this violence, too, was brought under control. Police expenditures rose precipitously, along with major crimes; the major

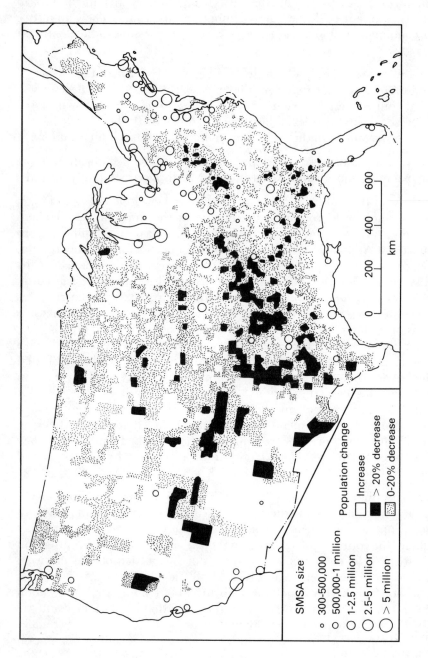

Figure 6.1 Population change between 1950 and 1960 (by county) (from B. J. L. Berry and F. E. Horton, 1970, p. 55).

poverty-fighter of the sixties, the Reverend Dr Martin Luther King, was assassinated; and Viet Nam and later Watergate pre-empted the available political energies of the nation. During the early seventies, economic recession became the national preoccupation and succeeded once again in focusing attention on overall growth rates and inflation.

Public interest in questions of urban poverty vanished as suddenly as it had arisen. With the shift of population from rural to urban areas essentially complete by 1970, there were faint murmurs about the declining economies of older metropolitan areas, such as Newark, Cleveland, St Louis, or Buffalo. But that decline was as much part of a general process of suburbanization (or the flight of white middle-class people from central cities), as it was the result of a continuing drift of population from the older settlement areas in the northeast to the sunbelt, from Florida to California (Morrison, 1972).

A doctrine for backward areas

The practice of economic and social planning for peripheral regions was far more prevalent in Europe than the United States. We have seen some of the reasons for this. Europe, however, produced no clear doctrine for backward areas. Planners emphasized instead the continuing political and technical problems. They showed little inclination to articulate a philosophical basis for regional planning and their approach was essentially pragmatic, a mixture of direct controls and incentives. For a while, French planners grew fond of *métropoles d'équilibres* and similar concepts, including *pôles de croissance*. Being overly rigid, however, these concepts hindered more than they helped and were eventually abandoned.

The only formal doctrine to evolve was Anglo-American in origin. Its principal tenets were first formulated by the British economist, E. A. G. Robinson (1969, chapter 1). Grounded in neoclassical economic theory, the doctrine was presented as transnational, as an expression of pure reason. In fact, it constituted an elaborate rationalization of why little, if anything, should be done to alleviate conditions of regional economic backwardness.

Four main reasons for this doctrine can be found either in the work of Robinson or in the larger body of related American writing on the subject:

(1) *Combating regional economic backwardness is an inefficient practice undertaken in the name of equity.* Such was the common refrain of nearly everyone writing on the subject, but especially of Alonso (1968, 1971) and Mera (1973, 1975). Robinson (1969, p. 19) formulated this principle as follows:

> If, for political or social reasons, there is a strong preference of local communities to retain their identity and achieve development within their own regions, there can be no economic objection to this, pro-

vided that it is recognized that the consequence may be the earning of lower efficiency-wages than could possibly be earned in an alternative more favourable location.... If a nation chooses to pay equal efficiency-wages and other rewards to workers working in an unfavourable location ... this represents in effect the acceptance of a non-optimal economic solution of its location problem.

Pouring labour or capital subsidies into 'backward' areas would thus slow down the overall rate of growth of the economy. The implication was that, other things being equal, overall productive efficiency and economic growth would be preferred to 'saving' the residual areas. In the exaggerated rhetoric of the debate, 'people prosperity' was thought to be a far more rational goal for society than 'place prosperity'. Labour, i.e. people, should accordingly move to efficient (and therefore also profitable) locations.

The advice to governments was very clear: only politically minimal efforts should be made to recover backward areas. Growth was preferable to choice. So long as high rates of economic growth could be maintained, the problem of regional backwardness could be ignored.

(2) *Regional poverty is not an imposed condition but a consequence of deficiencies inherent in the area itself.* This point was never made explicitly, but it affected the entire approach to economic backwardness and decline. An area *lacked* comparative advantage; it *lacked* locations that were favourable to industry; *its* industrial plant had become obsolete; *its* infrastructure was inadequate; *its* location was distant from expanding markets; *its* social structure was rigid; and so forth. Nothing seemed to have *caused* these conditions. The concentration of investments in major growth centres did not *lead* to the 'underdevelopment' of peripheral areas; the two conditions merely existed side by side. Peripheral locations were inefficient, central locations were not.

Technically speaking, economists understood the character of the relationship between the 'core' and its 'peripheries'. They understood that a semi-colonial relationship might be involved *even within the same country* (Hechter, 1975). That did not prevent them, however, from adopting a language that rendered this relationship invisible. Growth fetishism left them no other choice.

(3) *Regional backwardness is to be functionally interpreted.* Officially, it was defined according to certain criteria of unemployment and low income. In the United States, at least, little weight was put on cultural regionalism or what one might also call, in parallel with the economists' concept of time preference, *place* preference – a positive liking for a given area and for the socio-cultural patterns that endow it with that special sense and meaning that render it distinctive (Taylor and Townsend, 1976). Because place preference could not be measured by objective standards, such as the rate of interest, it was easy to push it out of mind.

The voices proclaiming Area Redevelopment seemed to conceive of the United States as a gigantic 'moveable feast'. Massive movements of workers to 'centres of growth and opportunity' were said to be the American Way. In order to 'solve' the economic problems of a region (i.e. to move its functional indices of unemployment and/or income within range of the national average), all that was required was to siphon off workers to near-by centres of industrial growth (Friedmann, 1966b; Hansen, 1973, chapter 12).

From a spatial perspective, formerly nucleated cities were rapidly yield-ing to 'urban fields' that reached outwards from major metropolitan centres for about two hours' travel distance by car (Friedmann and Miller, 1965). But if one plotted these fields, the economically depressed areas could be shown to lie in the 'troughs' between them, or precisely in the areas of least urban contact. This observation led to their designation as the *intermetropolitan periphery*. To solve the problems of this 'periphery', highways would be required to connect the backward area to the more rapidly growing metro-centres along their edges. The periphery would thus be opened up to core region populations and become progressively incorporated into the expanding structure of urban fields.

(4) *Areal dislocations will continue to occur, requiring an accompanying process of adjustment and adaptation.* According to this view, the space economy is continuously evolving. In the United States, labour-intensive industries were relocating from older industrial districts in the northeast to low-cost rural areas in the South; small enterprises, specializing in scientific research and development, were clustering near major universities; rapidly expanding petro-chemicals were finding optimal locations near vast reserves of oil and natural gas along the Gulf of Mexico; and aero-space industries flourished in southern California. But these were the exceptions. The bulk of market-oriented activities, which also comprised the bulk of employment, followed the movement of markets. For the first time in history, people had become relatively footloose. Wherever they chose to live, *jobs would follow them*. And, as it happened, they chose to live where sun, sea and space were plentiful, from Florida to southern California.

And when white middle-class people left central cities to move into the urban field, production followed them as well. Urban fields became a new kind of city: to start 'living', all one had to do was to 'plug-in'. Only headquarter offices might still prefer a central location; nearly everyone else could afford to live away from other people's problems – at least for a while.

Similar trends were beginning to be observed in Western Europe (Thorngren, 1970; Törnqvist, 1970; Rhodes and Kahn, 1971). As early as 1963 the United Kingdom had placed controls on office development. Applied only to London in the beginning, they were subsequently extended to the whole of the southeast and Midlands regions. Since the programme's inception as many as 10,000 office jobs were 'decentralized' each year, *but 75 per cent of the moves were less than 60 miles from the centre of London,* or well within the urban field, while development areas received only one per cent of the total number of jobs dispersed (European Free Trade Association, 1974, pp. 133–5).

More dramatic is Sweden's recent decision (1971–2) to relocate up to one-quarter of all national civil service jobs from Stockholm to selected smaller cities throughout the country, especially in the sparsely populated northern forest areas. In absolute numbers, however, this programme is somewhat less impressive. Because municipal authorities and county councils in Sweden are responsible for nearly two-thirds of public expenditures, the national government employs only 14 per cent of all Civil Service workers and of these, only 11,000 would be affected by the decision to decentralize (*ibid.*, pp. 173–206).

Summarizing, we may say that in the 1960s locational constraints were gradually giving way under the impact of the new technology. In the United States, the sixties saw the completion of the grandiose interstate highway system. Jet travel had become ubiquitous. Satellite telephones and direct distance dialling made international calling as easy, and only a little more expensive, than a trip to the corner grocery. McLuhanites waxed eloquent over the notion of a 'global village'. A little closer to the planning fraternity, Melvin Webber taught the *non-space urban realm* (Webber, 1964). 'An urban realm,' he wrote, 'is neither urban settlement nor territory, but heterogeneous groups of people communicating with each other through space' (p. 116). Place and space had all but dissolved. Everything seemed possible; choice was practically unlimited; the consumer's paradise was at hand. Computer networks and automated production had rendered the problem of optimum location trivial. The provision of so-called amenities, warm climate and high cultural, was becoming an increasingly important consideration in the decisions of families about where they should live. Jobs were expected to materialize later (Ullman, 1954; Klaassen, 1968).

Methods for implementing regional plans

The functional doctrine of planning for backward regions was conceived hand in hand with a certain approach to regional development. It was through the *national* planning of industrial location and settlement patterns that regional development was to be achieved (Klaassen, 1967; Advisory Committee on Intergovernmental Relations, 1968; Bussey, 1973; Sundquist, 1975). Such planning would deal specifically with the residual areas of the intermetropolitan periphery. Defined in terms of their weaknesses rather than strengths, these areas were not expected to respond creatively to problems as perceived by their own residents. The principal reason for attending to their needs was political. Most economists agreed that money spent on the periphery would have to be diverted from more productive uses elsewhere. Thus defined as a residual problem, the periphery could be dealt with in ways familiar to politicians, through 'giveaway' programmes and pork-barrelling.[7]

National regional planning relied heavily on location incentives for particular industries. One of the best short discussions of incentive methods, quite influential when it first appeared, was by Paul Rosenstein-Rodan (1963). A professor at MIT, Rosenstein-Rodan was a staunch advocate of planned industrialization and growth centre strategies. 'Programming in space,' he wrote, 'implies selection and planned discrimination in favour of higher yield districts, "poles" or zones, towns, or industrial estates' (p. 532). In particular, he favoured industrial estates that would create external economies for private industry.

> The establishment of industrial zones ... has proved to be a most effective instrument to induce the inflow of small (and medium-sized) industrial units into new areas.... Industrial estates can catalyze industrial investments which otherwise would not take place. [They] can be a most effective instrument for a national policy of industrial location, avoiding both overcrowding of certain areas which might cause increasing costs and an undue dispersion which would very soon, because of nonoptimum location, reduce the volume of industrial investment in the area [pp. 534-5].

Rather than summarize his brief incisive essay, we shall merely list the several methods out of which specific regional policies came to be fashioned. By the end of the 1960s, growth centre policies were being advocated almost universally. The remaining problems were thought to be primarily of a technical nature: how many centres should be the object of public sponsorship, how far down the urban hierarchy one should proceed in identifying them, on the basis of what criteria they might be chosen, and whether urban centres lying outside the depressed area should be assisted to accelerate their growth and so draw off the excess labour from the region (Hansen, 1970; 1973).

Once growth centres had been officially selected, their rapid and sustained growth had to be generated. One school of thought held that economic backwardness could be reversed by investing more heavily in urban and regional infrastructure (Youngson, 1967; Buhr, 1970, 1971). Industrial estates, praised by Rosenstein-Rodan and now in common use, were one attractive idea for investing public monies in ways that would reduce the costs to private capital. In many cases, however, completed estates might remain unused for years, not only because too many of them competed for a relatively small number of industries in search of sites, but also because most industries were not in the least anxious to shun the metropolis with its many seductions: high access to markets, experienced labour force, and accumulated finance capital. The other major infrastructure investment was in highways and, more generally, in transportation (Kraft, Meyer and Valette, 1971).

Financial incentives for location supplemented direct investments. In principle, it was as feasible to encourage people to move *out* of a region and into booming urban centres as it was to shift sources of employment to depressed regions (Klaassen and Drewe, 1973). Even in Europe, however, the actual number of migrant families assisted in this way was small. The bulk of subsidies went to capital rather than to labour. Generous financial aid was offered in the form of long tax-holidays, easy and low-cost credit, accelerated depreciation allowances, investment and building grants, and lowered tariff duties on imported machinery, raw materials, and semi-finished products. In some cases, employment premiums were also paid.

These positive inducements were supplemented, in Britain and France, by negative controls over the location of new, and the expansion of existing, industry. Manufacturing industries had to obtain specific permission from central government authorities to locate in the proscribed areas (chiefly the capital region). Nevertheless, the outright prohibition to locate there was not a very effective means of enticing industries into the more backward regions of the country. Financial incentives seemed to accomplish this purpose better (Alden and Morgan, 1974, chapter 4).[8]

Significantly, national measures for industrial location were most appropriate for firms that scanned the national territory for an optimal location. This automatically gave pride of place to the larger firms which also had a substantial headquarters staff. Though not officially excluded, smaller industries would be less likely to take advantage of the various incentive programmes.[9] Most planners were, in fact, quite hostile to the idea of small-scale plants and so-called rural industries. 'Any glorification of rural industrialization or of handicrafts as a panacea of development of underdeveloped areas must be recognized as a utopian dream' (Rosenstein-Rodan, 1963, p. 537). Significantly, these lines were written at a time when China was in the midst of a major drive to establish industries in rural areas (Sigurdson, 1975). Of course, rural industries were not a panacea for China either, but they represented a significant component of a balanced strategy that took development for the rural masses as its starting point (Paine, 1976). In the West, however, with its characteristic urban bias (Lipton, 1977), rural industries were considered not even a complement to urban-based industrialization. The dean of American agricultural economists, Earl O. Heady wrote in 1974 (p. 137):

The rural community, aside from programs for commercial farmers, drew little attention from national society during the 1950s and early 1960s. This was true even though rapid economic decay was beginning in the nonfarm sector of rural communities and some agricultural economists emphasized the need for a general economic and social policy for rural areas. It was simply assumed that the problems of the nonfarm rural economy would be automatically solved by programs which maintained a sufficient rate of national economic growth or through higher support prices and payments to commercial farmers. Neither of these policy orientations, as we now know, was a solution to the developing problems of the nonfarm rural community sector. More nearly, these two sets of national policies hurried the economic and social decay of rural communities.

Regional development policy, then, remained silent on questions of rural development. Urban-based planners had little insight into the nature of the rural problem (Morrison *et al.*, 1974, p. vii). Rural development would have required a territorial approach. Lacking this, local communities were pitted against national forces in a grossly uneven contest.

The term 'method' suggests technique, but it may also be understood as a way of organizing for the development of backward areas. We have already noted how, in western countries, regional policy became primarily a question of national planning. Martha Derthick (1974) has discussed the bewildering variety of ways through which Americans have attempted to bridge the gap between national policy and local programming. Other governments, such as Britain's, were no less ingenious in devising complex arrangements (Hall, 1975).

From all these experiences, two institutional innovations stand out: the regional development authority and the regional development bank. These institutions were made responsible for economic developments in specific areas, the former being primarily concerned with overhead investments and their co-ordination and the latter with loans to private enterprise. In the 1930s the United States had led the way with the Tennessee Valley Authority which, in time, became a model for multiple-purpose development corporations throughout the world (McKinley, 1950). Colombia was to have its Cauca Valley Authority, Venezuela its Guyana Development Corporation, and Brazil its Superintendencies for the Amazon region, the northeast, and other neglected parts of its vast territory. West African Ghana would create the Volta Dam Authority; India started up a similar agency in the Damodar River Valley. Charged with particular tasks, these organizations usually managed to invest heavily in economic and social infrastructure. Measured in terms of inputs, notable results were achieved. Economic results, however, were more ambiguous and, in any event, more difficult to judge.

The regional development bank, which worked more directly with the private sector, was a less favoured tool. The outstanding examples are the Cassa per il Mezzogiorno (Allen and Maclennan, 1970) and the Brazilian Bank for the Northeast (Robock, 1965). In no small measure, these banks owed their relative success to technical research staffs which helped to formulate loan criteria for the banks' operations and to distinguish them from the run-of-the-mill commercial banks which they were intended to supplement.

Banks and regional organizations were basically territorial organizations. They tended to identify with local interests and built up a political following among certain sectors of the regional population. It was feared that these powerful new institutions might put regional considerations ahead of national priorities. Regional authorities stood in danger of being co-opted by powerful regional interests (Selznick, 1949). But why was co-optation thought to be bad? Because the national interest would not always prevail? Because functional considerations might be subordinated to regional determination, as in Brazil? There was obviously no other than a political criterion to decide this issue.[10]

By the mid-1970s, functional-spatial integration had proceeded to the point where most problems of rural backwardness in the industrially advanced countries had become problems of urban growth. Rural poverty, it seemed, could best be dealt with by extending the living space of urban populations outward from central cities into the urban field. Here would be found the sporting grounds of the metropolis as well as the most desirable sites for second-home developments. Small towns would be converted into 'spontaneous growth centres' as more and more people moved into the urban field, taking manufacturing plants and offices with them.

This trend was observed in Europe as well. Jean-Claude Perrin (1974), for instance, wonders why France's settlement pattern might not become as decentralized as West Germany's. With the invasion of the countryside by the city, ecological considerations became suddenly important, recalling the ideas of the Regional Planning Association of America more than a generation earlier (McAllister, 1973). In February 1977 the International Research Centre on Environment and Development in Paris began publishing the *Ecodevelopment News*, serving a world-wide social movement in search of a general development process that would be in harmony with nature. How large-scale industrialism would be brought to heel was not explained. But then, social movements always believe in their ability to move mountains.

And so, the first traces of a new doctrine for regional planning were becoming visible. Before we look at them more closely, however, the literature that helped invalidate the reigning doctrine must be examined. This is the task of the following chapter.

Notes

1.   The main recommendation of the Commission was to create a central planning agency. Its job would be to help redevelop congested urban areas, to decentralize or disperse industries and population from such areas, and to encourage a reasonable balance and diversification of industrial development throughout the various regions of Great Britain. The Commission also proposed a number of specific measures. These included restrictions on the location of industry in London, the development of a greenbelt to limit the size of the city, and the encouragement of growth beyond the central area of London [Rodwin, 1970, pp. 117–18].

2. To what extent there was a 'lag' depends partly on how one interprets the evidence. The TVA, of course, was the best-known instance of regional planning and also the first. It had been the federal government's answer to endemic poverty in the South. But that was before a clear concept of 'depressed area' had been formed. During the New Deal period regional planning doctrine had been ideologically committed to territorial principles of history, culture, and natural resources. But the concern with the regional distribution of jobs and population emerged only in the post-war era. Its first statement actually appeared soon after America's entry into the war. (See Hansen and Perloff, 1942.) It is only with respect to this new emphasis that we can speak of a European edge on American practice. Paradoxically, it was Europe's cultural regionalism which provided the political impetus for regional planning in the new vein. America's more functional civilization found it difficult to arouse public support for regional development in any form.

3. Resurgence of the post-war economy was everywhere interpreted as a 'miracle'. Right up to the end of the war, dominant professional opinion expected a resumption of massive unemployment, and designs for the peacetime economy were to ensure that the conditions of the 1930s would never recur. The spontaneous upsurge of production which followed the war took most economists by surprise and appeared to spell an end to material poverty. Planning in the sense of a central allocation of investment resources seemed superfluous under American conditions. Who could be certain that government bureaucrats knew how to out-perform the private sector?

4. According to Hansen (1975, p. 143), 'During their first six years of operation, federal expenditures for all of the Title V commissions amounted to a little over $100 million, while those for Appalachia came to $1.3 billion.' Clearly, the Title V commissions subsisted on political crumbs.

5. Of the initial $1.1 billion authorized by the Appalachian Redevelopment Act, $840 million (or 76 per cent) were allocated for highway construction over a period of five years (Hansen, 1975, p. 142). For a very thorough study of the Appalachian Commission's early years, see Rothblatt, 1971.

6. The small band of American regional planners who made major commitments to work outside the United States included Charles Abrams, Charles Boyce, John Dyckman, John Friedmann, Ralph Gakenheimer, William Goldsmith, Lawrence Mann, Harvey Perloff, Lisa Peattie, Malcolm Rivkin, Lloyd Rodwin, Stefan Robock, Anatole Solow, Thomas Vietorisz and Francis Violich.

7. Would any other solution be possible? Regional development requires a shift in resource allocation. Could sufficient resources be made available for this purpose, without political support? Central planners sometimes like to think that politics, operating according to a logic of its own, is dispensable. Because, in fact, it is not, the bulk of resources spent on Appalachian development went towards the construction of highways. Ever popular in the United States, the building of highways is readily organized, and the effect on employment is immediate. And who was to say that the highways were not needed? It would be another decade before the environmental movement managed to put a stop to further highway construction in the United States.

8. After 1954 the French government proscribed further factory construction in the Paris region. Results in this case were dramatic. 'The capital region's share of new factory construction in France was brought down from 33 per cent in 1949–55 to 27 per cent in 1956, 20 per cent the next year, and to 10 per cent by 1963. Moreover, a considerable amount of existing factory space was being abandoned or converted to other uses in the Paris region.... Between 1960 and 1963 the region saw a net loss of factory space ...' (Sundquist, 1975, p. 99). Factory flight from Paris would probably have occurred in any event. Government incentives merely hastened a trend towards industrial dispersion. Office space continued to concentrate in the nation's capital.

9. In no western country did it occur to policy-makers that development could also be promoted *from within* a region. Defined as 'backward', regional populations were

supposed to be incapable of generating investments which would obviate the need for outsiders to make locational commitments in areas where they did not care to be. Developments from within would have had to start with small industries and relatively modest investments. But these were thought to be incapable of carrying a dynamic development process forward. Here as in other cases, so much planning appears to be concerned more with symbolic actions than with reality directly.

10. As Norman Wengert has pointed out, 'Co-optation is reciprocal and mutual. It must recognize the role of reason and rationality in human motivation.... A balanced portrayal would have to put into the scales those instances where TVA's influences on individuals and groups in the region resulted in "co-opting" them in the directions that TVA thought sound' (Wengert, 1952, p. 13).

Bibliography

Advisory Committee on Intergovernmental Relations, 1968: *Urban and rural development: policies for future growth.* Washington, DC: Government Printing Office.

Alden, J. and Morgan, R. 1974: *Regional planning: a comprehensive view.* New York: John Wiley & Sons.

Allen, K. and Maclennan, M. C. 1970: *Regional problems and policies in Italy and France.* Beverly Hills, Ca.: Sage Publications.

Alonso, W. 1968: Urban and regional imbalances in economic development. *Economic Development and Cultural Change* **17**, 1–14. Reprinted in Friedmann, J. and Alonso, W., editors, 1975, 622–35.

— 1971: Equity and its relations to efficienty in urbanization. In Kain, J. F. and Meyer, J. R., editors, 1971, 40–57.

Buhr, W. 1970: A retrospective view of criteria for investment planning in developing countries. *Theorie und Praxis der Infrastrukturpolitik.* Schriften des Vereins für Sozialpolitik, Neue Folge **54**, 153–76.

— 1971: Die Abhängigkeit der räumlichen Entwicklung von der Infrastrukturausstattung. *Grundfragen der Infrastrukturplanung für Wachsende Wirtschaften.* Schriften des Vereins für Sozialpolitik, Neue Folge **58**, 103–67.

Bussey, E. M. 1973: *The flight from rural poverty: how nations cope.* Lexington, Mass.: Lexington Books.

Cameron, G. C. 1970: *Regional economic development: the federal role.* Baltimore: Johns Hopkins University Press.

Chenery, H. B. 1962: Development policies for southern Italy. *Quarterly Journal of Economics* **76**, 515–48. Reprinted in Friedmann, J. and Alonso, W., editors, 1964, 668–700.

Committee for Economic Development 1961: *Distressed areas in a growing economy: a statement on national policy.* New York: Committee for Economic Development.

Cumberland, J. H. 1971: *Regional development: experiences and prospects in the United States of America.* Paris: Mouton.

Derthick, M. 1974: *Between state and nation: regional organizations of the United States*. Washington, DC: Brookings Institution.

European Free Trade Association 1974: *National settlement strategies: a framework for regional development*. Geneva: European Free Trade Association.

Friedmann, J. 1966a: *Regional development policy: a case study of Venezuela*. Cambridge, Mass.: The MIT Press.

1966b: Poor regions and poor nations: perspectives on the problem of Appalachia. *Southern Economic Journal* **32**, 465–73.

Friedmann, J. and Alonso, W., editors 1964: *Regional development and planning. A reader*. Cambridge, Mass.: The MIT Press.

editors 1975: *Regional policy. Readings in theory and application*. Cambridge, Mass.: The MIT Press.

Friedmann, J. and Miller, J. 1965: The urban field. *Journal of the American Institute of Planners* **31**, 312–19.

Gilmore, D. R. 1960: *Developing the 'little' economies. A survey of area development programs in the United States*. Committee for Economic Development, Supplementary Paper 10. New York.

Hall, P. 1975: *Urban and regional planning*. London: Penguin.

Hansen, A. and Perloff, H. 1942: *Regional resource development*. Washington, DC: National Planning Association.

Hansen, N. M. 1970: *Rural poverty and the urban crisis. A strategy for regional development*. Bloomington: Indiana University Press.

1973: *The future of nonmetropolitan America: studies in the reversal of rural and small town population decline*. Lexington, Mass.: Lexington Books.

editor 1974: *Public policy and regional economic development: the experience of nine Western countries*. Cambridge, Mass.: Ballinger.

1975: Regional policies in the United States: experience and prospects. In Kuklinski, A., editor, 1975, 139–52.

Harrington, M. 1962: *The other America*. New York: Macmillan.

Harris, C. D. 1954: Market potential as a factor in industrial location in the United States. *Annals of the Association of American Geographers* **44**, 315–48.

Heady, E. O. 1974: Rural development and rural communities of the future. In North Central Regional Centre for Rural Development, 1974, 136–50.

Hechter, M. 1975: *Internal colonialism: the Celtic fringe in British national development, 1536–1966*. London: Routledge & Kegan Paul.

Hirschman, A. O. 1963: *Journeys toward progress: studies of economic policy making in Latin America*. New York: The Twentieth Century Fund.

Joint Economic Committee, Congress of the United States, 1975; *China: a reassessment of the economy*. Washington, DC: Government Printing Office.

Kain, J. F. and Meyer, J. R., editors 1971: *Essays in regional economics*. Cambridge, Mass.: Harvard University Press.

Klaassen, L. H. 1965: *Area economic and social redevelopment: guidelines for programmes.* Paris: OECD.

1967: *Methods of selecting industries for depressed areas: an introduction to feasibility studies.* Paris: OECD.

1968: *Social amenities in area economic growth: an analysis of methods for defining needs.* Paris: OECD.

Klaasen, L. H. and Drewe, P. 1973: *Migration policy in Europe: a comparative study.* Lexington, Mass.: Lexington/Heath.

Kraft, G., Meyer, J. R. and Valette, J.-P. 1971: *The role of transportation in regional economic development.* Lexington, Mass.: Lexington Books.

Kuklinski, A., editor 1975: *Regional development and planning: international perspectives.* Leyden: Sijthoff.

Levitan, S. A. 1964: *Federal aid to depressed areas.* Baltimore: Johns Hopkins University Press.

Lipton, M. 1977: *Why poor people stay poor: urban bias in world development.* Cambridge, Mass.: Harvard University Press.

McAllister, D. M. 1973: *Environment: a new focus for land-use planning.* Washington, DC: National Science Foundation.

McKinley, C. 1950: The Valley Authority and its alternatives. *American Political Science Review* **44**, 607–30. Reprinted in Friedmann, J. and Alonso, W., editors, 1964, 554–78.

McLaughlin, G. E. and Robock, S. 1949: *Why industry moves south.* Washington, DC: National Planning Association.

Mera, K. 1973: On the urban agglomeration and economic efficiency. *Economic Development and Cultural Change* **21**, 309–24.

1975: *Income distribution and regional development.* Tokyo: Tokyo University Press.

Morrison, P. A. 1972: *Population movements and the shape of urban growth: implications for public policy.* Santa Monica, Ca.: the Rand Corporation.

Morrison, P. A., *et al.* 1974: *Review of federal programs to alleviate rural deprivation.* Santa Monica, Ca.: the Rand Corporation.

Nicholls, W. H. 1960: Southern tradition and regional economic progress. *Southern Economic Journal* **26**, 189–98. Reprinted in Friedmann, J. and Alonso, W., editors, 1964, 462–73.

North Central Regional Centre for Rural Development, 1974: *Rural industrialization: problems and potentials.* Ames: Iowa University Press.

Paine, S. 1976: Balanced development: Maoist conception and Chinese practice. *World Development* **4**, 277–304.

Perrin, J.-C. 1974: *Le développement régional.* Paris: Presses Universitaires de France.

The President's Water Resources Policy Commission 1950: *A water policy for the American people*, 3 vols. Washington, DC: Government Printing Office.

Report of the Royal Commission on the Distribution of the Industrial Population 1940. London: HMSO.

Rhodes, J. and Kahn, A. 1971: *Office dispersal and regional policy*. Occasional Papers no. 30, Department of Applied Economics. Cambridge University Press.

Robinson, E. A. G., editor 1969: *Backward areas in advanced countries*. Proceedings of a conference held by the International Economic Association. London: Macmillan.

Robock, S. H. 1965: *Brazil's developing north-east. A study of regional planning and foreign aid*. Washington, DC: Brookings Institution.

Rodwin, L. 1970: *Nations and cities: a comparison of strategies for urban growth*. Boston: Houghton Mifflin Co.

Rosenstein-Rodan, P. N. 1963: Reflections on regional development. *Estratto da Scritti di Economia e Statistica in Memoria di Alessandro Molinari*. Milan: Dott. A. Giuffrè, 525–47.

Rothblatt, D. R. 1971: *Regional planning: the Appalachian experience*. Lexington, Mass.: Heath Lexington Books.

Selznick, P. 1949: *TVA and the grass roots*. Berkeley: University of California Press.

Sigurdson, J. 1975: Rural industrialization in China. In Joint Economic Committee, Congress of the United States, 1975, 411–35.

Sundquist, J. C. 1975: *Dispersing population: what Americans can learn from Europe*. Washington, DC: Brookings Institution.

Taylor, C. C. and Townsend, A. R. 1976: The local 'sense of place' as evidenced in north-east England. *Urban Studies* **13**, 113–46.

Thorngren, B. 1970: How do contact systems affect regional development. *Environment and Planning* **2**, 409–27.

Törnqvist, G. 1970: *Contact systems and regional development*. Lund Studies in Geography, Series B, no. 35. Lund: Gleerup.

Ullman, E. 1954: Amenities as a factor in regional growth. *Geographical Review* **44**, 119–35.

Webber, M. M. 1964: The urban place and the nonplace urban realm. In Webber, M. M., *et al.*, editors, 1974, 79–153.

Webber, M. M., *et al.*, editors 1964: *Explorations into urban structure*. Philadelphia: University of Pennsylvania Press.

Wengert, N. I. 1952: *Valley of tomorrow: the TVA and agriculture*. Bureau of Public Administration, The University of Tennessee, Knoxville.

Youngson, A. J. 1967: *Overhead capital: a study in development economics*. Edinburgh University Press.

Part III: The crisis in development

Chapter 7
Towards a paradigm shift in regional planning

New streams of development doctrine

Regional planners are passing through a period of deep self-examination. Their tasks, after all, are not independent of the historical flow of events. Since the end of the 1960s, a widespread loss of confidence has descended on Western intellectuals. Books with darkly foreboding titles began to appear: *The Pentagon of Power* (Mumford, 1970); *Doomsday Book* (Taylor, 1970); *Limits to Growth* (Meadows *et al.*, 1972); *A Blueprint for Survival* (Editors of *The Ecologist*, 1972); *Mankind at the Turning Point* (Mesarovic and Pestel, 1974); *Inquiry into the Human Prospect* (Heilbronner, 1974); *Legitimation Crisis* (Habermas, 1975); *Late Captialism* (Mandel, 1975). Just what they signified is not very clear. Ernest Mandel heard the death rattles of capitalism; others foresaw the end of the world. Only one thing is certain. Confidence in the old ways of doing things was rapidly vanishing. Traditional answers to traditional problems were viewed with suspicion. Old problems were reinterpreted, new ones were added. People in the management sciences speak of a 'turbulent' environment. What makes an environment turbulent, they say, is its malevolence. You throw a pebble in the stream and it comes hurtling back at you, aimed at your forehead. Deadly.

Towards the end of the sixties, then, people were beginning to take stock of their affairs, and development specialists were no different from others. The First United Nations Development Decade (1960–70) had given little evidence that expectations were going to be met (Faber and Seers, ed., 1972). Meanwhile, the Great Proletarian Cultural Revolution was in full swing in China; an imperialist war was raging in Vietnam; French students and workers erupted for one brief moment of revolutionary glory into the streets of Paris; a world-wide radical movement was gaining adherents.

Towards the end of 1969 Dudley Seers, then Director of the Institute of Development Studies at the University of Sussex in England, addressed a gathering of the Society for International Development. In his speech, he raised some fundamental questions concerning the 'meaning' of development. The GNP standard was not enough, he said. Planners must also take account of income distribution and employment. The basic thrust of development had to be redirected (Seers, 1969, p. 3):

> The questions to ask about a country's development are therefore: What has been happening to poverty? What has been happening to unemployment? What has been happening to inequality? If all three of these have declined from high levels, then beyond doubt this has been a period of development for the country concerned. If one or two of these central problems have been growing worse, especially if all three have, it would be strange to call the result 'development', even if per capita income doubled.

Seers' speech marked the beginning of a very serious search for ways of ameliorating the consequences of unequal development and, ultimately, for replacing the conventional models. A whole new vocabulary was invented to express this purpose. In Figure 7.1 we have attempted to summarize some of these streams of thinking about development. We do so because it is within this context that we shall have to forge the new doctrine of regional planning, whose point of departure is no longer 'polarized development' but an altogether different concept.

Our diagram represents a *policy response space* that is structured by two persisting world-historical forces. The first of these is China, whose very different path to national development was dramatically brought to the attention of the world during the Cultural Revolution. Considering the comparatively long period which had elapsed since the defeat of the Kuomintang Government in 1949, Western experts had been rather slow in drawing the appropriate lessons from China's history (Dumont, 1973, orig. 1969; Joint Economic Committee, 1975; Keesing, 1975; Weiss, 1975; Gurley, 1976; Slater, 1976; Wong, 1976; Sawers, 1977). China, they discovered, was 'walking on two legs': the modern and the traditional were both found useful in development. China was self-reliant: it required only a minimum of outside help. China gave priority to rural development. China was attempting to overcome the contradictions between town and countryside (Schenk, 1974; Hahn, 1977).

After 1968, a growing trickle of visitors to China brought back stories of impressive achievement. China had discovered a way of bringing material progress to the masses. All people were entitled to the satisfaction of their basic needs. And social solidarity, it seemed, was high.[1]

China did not really have a 'model' of development for export, though some people liked to speak of such a model. Her example was chiefly moral. If one looked at China, it seemed possible, after all, to combine economic progress with a measure of social justice. The contrast with the American doctrine of unequal development, in which efficiency calculations drowned out all thoughts of equity and justice, could not be more dramatic. China's way had been achieved without much outside help. If China could do this, why should it be out of reach for other countries?

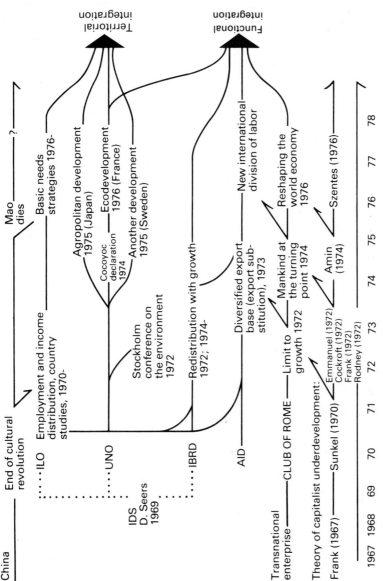

Figure 7.1 New streams of development doctrine: 1969–77

China's example fired the imagination of those who saw in national development a struggle for human liberation.

The second world-historical force giving structure to the policy response space of Figure 7.1 is the emergence of the transnational corporation and the recognition of an emerging world economy under its tutelage. The ideology of this new phase of development was fashioned in a series of reports sponsored by the Club of Rome, a somewhat loosely organized but potentially very powerful group of international consultants, techno-crats, and senior academics whose linking was global and whose work was backed with generous grants from international foundations. The first two studies sponsored by the Club of Rome conjured up the spectre of a world that was diligently working its way towards self-destruction. Either material resources would be used up, they insisted, or the world would suffocate in a mountain of pollutants, or millions would die from starvation. What dramatized these conclusions was, first, the magic of computerized models which made the forecasts assume an aura of inevitability and, second, the timetable attached to them. Doomsday was set for the early part of the twenty-first century, a mere fifty years hence.

The first report to the Club of Rome (Meadows *et al.*, 1972) coincided with the UN Stockholm Conference on the Environment. Following a carefully thought-out plan, it received world-wide distribution. Not un-expectedly, its startling conclusions engendered a good deal of debate.[2] Most critics thought the model too simplistic and its prospects too gloomy.[3] The second report (Mesarovic and Pestel, 1974) had a less dramatic critical reception. Not only was its model regionally disaggregated, sug-gesting the serial disintegration of the world in place of one catastrophe, but the authors also made extensive use of alternate future scenarios, or imaginary renderings of things to come. After drawing graphic images of mass starvation, the authors concluded with what has become an article of faith with the transnationals. 'In summary,' the authors wrote, 'the only feasible solution to the world food situation requires: (1) a global approach to the problem; (2) investment aid rather than commodity aid, except for food; (3) a balanced economic development of all regions; (4) an effective population policy; (5) worldwide diversification of in-dustry, leading to a truly global economic system' (p. 127). Mesarovic and Pestel underlined the urgency of their message: 'If we wait twenty years to implement a policy with a transition period of 15 years, there will be, between 1975 and 2025, an increase in child deaths of 300 per cent' (p. 129).

The same ideology is encountered in the third and, in a way, most fascinating report to the Club of Rome (Tinbergen, 1976). The report was co-ordinated by (and bears the imprint of) Jan Tinbergen, the Dutch Nobel Prize Winner in economics. Tinbergen was deeply disturbed by the world's condition and prospects. Much of his work therefore mirrors approaches that are characteristic of the upper part of Figure 7.1, labelled 'basic needs' and 'territorial'. But elsewhere, the rhetoric of the report

reveals its sponsorship. In a chapter entitled 'The Need of a Reinterpretation of National Sovereignty', the ideology of the transnationals is bluntly
stated (pp. 83-4);

> Participation and social control suggest a functional rather than a
> territorial interpretation of sovereignty, or jurisdiction over deter-
> mined uses rather than geographic space. Conceptually, this inter-
> pretation will make possible the progressive internationalization and
> socialization of all world resources – material and non-material –
> based upon the 'common heritage of mankind' principle. It also
> permits the secure accommodation of inclusive and exclusive uses
> of these resources or, in other words, the interweaving of national
> and international jurisdiction within the same territorial sense....
>
> Acceptance of the concept of functional sovereignty will require the
> creation of new kinds of international institutions comprising a
> balanced system of functional interests. The aim should be functional
> confederations of international organizations, decentralized at the
> operational level and centralized at the policy making level. Ulti-
> mately, we must aim for *decentralized planetary sovereignty* with the net-
> work of strong international institutions which will make it possible.

The gentlemen of the Club of Rome could be counted upon to take this
message to heart. Did it not bear the stamp of approval from the very
highest academic quarters?

The authors of the report were not unconscious of the contradictory
character of their conclusions. For instance, in a technical appendix
concerning the transnationals, we read (*ibid.*, p. 280):

> Many of the objectives of self-reliant development described in Part
> II of this report collide with the present rationale of transnational
> enterprises. Self-reliance is a style of development based on a recog-
> nition of cultural diversity and, as such, is an instrument against the
> homogenization of cultures. Transnational enterprises' rationale, on
> the contrary, is based on the proposition that most products can be
> profitably marketed in almost all of the countries where they operate,
> taking due account of their development levels. Selling the same,
> or substantially similar, products everywhere is a foundation of their
> strength. To the extent they can homogenize the markets of
> the world, they attain their own maximum efficiency.
>
> If their markets were to be disaggregated and made increasingly
> responsive to local cultural and taste determinants, their *raison d'être*
> may be jeopardized. Their interest lies not in maximum response
> to local requirements, but in incorporating local capacity into global
> consumption models where they are the predominant producers.
> Their 'efficiency' in terms of their own objectives lies in the fact that
> their subsidiaries or representatives are producing basically the same
> or related products, not different products. Should local investments

adopt production policies geared to the satisfaction of local needs, the economies of scale on which their global cost structures are based would be adversely affected.

Authored by I. Jazairy, P. Kuin and J. Somavia, this technical paper concludes with the following 'policy' proposals (*ibid.*, p. 283):

> Transnational enterprises should ... comply with the aims of the host countries' development plans. They should be aware in particular of the overwhelming importance of maximizing employment and value added in the developing countries. They should ... refrain from all forms of political interference in the affairs of host countries and avoid restrictive business practices. They should co-operate in the study of alternative tasks ... such as shifting towards advisory, management and training contracts with governments of developing countries.

One can only wonder to what extent transnationals would honour this 'boy-scout code' of conduct, or why, indeed, they should.[4] A truly global force in structuring the world economy, they have begun to break out of their national cocoons. The spatial structure into which they are inserted (and which they helped to bring about) consists essentially of *enclaves* in a global network of locations and associated market (or resource) areas, *unbound by any loyalties to place* (Sunkel, 1970, 1973; Vernon, 1971; Murray, 1975; Froebel, Heinrichs and Kreye, 1976; Feder, 1976).

The transnational role had been made the centrepiece of what Samir Amin has called the 'theory of underdevelopment' (Amin, 1974). Indeed, a third pervasive influence on the response-space of the diagram was a substained neo-Marxist critique of capitalistic development doctrine and practice. New terms entered the common vocabulary through this door: dependency, marginality, unequal development, the development of underdevelopment, accumulation on a world scale (Frank, 1967; Sunkel, 1970, 1973; Emmanuel, 1972; Cockroft *et al.*, 1972; Rodney, 1972; Amin, 1974). With one notable exception, the cited works and the stream of literature that followed in their wake were accusatory more than analytical. Their major purpose was to raise the consciousness of development specialists, particularly in Latin America where the process of 'underdevelopment' (i.e. unequal development) had proceeded the furthest.[5] The exception was Tamás Szentes, a Hungarian economist who had worked as an adviser to the government in Tanzania and whose widely read text *The Political Economy of Underdevelopment* (3rd edition 1976) included, in addition to a devastating critique of the standard development doctrine, carefully thought-out guidelines for what the author called 'the overcoming of underdevelopment'.

The resulting policy response space of Figure 7.1 includes references to several of the most important international agencies. The first to respond was the International Labour Office which, as early as 1969, declared a World Employment Programme for the explicit purpose of getting national governments to adopt full-employment policies as a major development objective. As a means for promoting this idea, the ILO organized a series of country missions, the first of which was sent to Colombia, followed by others to Kenya, Sri Lanka, and the Philippines. The first group of three was contracted with Dudley Seers' Institute of Development Studies at Sussex. The reports that were subsequently published, propounded this simple message: to the traditional objective of increasing per capita gross national product, governments should add objectives of full employment and a more equal income distribution. Poverty was seen to be increasing everywhere. To reverse this trend, a fraction of the annual increment of economic growth should be diverted to 'investments in the poor' (Thorbeck, 1973).

The Philippines report (International Labour Office, 1974) took a somewhat different approach. Its principal authors, notably Mission Chief Gustav Ranis, were members of the Yale University Economic Growth Center. In their policy recommendations, they argued that a country such as the Philippines had reached the critical point in its development where it would have to begin diversifying its export-base by encouraging manufacturing destined for European and American markets (Paauw and Fei, 1973). To achieve this would require 'wage restraint' and an 'open door' policy for transnational enterprise.

It was clear that here was a report that championed the 'new international division of labour' according to which the developing countries would participate in the world economy on the strength of their comparative labour advantage, while the already industrialized countries would specialize in staple food production and high technology, assuring their hegemony over the entire process.

The World Bank (full title: the International Bank for Reconstruction and Development), meanwhile, was playing a very difficult game. On one hand, its membership was composed of *territorial* entities or countries that could be expected to be fundamentally at odds with transnational imperialism. On the other hand, its *money* came primarily from the world's bankers and was, in principle, transnational. The Bank resolved its dilemma by using a *rhetoric* which suggested great affinity with radical, territorially based policies (Ul Haq, 1971; McNamara, 1975), but adopting *policies and programmes* that, on closer inspection, were more in line with the evolving doctrine of transnationals.

This stance became eminently clear in a book whose principal author was IBRD vice president for research and policy, Hollis B. Chenery, an American economist with a lifetime of development experience. His co-authors were drawn partly from the Bank and partly from the Sussex Institute of Development Studies (Chenery *et al.*, 1974).

Chenery looked more deeply into the strategy doctrine which the IDS had formulated in its Report on Kenya (International Labour Office, 1972). The title also announced the basic intention of the book: *Redistri-*

bution with Growth. The basic problem was simply stated: wealth redistribution might be politically difficult; growth was essential; poverty was
inconveniently embarrassing. The Chenery report claimed that the
poverty problem might be brought under control in a period of one or
two decades (p. 47). Towards this end, it might be necessary to practice
a little growth restraint and a fraction of the annual increment of production should be diverted to 'investment in the poor'. The poor themselves, who were to be the 'target group' of this new policy, were defined
according to an income criterion. By holding the threshold sufficiently
low ($75 per capita a year), the authors could pretend that they were
dealing with only a minority problem, the 'rich' being defined as *anyone*
above that threshold. Had the income criterion been raised even slightly,
however, the special target-character of the population would have
evaporated. Chenery *et al*. would then have had to contemplate radical
strategies for transforming the entire economy instead of diddling only
with the margins.

Let us, however, return to the upper part of our diagram (Figure 7.1),
specifically to the activities of the International Labour Office which
continued to play an outstanding role in advancing development thinking
during the entire period. By 1974 many ILO economists in Geneva had
become disillusioned with the results of the 'redistribution-with-growth'
proposals which they themselves had helped to spawn. The Green Revolution on which so much hope had been staked for 'solving' the food problems
of densely populated, agrarian countries turned out to be primarily a
means for the proletarianization of the peasantry (Griffin, 1974). And
contrary to expectations, the poverty of many rural people was increasing
not only in relative but in absolute terms (Griffin and Khan, 1976). The
Philippines report had proposed a doctrine that would have played
directly into the hands of the transnationals. It offered no chance
whatever to meet the ever more distressful problems of joblessness and
landlessness in countries such as Bangladesh and India. A more drastic
solution was needed.

The response was an emphasis on *self-reliance in development*, a cutting
or at least a weakening of the umbilical cord that tied a country's fate
to the world economy of the transnationals. This implied a territorially
based, autonomous development that would give priority to raising agricultural production and to the *basic needs* of the masses of the people
(International Labour Office, 1976). A World Employment Conference
was convened in 1976 which brought together representatives from the
first, second, and third worlds, as well as from capital and labour.
Although broad agreement was obtained on a 'basic-needs' approach to
development planning, much controversy remained concerning particular
aspects such as the role to be assigned to transnational enterprise in
national development (International Labour Office, 1977).

At about the same time as the ILO was preparing its conference, a
series of independently written reports was published, related in one way

or another to the United Nations. They all told more or less the same story. Development should be increasingly self-reliant, declared a group of internationally famous scientists (Cocoyoc Declaration, 1974). There had to be 'another development', argued the Swedish Dag Hammarskjöld Foundation (*What Now*, 1975), by which they meant a strategy of basic needs. At about the same time, at a United Nations conference in Nagoya, Friedmann and Douglass (1975) proposed an 'agropolitan' strategy. Their intention was to integrate rural with urban development, the countryside with cities. Towards this end, they considered the creation of a parallel economy: a wage-goods economy in the domestic market would exist side by side with an export-oriented, internationally competitive economy. Basic needs were taken as a starting point for organizing the domestic economy according to a cellular principle whose smallest, self-governing unit was the agropolitan district.

Finally, the following year, Ignacy Sachs helped to popularize the concept of *ecodevelopment* (Sachs, 1976), which combined basic needs strategies with an environmental ethics gleaned from such sources as the UN Stockholm Conference of 1972, the Club of Rome reports, and a report which had just been prepared at the Bariloche Foundation in Argentina by a group of Latin-American scientists (Herrera *et al.*, 1976). Ecodevelopment focused primarily on rural aspects of development, remaining silent on the burning questions of industrialization, urbanization, transnational enclaves, and export diversification. Because of this omission (which was partly a consequence of not adopting an explicit spatial framework for development), ecodevelopment lent itself to being 'captured' by transnational interests for their 'new international division of labour', with its emphasis on export-diversification. In this context, ecodevelopment would appear as a noble gesture, directed at the rural poor in whom the transnationals had, at any rate, only minimal interest.

The new streams of development since 1969, though they are clearly interrelated, converge upon two principal forms of social integration: territorial and functional. A unity of opposites, these forms not only complement but also contradict each other.

Every national economy is, to a degree, both functional and territorial, but the actions to which these principles of social cohesion give rise often result in bitter struggle. In any event, the complexity of the response space does not allow of ideologically 'pure' answers. Territory and function are both needed for development. The real question is which principle is to be master: shall function prevail over territory, or territory over function. At the moment the transnationals appear to be gaining in this contest for dominion, but the arguments favouring the territorial principle are very strong, and territorial systems are, in any case, essential to the survival of corporate (functional) power. Without territory, corporate power could not shift the burdens of production on society (Murray, 1975, pp. 63–77).

Regional development doctrine will have to find accommodation within the policy response space we have described. Current doctrine, which is based on the theory of polarized development, is fully consistent with the transnational ideology of development; it is a willing instrument in the hands of the managers of unequal development. Opposed to trans- national ideology, and in struggle against it, is the territorial strategy of basic needs. The question is, what changes in regional development doctrine are required to make it serve the interests of equal territorial development.

Before proceeding to sketch an answer in the final chapter, we must look more closely at growth centre doctrine and the criticisms which have been brought against it. Both technical and ideological arguments will be considered.

Critiques of the growth centre doctrine

Regional planning doctrine in the 1950s and 1960s revolved essentially around the idea of growth centres. It was, basically, an entrancing notion that had gained plausibility from its common-sense appeal. Wasn't economic growth a result of industrialization? And weren't industries found concentrated in locations that favoured further accumulation? And wasn't it true that these burgeoning centres of progress helped to spread jobs and income over wider and wider areas, until the entire national space was integrated into a single market area?

Many economists and planners thought the answers to these questions self-evident and thus unworthy of their further attention. To be sure, there were the developing countries, but most planners assumed that their historical trajectory would be structurally quite similar to the course which the already industrialized countries had taken. The process of their spatial development might be speeded up through effective regional planning, but it was inconceivable that planning might itself initiate an altogether different process. In the 1930s, Arthur E. Morgan had dreamed of creating a new civilization in the Tennessee Valley and had failed. Three decades later some of the social planners in the Guayana area of Venezuela had the same dream. They, too, wanted to shape another Venezuela in the empty lands of the lower Orinoco Basin. What they in fact produced was simply another bit of the old Venezuela. Regional planning, then, could serve as midwife to a spatial pattern in the ordering of activities that would in any event occur; it could not change that pattern. Any dramatic departure from familiar forms would require a very different kind of politics.

One trouble with this popular fashion was that it spread much faster than it was possible to test its performance in practice. The earliest critical observations were made by Harry W. Richardson, a British economist, in 1971, in a review of Spanish experience. Richardson argued that two conditions had to be fulfilled for a successful application of growth centre doctrine: the number of designated centres had to be kept small, and spatial priorities had to be maintained unaltered over long periods of time. Spanish planners appeared, by these criteria, both spendthrift and inconstant. Too many centres had been selected for special treatment, and their designations had frequently changed. The result was that Spanish planners had become disenchanted with growth centres as an instrument of regional policy.

Malcolm Moseley's major synthesis of the doctrine followed three years later, in 1974, succeeded by Niles M. Hansen's critical assessment (1975a, b), Friedmann and Douglass' review of Asian experience (1975), and then, in 1976, by a veritable flood of essays which, in one way or another, all expressed their disenchantment with the doctrine (Gilbert and Goodman, 1976; Pred, 1976, Stöhr and Tödtling, 1976; Schilling-Kaletsch, 1976). Growth centres were ceasing to be an 'idea in good currency'.

We shall not attempt to summarize these criticisms individually. It is fair to say, however, that most critics would agree on the following observations. To begin with, growth centre doctrine had always been in a conceptual muddle. Planners applied the term indifferently to major urban-industrial complexes (core regions) and to small central places in rural areas (growth points). Moreover, it was not always clear whether the term referred descriptively to centres that were undergoing a major phase of growth ('spontaneous' centres in the language of Alonso and Medrich) or cities designated for their potential role instead of actual performance.

Other aspects of the concept were no less ambiguous. How was growth, for instance, to be measured? What were the appropriate indicators? Jobs in the corporate sector or total employment, including the so-called informal sector? Or was population the more relevant measure? And why shouldn't income be used, together with a measure of its distribution (except that it was difficult to account for income at the urban level)? With these questions treated gingerly and without intellectual depth, it was unclear what operational meaning might be attributed to the phrase that was also the doctrine's centrepiece and glory: 'self-sustaining growth'. Although no planner could really answer what that meant, it was precisely 'self-sustaining growth' that their policies were to achieve. Finally, there was a good deal of confusion concerning the ways in which growth centres might be used to help in the spatial allocation of invest-ment resources. Operationally speaking, how were they to be 'activated'? Except where heavy industrial complexes were being built, as in Ciudad Guayana (Venezuela) and Las Truchas (Mexico), the means for activation were generally too weak to divert manufacturing industries from the 'natural' growth centres of the national economy. The tendency of capitalist systems is to reproduce patterns of inequality. The financial inducement offered by governments to private enterprise are usually much too weak to achieve a permanent restructuring of spatial organization.

This point has recently been stressed by another British economist, Stuart Holland (1976), in his excellent study of the relation between what he called the meso-economic sector (or Big Business) and regional development. Before a firm in the meso-economic sector will set up shop in Scotland, for example, it will prefer to build a branch plant in Portugal or in Morocco, where wages are much lower, labour relations pose few problems, and taxes are practically nonexistent. Holland suggested a number of drastic measures by which the State could gain virtual control over the investment policies of this sector. In general terms, he proposed *to subordinate corporate to territorial power*. With this proposal, he stated what is likely to become the major theme in regional development during the coming decades.

One essential aspect of growth centre doctrine is that employment multipliers of initial investments are 'internalized' within the growth centres themselves. But this assumption is more wishful thinking than known fact. Probabilities are against it, and multipliers are more likely to be 'captured' by the largest cities in either region or nation, or, in the case of many smaller nation-states, by the major production centres of the world economy beyond their boundaries.

These 'leakages' are very common in regional development. In advanced economies, they result from the high degree of spatial inter-dependence (Pred, 1976). In poor countries, the reason is often the absence of complementary business firms in the newly expanding region. The additional demand produced by one or two new industrial plants is generally insufficient to reach that minimum demand threshold that would permit a business to be locally established. It is far more economical to expand production in existing facilities located in the primate cities of the country, or even overseas. In cases where new invest-ments are required to accommodate increased demand, several reasons conspire to lead once more to the choice of primate cities, including the conservatism of financial institutions and the geographical distribution of the national market, a major share of which is concentrated in these cities.

As the discussion above suggests, the spatial dimension of growth centre doctrine rests on a number of doubtful propositions. In addition to unwarranted assumptions about the spatial incidence of multiplier effects, a good deal of nonsense has been written (including by the present senior author) about the *spatial diffusion* of economic growth. The most succinct formulation of diffusion theory in its application to growth centres is by Brian Berry (1972). According to Berry, 'the developmental role of growth centres involves the simultaneous *filtering* of innovations that bring growth down the urban hierarchy and the *spreading* of the benefits accruing from the resulting growth, both nationally from core to hinterland regions and within these regions from their metropolitan centres outwards to the intermetropolitan periphery' (p. 108). Berry concludes his essay with these words: 'Diffusion theory provides a second conceptual base for the growth centre idea' (p. 136).

Central to Berry's hypothesis was the rather fuzzy notion of bringing 'growth' *down* the urban hierarchy. In truth, it would be difficult to attach specific and theoretically valid meaning to this phrase. Berry's main mistake was to base his conclusions on an analysis of the diffusion of consumer goods (specifically of television) rather than on facilities for production. Had he concentrated his research on the latter, his conclusions about hierarchical filtering might have been very different.

In small and relatively poor countries, for example, major industrial branches are represented by only one or two plants, such as an oil refinery or aluminium smelter. Thus, it is, in principle, impossible for innovations to 'diffuse', whether through urban hierarchies or not. More finely articulated activities, such as bakeries, do 'filter' down, if that is the right word for it, but they are not generally the so-called propulsive industries or sectors. They only follow in the wake of general development; they do not lead it.

The hypothesis of horizontal spread fares little better. The idea is closely related to central place theory in geography, combined with certain ideas from economics which assert that the operation of capital and labour markets is more efficient in the vicinity of large cities than it is further away (Schultz, 1953).[6] What growth centre planners tend to overlook is that central place theory requires a more or less homogeneous market economy of small producers who would make use of central places for their daily or weekly transactions. This may be a fair assumption in southern Germany or Iowa. In the developing world, however, small-scale, commercial farming is a rarity. For the most part, peasants live outside the exchange economy. Local towns are therefore rather sleepy affairs that spring to life only on days when a periodic market is set up.

As for the vaunted operation of labour and capital markets near large cities, their efficiency in developing countries tends to decline rather steeply with distance from the centre, so that only a few miles out of town urban impacts may become virtually unmeasurable. On the whole, growth centre thinking reveals a distinctive *urban bias* in development (Lipton, 1977). In the case of lower-ranking central places, it would be more appropriate to say that economic growth filters *upward*, in response to agricultural developments in their vicinity, rather than down the urban hierarchy and outwards into the surrounding countryside.

In summary, growth centre doctrine is quite useless as a tool for regional development. It is even questionable whether historical accounts of capitalist regional development are best approached through the growth centre hypothesis. An answer hinges largely on the role of cities in development, and this still remains an unresolved issue (Abu-Lughod and Hay, 1977).

But growth centre doctrine is not only technically deficient. For about a decade it has come under serious ideological attack. The critique originated in South America, a continent frustrated in its aspirations and living in the shadow of North American economic and military power. South America had been a pioneer in regional policies and in creating an appropriate institutional framework for them, but spatial inequalities had not diminished. On the contrary, in most places they had only grown worse (Stöhr, 1975). Growth centre policies were introduced in the mid-1960s, initially in Chile, a country with a very high degree of economic primacy. At roughly the same time what had come to be known as 'dependency theory' was formulated as a specific Latin-American answer to the question of why the masses living in the twenty-odd republics of the continent were all but excluded from the benefits of industrialization, which were accumulating more and more in the hands of the new urban elites. Dependency theory tried to account for the observed facts of economic growth and underdevelopment by reference to the hegemony of the United States.

The application of this theory to the phenomenon of spatial development was carried out, for the first time, by Aníbal Quijano (1968), a Peruvian anthropologist working for the United Nations in Santiago. The argumentation was long and involved, concentrating on the role of the power elites who themselves had been co-opted into the North American-dominated industrial system. Already at that time the radical wing of urban and regional planners in Latin America could be heard to advocate the thesis that only a reduction in dependency to the United States would allow Latin American governments to devise a different spatial order in which both the peasant masses and workers would be able to share fully in the modern transformations of the economy. Agrarian reform would have to spearhead such a transformation, followed by a much more decentralized utilization of regional resources for the benefit of the country as a whole (Lehman, 1974). What was needed was a social revolution. But the attempt at a peaceful revolution in Chile was brutally suppressed with the help of North American imperial power.

The most complete formulation of the dependency hypothesis in relation to spatial development was worked out by the Chilean economist Osvaldo Sunkel (1970, 1973), until recently in exile as a Research Fellow at the Institute of Development Studies, Sussex University. Sunkel focused on the disruptive effects which industrialization based on the transnational corporation (which, for short, he called TRANCO) had on national social and economic structure. He concluded as follows (1973, pp. 168 and 170):

> The capitalist system of world economy is in the process of being reorganized into a new international industrial system whose main institutional agents are the TRANCOS, increasingly backed by the governments of the developed countries; this is a new structure of domination sharing a large number of characteristics of the mercantilist system, which concentrates the planning of the development of natural, human, and capital resources and the development of science and technology in the 'brain' of the new industrial system (i.e. the

technocrats of the TRANCOS, international organizations, and governments of developed countries), and which tends to reinforce the process of economic, social, political, and cultural underdevelopment of the Third World, deepening foreign dependence and exacerbating internal disintegration. . . .

In this process, some national entrepreneurs are incorporated as executives into the new enterprises or those absorbed by the TRANCO, and others are marginalized; some professionals, forming part of the technical staff and the segment of employees are incorporated, and the rest are marginalized; part of the qualified labour supply and those that are considered fit to be upgraded are incorporated, while the remainder are marginalized.

Sunkel called this a process of social disintegration. And rightly so. An artificial dualism is created and maintained by force, establishing a social class that is tied into and identifies with the transnational system, reaping its material advantages, while another, and very much larger class, is marginalized, serving as little more than a cheap labour reserve for the transnational sector (Stuckey, 1977). The 'marginalized' population either becomes a landless rural proletariat or moves into the cities where it is absorbed into the 'lower circuits' of the urban economy at levels of productivity that remain close to physical survival (Santos, 1971, 1974, 1975; Friedmann and Sullivan, 1974; McGee, 1974).

What lent weight to this analysis was the actual experience of socialist Cuba (Barkin and Manitzas, eds, 1973; Garnier, 1973; Susman, 1974). Cuba had managed to develop her regions much more equitably than any other Latin American country. The growth of Havana had been effectively contained; smaller urban centres had received preferential treatment in government expenditures; and social programmes had been extended to urban and rural workers alike. How different this all seemed to David Barkin's conclusions from a case study of regional development in Mexico (1972, pp. 92–3):

The investments in the Tierra Caliente clearly led to the amassing of great wealth in the zone, but its benefits were highly concentrated in the hands of a small number of people. . . .

Recent development in Mexico has been characterized by an accelerating rate of geographical and personal concentration of economic activity. It seems apparent that when regional development programmes are undertaken they are selected on the basis of their contribution to national economic growth and that, in most cases, none of the special developmental incentives necessary for regional growth are provided. Such programmes as the Tepaltepec river basin project may respond to the genuine needs of people in the region, but the design of the programme relegates most of them to the position of recipients of a minor 'trickle-down' effect, such as the improvement of the sanitary conditions in the region, while systematically canalizing most of the benefits to a small group of private investors who already participate in the elite structure of the society.... This situation is the result of a series of governmental measures which have favoured capital and tended to tax labour in the production processes.... The educational system further reinforces this process.... As a result, income has become more concentrated in Mexico, and a large proportion of the population has become marginal to the modernization effort.

In the same year that Barkin published his structuralist account of the economic and social consequences of regional development in Mexico, José Luis Coraggio (1972) came out with the first explicitly ideological critique of the growth centre doctrine. Coraggio had received his Ph.D. at Walter Isard's Regional Science Program at the University of Pennsylvania and had subsequently joined one of Latin America's foremost urban research centres, the Centro de Estudios Urbano-Regionales at the Torcuato di Tella Institute in Buenos Aires. His critique centred largely on the writings of François Perroux, but it was clear that he had in mind the *application* of Perrouvian growth centre doctrine in Latin America. The purpose of his critique was to demonstrate that, far from being an instrument for equalization, growth centre doctrine expressed the theory and practice of unequal capital accumulation and served as a tool for spatial domination.[7] His theoretical analysis was subsequently incorporated into a broader historical perspective by two colleagues at the Torcuato di Tella Institute, Marcos Kaplan (1973) and Alejandro Rofman (1974a, b).[8]

After 1974 growth centre doctrine was generally rejected by neo-Marxist planners and economists (Mønsted, 1974; Kongstadt, 1974; Rochefort, ed., 1975; Slater, 1975a, b, 1976; Stuckey, 1975). Unfortunately it was not clear in the name of what *alternative* policies they rejected it. Soviet authors, for instance, were much less violent in their critique. They perceived a direct analogy between growth centres and their own concept of *territorial production complex* which formed the backbone of industrial location planning in the Soviet Union. But the absence of a market economy lends a realism to Soviet discussions of this concept which is generally missing in the West. What western regional economist or planner has ever written a sentence so matter-of-fact as the following: 'The process of forming large-scale Complexes usually takes several decades and is carried out in stages' (Bandman, 1975, p. 207; see also Gokham and Karpov, 1972; Nekrasov, 1974). While the Soviets went ahead and built their Complexes, western theorists debated the merits of innovation diffusion from hypothetical growth centres.[9]

Notes

1. Mao Tse-Tung died in 1976, and a new group of leaders rose to power. It appears that major changes in development priorities are in the offing. Industrialization is to be speeded up, help from abroad is to be increased. The basic goals, however, will apparently remain the same.

2. According to certain reports, 15,000 copies were dispatched to political and social leaders throughout the world.

3. Only a few critics attacked the report for ideological reasons. Thus Johan Galtung (1972): '. . . the book gives the message of the finiteness of nature, of increasing pollution and decreasing resources in a way completely acceptable to the elites of the world' (p. 101). For an extremely interesting, if somewhat idiosyncratic socialist view, see Harich (1975). Harich, an East German philosopher, takes the *Limits to Growth* report seriously, arguing that it calls for a revision of traditional communist doctrine concerning the 'dissolution of the state'. A 'limited' world, says Harich, requires an increasingly powerful state to manage resources for the common good and to enforce equality in distribution.

4. In a Congressional Committeee Staff Study (Joint Economic Committee, 1977, p. 28), we read the following bland statement concerning US policy on the operation of transnationals: 'The United States has been receptive to the idea of an international code of conduct . . . but opposes any mandatory standards. An admonitory – not mandatory – code of conduct was recently developed by the Organization for Economic Coordination and Development (OECD). The code has received US endorsement.' See also the detailed report on this issue in International Labour Office, 1977.

5. In the early 1970s, Latin American 'dependency theory' leaped the Atlantic to Africa where it inspired a similar critical, but more explicitly neo-Marxist, school of writings.

6. Divergencies in economic development are related to location, according to Schultz (1953, p. 147). On this assumption, the following hypothesis, consisting of three parts, may be advanced: '(1) Economic development occurs in a specific locational matrix. . . . (2) These locational matrices are primarily industrial-urban in composition. . . (3) the existing economic organization works best at or near the centre of a particular matrix of economic development, and it works best in those parts of agriculture which are situated favourably in relation to such a centre. . . .'

7. Some of Coraggio's views were further elaborated in articles available in English (see Coraggio, 1975, 1976). A similar critique of growth centre doctrine was elaborated by Per Kongstadt (1974, with reply by Friedmann) and Barbara Stuckey (1975, also with a reply by Friedmann).

8. At the time of this writing (1977), Kaplan and Rofman, like Sunkel and Coraggio, are living in exile.

9. The abandonment of growth centre doctrine as defining for regional planning does not, of course, mean that the concept of centrality as such is no longer useful. As a quick review of its possible uses will show, it has merely been reduced to the status of an ordinary work-a-day concept.

   Let us begin with lower-order rural centres. By themselves, they do not *generate* socio-economic development; rather, they *respond* to changes in agricultural production within their area of general accessibility. Nevertheless, they may be useful in helping to articulate the spatial organization of the rural economy through the location of services, the lay-out of transport and communication networks, the establishment of public offices and governmental institutions and the development of rural industries. These very practical problems of development planning must be considered in the context of revitalizing the rural economy as a whole. Lower-order centres cannot function as instigators of 'spontaneous' growth processes that are described in such metaphysical terms as 'filtering down' and 'diffusion'.

Another important use of 'centrality' is in conjunction with planned urban-industrial complexes. These, of course, must correspond to both resource availability and the existence of technical complementarities. By definition, industrial complexes are 'massed' and become the nucleus for associated urban developments. It is also clear, however, that within a given country there will be very few potential developments of this sort, and each of these will present unique problems for planning and implementation. For instance, the Ciudad Guayana project in Venezuela's eastern Orinoco region is very different in character from the new urban-industrial zone in the southeast corner of the Republic of Korea. Both efforts, no doubt, are having major impacts upon their respective regions (and indeed upon the national economy), but it would be misleading to regard their primary purpose as that of 'spreading economic growth impulses' as the growth centre literature would have us believe. The broader regional impacts may constitute an appropriate subject for empirical research, but that is an altogether different matter.

A third possible use of 'centrality' arises in conjunction with so-called intermediate cities. These have been the subject of special attention by regional economists such as Niles Hansen. According to growth centre doctrine, a combination of public infrastructure investments and locational subsidies can turn the economy of these cities around, accelerating their growth and bolstering the regional economies they dominate. Attempts to implement such policies have met with indifferent success. More to the point, it is probably true that intermediate urban centres do better when they are administrative capitals in a multi-regional (federal) country than when their function is purely economic. Intermediate centres have done reasonably well in Brazil, Malaysia, Nigeria, and Colombia; they have stagnated in countries with unitary governments such as Chile, Argentina, Thailand, and Egypt. This suggests that a solution may have to be looked for in political and administrative changes rather than in economic policy.

Finally, there is the possible use of 'centrality' in connection with the principal core regions of a country. According to growth centre doctrine, the purpose of regional policy should be to hold back the further growth of these regions. But experience has shown that this can only be done, if at all, with far-reaching state intervention in overall national development. In China, millions of young urbanites have been forced to resettle in the countryside (and even there it is not clear how much of this constitutes a permanent resettlement, how much involves short- as opposed to long-distance moves, and to what extent the policy has any but temporary effects on the long-term rate of urbanization); in Cuba, it has been official policy of the government to allow the capital city of Havana physically to deteriorate while the government devoted its energies to building up provincial centres; and for Great Britain, Stuart Holland (1976) has advocated the nationalization of selected dynamic industries as a lever for imposing the will of the state upon a recalcitrant but powerful private sector. State intervention on this scale makes sense only if there exists a political commitment to carrying out a comprehensive location and settlement policy, most likely for geo-political rather than for purely economic reasons.

In short, 'centrality' continues to be a useful concept. But it would be dangerous to blow up this limited usefulness to the full scale of a regional planning doctrine. It is this which has been wrong about the regional planning work of the last two decades; it is this mistake which has to be corrected.

Bibliography

Abu-Lughod, J. and Hay, R., Jr 1977: *Third world urbanization.* Chicago: Maaroufa Press.

Amin, S. 1974: *Accumulation on a world scale: a critique of the theory of underdevelopment.* 2 vols. New York: Monthly Review Press.

Bandman, M. K. 1975: Scheme and composition of optimization models of forming spatial production complexes. In Kuklinski, A., editor 1975, 201–18.

Barkin, D. P. 1972: A case study of the beneficiaries of regional development. *International Social Development Review* (UN) No. 4, 84–94.

Barkin, D. P. and Manitzas, N. R., editors 1973: *Cuba: the logic of revolution.* Andover, Mass.: Warner Modular Publications.

Berry, B. J. L. 1972: Hierarchical diffusion: the basis of development filtering and spread in a system of cities. In Hansen, N. M., editor 1972, 108–38.

Chenery, H., *et al.* 1974: *Redistribution with growth.* Oxford University Press.

Cockroft, J. D., Frank, A. G. and Johnson, D. L., editors 1972: *Dependence and underdevelopment: Latin America's political economy.* Garden City, N.Y.: Anchor Books.

The Cocoyoc Declaration 1974: *Development Dialogue* **2**, 88–96.

Coraggio, J. L. 1972: Hacia una revisión de la teoría de los polos de desarrollo. *Revista Latinoamericana de Estudios Urbano Regionales* **2**, 25–40. An English translation appeared in *Viertel Jahres Berichte* (Bonn) **53**, September 1973.

— 1975: Polarization, development and integration. In Kuklinski, A., editor 1975, 353–74.

— 1976: Preliminary notes on the possibilities and difficulties of radical spatial analysis. Paper for the Latin American Studies Association (LASA), Atlanta.

Diamond, D. and McLoughlin, J. M., editors 1975: *Progress in planning.* Vol. 4, Part 2. Oxford: Pergamon Press.

Dumont, with Mazoyer, M. 1973 (orig. 1969): *Socialisms and development.* London: Andrew Deutsch.

Editors of *The Ecologist* 1972: *A blueprint for survival.* London.

Emmanuel, A. 1972: *Unequal exchange: a study of the imperialism of trade.* New York: Monthly Review Press.

Faber, M. and Seers, D., editors 1972: *The crisis in planning.* 2 vols. London: Chatto and Windus.

Feder, E. 1976: How agribusiness operates in underdeveloped agricultures. *Development and change* **7**, 413–44.

Frank, A. G. 1967: *Capitalism and underdevelopment in Latin America.* New York: Monthly Review Press.

— 1972 (orig. 1970): *Lumpenbourgeoisie: Lumpendevelopment. Dependence, class, and politics in Latin America.* New York: Monthly Review Press.

Friedmann, J. and Alonso, W., editors 1975: *Regional policy: readings in theory and applications*. Cambridge, Mass.: The MIT Press.

Friedmann, J. and Douglass, M. 1975: Agropolitan development: towards a new strategy for regional planning in Asia. In United Nations Centre for Regional Development, 1975, 333–87.

Friedmann, J. and Sullivan, F. 1974: Labor absorption in the urban economy: the case of the developing countries. *Economic development and cultural change* **22**, 385–413.

Froebel, F., Heinrichs, J. and Kreye, O. 1976: Tendencies towards a new international division of labour. *Economic and Political Weekly* (Bombay) February, 159–70.

Galtung, J. 1972: 'The limits to growth' and class politics. PRIO – publication no. 27–7. Oslo: International Peace Research Institute.

Garnier, J.-P. 1973: *Une ville, une revolution: la Havane*. Paris: Anthropos.

Gilbert, A., editor 1976: *Development planning and spatial structure*. London: John Wiley & Sons.

Gilbert, A. P. and Goodman, D. E. 1976: Regional income disparities and economic development: a critique. In Gilbert, A., editor 1976, 113–42.

Gokham, V. M. and Karpov, L. N. 1972: Growth poles and growth centres. In Kuklinski, A., editor 1972, 125–34.

Griffin, K. 1974: *The political economy of agrarian change: an essay on the green revolution*. London: Macmillan.

Griffin, K. and Khan, A. R. 1976: Rural poverty: trends and explanation. MS. Geneva. International Labour Office.

Gurley, J. G. 1976: *China's economy and the Maoist strategy*. New York: Monthly Review Press.

Habermas, J. 1975: *Legitimation crisis*. Boston: Beacon Press.

Hahn, E. 1977: Raumplanung und Siedlungs politik in der Volksrepublik China. *Raumforschung und Raumordnung* **7**, 293–304.

Hansen, N. M., editor 1972: *Growth centers in regional economic development*. New York: The Free Press.

1975a: An evaluation of growth center theory and practice. *Environment and Planning* **7**, 821–32.

1975b: Growth strategies and human settlement systems in developing countries. In United Nations Centre for Regional Development, 1975, 309–28.

Harich, W. 1975: *Kommunismus ohne Wachstum? Babeuf und der 'Club of Rome.'* Hamburg: Rowohlt.

Heilbronner, R. 1974: *An inquiry into the human prospect*. New York: Norton.

Herrera, A., *et al*. 1976: *Catastrophe or new society? a Latin American world model*. Ottawa: International Development Research Center.

Holland, S. 1976: *Capital versus the regions*. London: Macmillan.

International Labour Office 1972: *Employment, incomes, and equality: a strategy for increasing productive employment in Kenya*. Geneva: ILO.

1974: *Sharing is development: a programme of employment, equity, and growth for the Philippines.* Geneva: ILO.

1976: *Employment, growth, and basic needs.* Geneva: ILO.

1977: *Meeting basic needs: strategies for eradicating mass poverty and unemployment.* Geneva: ILO.

Joint Economic Committee, Congress of the United States 1975: *China: a reassessment of the economy.* Washington, DC: Government Printing Office.

1977: *The United States response to the new international economic order: the economic implications for Latin America and the United States.* Washington, DC: Government Printing Office.

Kaplan, M. 1973: La ciudad Latinoamericana como factor de transmisión de poder socioeconómico y político hacia el exterior. In Schteingart, M., editor 1973, 132–76.

Keesing, D. E. 1975: Economic lessons from China. *Journal of Development Economics* **2**, 1–32.

Kongstadt, P. 1974: Growth poles and urbanization: a critique of Perroux and Friedmann. *Antipode* **6**, 114–22.

Kuklinski, A., editor 1972: *Growth poles and growth centres in regional planning.* The Hague: Mouton.

editor 1975: *Regional development and planning: international perspectives.* Leyden: Sijthoff.

Lehman, D., editor 1974: *Agrarian reform and agrarian reformism. Studies of Peru, Chile, China, and India.* London: Faber and Faber.

Lipton, M. 1977: *Why poor people stay poor: urban bias in world development.* Cambridge, Mass.: Harvard University Press.

Mandel, E. 1975: *Late capitalism.* London: NLB.

McGee, T. G. 1974: *The persistence of the proto-proletariat: occupational structures and planning for the future of Third World cities.* Comparative Urbanization Studies, School of Architecture and Urban Planning, University of California, Los Angeles.

McNamara, R. S. 1975: Address to the Board of Governors. Washington, DC: International Bank for Reconstruction and Development.

Meadows, D. H., *et al.* 1972: *The limits to growth.* A report to the Club of Rome. New York: Universe Books.

Mesarovic, M. and Pestel, E. 1974: *Mankind at the turning point.* The second report to the Club of Rome. New York: E. P. Dutton.

Mønsted, M. 1974: François Perroux's theory of 'growth pole' and 'development' pole: a critique. *Antipode* **6**, 106–14.

Moseley, M. J. 1974: *Growth centres in spatial planning.* Oxford: Pergamon Press.

Mumford, L. 1970: *The pentagon of power.* New York: Harcourt, Brace, Jovanovich.

Murray, R. 1975 (orig. 1971): *Multinational companies and nation states: two essays.* London: Spokesman Books.

Nekrasov, N. 1974: *The territorial organization of Soviety economy.* Moscow: Progress Publishers.

Paauw, D. S. and Fei, J. C. H. 1973: *The transition in open dualistic economies: theory and Southeast Asian experience.* New Haven: Yale University Press.

Pred, A. 1976: *The interurban transmission of growth in advanced economies: empirical findings versus regional planning assumptions.* International Institute of Applied Systems Analysis, Research Report No. 76–4. Laxenburg, Austria.

Quijano, A. 1968: Dependencia, cambio social y urbanización en Latino América. *Revista Mexicana de Sociología* **30**, 525–71.

Richardson, H. W. 1971: Regional development policy in Spain. *Urban Studies* **8**, 39–54. Reprinted in Friedmann, J. and Alonso, W., editors 1975, 712–26.

Rochefort, M., editor 1975: *Organisation de l'espace.* Special issue of *Revue Tiers-Monde* **8** (January–March).

Rodney, W. 1972: *How Europe underdeveloped Africa.* Dar-es-Salaam: Tanzania Publishing House.

Rofman, A. 1974a: *Desigualdades regionales y concentración económica: el caso Argentino.* Buenos Aires: Ed. SIAP-Planteos.

— 1974b: *Dependencia, estructura de poder y formación regional en América Latina.* Buenos Aires: Siglo XXI.

Sachs, I. 1976: Ecodevelopment. *Ceres* (Rome) no. 42, 8–12.

Santos, M. 1971: *Les villes du tiers monde.* Paris: M.-Th. Genin.

— 1974: Sous-développement et poles de croissance économique et sociale. *Revue Tiers-Monde* **25**, 271–86.

— 1975: *The shared space: the two circuits of urban economy in underdeveloped countries and their spatial repercussions.* London: Methuen.

Sawers, L. 1977: Urban planning in the Soviet Union and China. *Monthly Review* March, 39–48.

Schenk, H. 1974: Concepts behind urban and regional planning in China. *Tijdschrift voor Economische en Sociale Geografie* **65**, 381–9.

Schilling-Kaletsch, I. 1976: *Wachstumspole und Wachstumszentren: Untersuchungen zu einer sektoral und regional polarisierten Entwicklung.* Wirtschaftsgeographische Abteilung des Instituts für Geographie und Wirtschaftsgeographie der Universität Hamburg.

Schteingart, M., editor 1973: *Urbanización y dependencia en América Latina.* Buenos Aires: Ed. SIAP.

Schultz, T. W. 1953: *The economic organization of agriculture.* New York: McGraw-Hill.

Seers, D. 1969: The meaning of development. Paper presented at the 11th World Conference of the Society for International Development, New Delhi, 14–17 November. *International Development Review* 2–6 December.

Slater, D. 1975a: El capitalismo sub-desarrollado y la organización del espacio: Perú, 1920–1940. *Revista Interamericana de Planificación* **9**, 87–106.

   1975b: Underdevelopment and spatial inequality: approaches to the problem of regional planning in the Third World. In Diamond, D. and McLoughlin, J. M., editors 1975, 97–167.

   1976: Radical approaches to the urban and regional analysis of peripheral capitalist social formations: a bibliography. Amsterdam: Center for Latin American Research and Documentation.

Stöhr, W. 1975: *Regional development: experiences and prospects in Latin America.* The Hague: Mouton.

Stöhr, W. and Tödtling, F. 1976: Spatial equity: some antitheses to current regional development doctrine. MS. Vienna: Interdisciplinary Institute of Urban and Regional Studies, Wirtschaftsuniversität.

Stuckey, B. 1975: Spatial analysis and economic development. *Development and Change* **6**, 89–101.

   1977: The spatial distribution of the industrial reserve army. MS. Starnberg: Max Planck Institute.

Sunkel, O. 1970: Desarrollo, subdesarrollo, dependencia, marginación y desigualdades espaciales: hacia un enfoque totalizante. *Revista Latinoamericano de Estudios Urbanos y Regionales* (EURE) **1**, 13–51.

   1973: Transnational capitalism and national disintegration in Latin America. *Social and Economic Studies* **22**, 132–76.

Susman, P. 1974: Cuban development: from dualism to integration. *Antipode* **6**, 10–30.

Szentes, T. 1976: *The political economy of underdevelopment.* Third edition, revised. Budapest: Akademiai Kiadó.

Taylor, G. R. 1970: *Doomsday Book.* London: Thames and Hudson.

Thorbeck, E. 1973: The employment problem: a critical evaluation of four ILO comprehensive country reports. *International Labour Review* **107**, 393–423.

Tinbergen, J., co-ordinator 1976: *RIO: reshaping the international order.* A report to the Club of Rome. New York: E. P. Dutton.

Ul Haq, M. 1971: Employment in the 1970s: a new perspective. *International Development Review* 9–13 December.

United Nations Centre for Regional Development 1975: *Growth pole strategy and regional development planning in Asia.* Proceedings of a seminar. Nagoya, Japan: UNCRD.

Vernon, R. 1971: *Sovereignty at bay.* New York: Basic Books.

Weiss, U. 1975: Das chinesische Entwicklungsmodell. *Berichte des Osterreichischen China-Forschungsinstitutes* (Vienna) **1**, 63–114.

What Now. The 1975 Dag Hammarskjöld Report on Development and International Cooperation. Special issue of *Development Dialogue* 1975, No. 1/2.

Wong, J. 1976: Some aspects of China's agricultural development experiences: implications for developing countries in Asia. *World Development* **4**, 485–95.

Chapter 8
The recovery of territorial life

Global growth management

With the growth centre doctrine as its principal tool, spatial development planning became the handmaiden of transnational capital.[1] The historical overlap between functional and territorial integration had initially obscured this relationship. Planning was a function of territorial governance, and its spatial component presumably had the task of securing a balanced interregional pattern of production and consumption. Spatial planning was thus intended to reflect a public purpose. But speaking practically, efficiencies were almost always calculated on private account. The question most frequently addressed was by how much private capital should be subsidized.

Given its context, the question was a perfectly reasonable one. Yet it could only arise under conditions of unequal development, where efficiency and equity, production and distribution were treated as separate and independent issues.[2] Spatial planners might retain the territorial concept of region, though all that remained of it now was a convenient designation for a functionally integrated area. Their ultimate aim was to integrate the spatially articulated national economy, by subordinating its smaller, local economies to the reason of the national market.

In a widely read text, Friedmann (1966, p. 54) had formulated the main objectives of this doctrine:

1. The gradual elimination of the periphery on a national scale by substituting for it a single, interdependent system of urban regions.
2. The progressive integration of the space economy by the extension, on a national scale, of a system of efficient commodity and factor markets.

The second objective was further explained (p. 55):

> The goal of integration ... is essential for a nation that is initiating its drive to maturity. It has in view the breakdown of a pattern of regionalized economies partly closed to commerce with one another and holding on a steady course towards an interdependent national system, based on the principle of comparative advantage.

At the time these lines were written, no one questioned that the developing entity was, indeed, the nation. It was therefore reasonable to assume that the nation would be strengthened by the full articulation of its regional economies defined according to an urban-based node-linkage model.[3]

In the United States the cultural region had long ago ceased to be significant. This had even been true at the outset of regional planning, when Mumford and Odum wrote their major polemical works.[4] In Europe the cultural region lingered as a political reality. But the immediate consequences of World War II was not a resurgence of regionalism. In the case of the newly formed countries of the world periphery, it was the attempted political and economic integration of economies on a *national* scale and, in Western Europe, the integration of the *multi-national* economy of the EEC (Lindberg and Scheingold, eds., 1971).

A mere twenty years later, however, even the national and multi-national scales had grown too small. The imperative of growth required the further integration of the economy on a world scale (Wallerstein, 1974). International resources and markets had to be marshalled to sustain the expansion of capital. A new division of labour had to be imposed. The question was how to organize the world efficiently for production. As Aurelio Peccei (1969, p. 219) put it in describing the future activities of the Club of Rome, 'This project is intended to be a multi-nationally sponsored feasibility study on systematic, long-term planning of world scope.'

From the vantage point of the Club of Rome, there were, in fact, no inherent 'limits to growth'. *But there would have to be growth management on a global scale.* Prudent planning would allow the world economy to expand its productive forces into the foreseeable future. It was this belief in a managerial economy that lay behind Peccei's hope of eventually obtaining the co-operation of the Soviet Union and even China in his scheme.[5]

As discussed in the preceding chapter, the third report to the Club of Rome (Tinbergen, 1976) represents the first serious attempt to come to grips with the question of world-wide growth management. It makes explicit the requirement for a reduction in the sovereign powers of the nation-state and thus for the further dissolution of territorial power. Simultaneously, of course, functional powers would have to be strengthened at the next higher, or world level of integration.

Aurelio Peccei is very open about this ultimate objective. He writes (1969, p. 245):

> It is the task of our press, techno-structure, academia, and also political class – a few new leaders, after all, are enough – to keep public opinion informed of the reality of one world, and of the repercussions its macroproblems have on every country, and indeed, every family. If this is done, I am sure that our peoples will prove mature enough to support with their vote, and if necessary with their own sacrifice, not only this new thinking and this new approach, but also the strategy and policy decisions they will require.

To Peccei it seems all very simple: 'a few new leaders, after all, are enough'. There will be no attempt to make the future planners of the world accountable to anyone other than themselves. The transnational dream is a benevolent world tyranny. Because national sovereignty stands in the way of this project, it must be restrained – of course, in the name of high-sounding phrases, such as Tinbergen's 'common heritage of mankind' principle.[6]

This short detour to consider the historical divergence in the structure and purposes of national societies and transnational corporations will perhaps clarify the statement with which we began this chapter: spatial development planning has unwittingly become the handmaiden of transnational capital. *The growth centre doctrine is completely attuned to the ideology and planning approaches of transnational corporations.*

An urban-based rural development

As we saw in chapter 7, transnational ideology has recently modified its doctrine of development: redistribution with growth has become fashionable. International agencies, such as the World Bank, have pushed the rural and the urban 'poor' a few notches higher up the scale of official attention. Traditional growth centre doctrine had to be extended and modified accordingly. In their recent report to the United States Agency for International Development (AID), Rondinelli and Ruddle (1976) join in the chorus of criticism of this doctrine. In the end, however, they turn around and replace it with a model that is virtually identical.

On the technical side, Rondinelli and Ruddle lean heavily on the work of E. A. J. Johnson (1970), an economic historian who had worked for many years as an adviser to the Indian government. Johnson was an ardent advocate of the growth centre approach to regional development. So convinced was he of its validity, that he carried it down the urban hierarchy to individual village centres. His immediate aim was to build up district towns as 'poles' for a dynamic rural development. These poles would come into existence through the judicious placement of services and through appropriate linkages of towns to both their service areas and higher-order metro-centres.[7]

Adopting Johnson's model, Rondinelli and Ruddle call their policy one of integrated spatial development by which they mean a development that encompasses both rural and urban areas. Unfortunately, but not surprisingly, their report is as strong on analysis as it is weak on measures for implementation. In the context of transnational development, an integrated process of rural-urban development that will consistently favour rural populations (instead of destroying the basis of their survival economy by replacing it with alien corporate structures) is not possible. Planners with an experienced grasp of the realities of agricultural development in a transnational context have recognized this for some time (Ruttan, 1975).

Basic needs:
A new approach to territorial development

As members of many different territorial communities, we are confronting the following historical situation:

1. Transnational corporations continue to have some need of territorial power – for example, to absorb the social costs of production; but territorial power cannot rely on purely utilitarian and coercive means of persuasion. In the longer term, the legitimacy of territorial governments derives from an historical and self-transcending sense among the people that they are joined by threads of common destiny, that they are more to each other than to those who do not share their history.

2. The managers of transnational power are ultimately responsible to no one but themselves. Unchecked by territorial and, indeed, by any other power, they wish to totalize their grasp upon the world. The exclusive interest they have is to retain and to enlarge the bases of their power. Those who are integrated into their system will be materially rewarded; those who are not – a majority of the world's population – must be controlled by force.

3. Transnational development occurs according to the principles of an exchange economy in which efficiency in production and equity in distribution are structurally separated in theory as well as fact. Given the global approach of the transnationals, this implies that a majority of the world's population is destined to remain outside the system of transnational power and, therefore, poor, exploited, and coerced. But even those who are *within* the system will be exploited to serve the transnational managers whose power to decide is absolute and knows no interest beyond its further aggrandizement.

Keeping this situation in mind, it would be the height of folly to accept transnational claims for hegemony and acquiesce in the further weakening of territorial powers as demanded by the Club of Rome. The seduction held out to us is material reward. If we play the transnational game, we are told, we shall be able to purchase our happiness. '*Far too many people have now seen what the global shopping centre holds in store for them,*' said the Chairman of Citicorp, Walter B. Wriston (1976), to a London audience of bankers. '*They will not easily accept having the doors slammed shut by nationalism.*'

If we wish to reject the hegemonic claims of the transnationals in favour of a development guided by territorial power, we must begin with five assumptions. *First*, most of the world's population live at unacceptably low levels of material consumption. *Second*, most of the world's population are engaged in the production of use values outside the exchange economy. *Third*, every territorially integrated national community must be able to meet the basic needs of its members or eventually lose its claims to legitimacy. *Fourth*, the strengthening of territorial power that is implied in a basic needs approach to development does not exclude the necessity of judiciously using transnational power in meeting national needs. *Fifth*, the basic-needs approach is intended as a general model of development in which production and distribution are treated as facets of the same process of *equal development*. It is not meant to be an instrument for containing poverty in a context of transnational development.[8]

Basic needs refer to the sum of reciprocal claims in a territorially integrated society. In such a society, everyone is regarded as simultaneously a producer and consumer.[9] Needs are basic to the extent that their satisfaction is regarded as essential for a dignified human existence (Ghai and Alfthan, 1977).[10] As such, they represent an entitlement: each member has a rightful claim on his community for their satisfaction. But this entitlement implies a reciprocal claim. The community can ask for useful contributions from each member of its work.[11]

Basic needs, in the sense of survival, may be further regarded as a variable subset of a more general category of *human needs*. Two additional types of need may be distinguished: social and individualized. *Social* needs are needs of the collectivity (they are regarded as essential for the collectivity's survival and well-being). Transportation, for instance, is such a need and requires an allocation of resources. So are universities, even though not everyone may be able to attend one; they are not yet a survival need. Finally, *individualized* needs are those for which the collectivity assumes no specific responsibility. They remain each person's own concern, such as his/her choice of companionship, travel, or taste in food and clothes. Within certain bounds, intended to safeguard the wider interests of the collectivity, they are an expression of personal preference, and the collectivity remains silent about them.

These distinctions are derived from the historical experience with resource allocation in the Jewish kibbutz (Helman, 1974). There the historical path in the evolution of human needs may be briefly described as follows. In the early days of the movement, nearly all the needs of kibbutzim members were those of survival, thus they were satisfied collectively. As the kibbutzim movement grew more prosperous, a category of *social* needs was added, expanding more rapidly than basic or survival needs, which tended to level off. Operationally speaking, social needs were those whose satisfaction was hedged in by certain rules and procedures, reflecting communal preferences. Individual members had to apply for them to the kibbutz. But as the movement became still more prosperous, *individualized* needs began to appear and to establish their own claim on the community's resources. Provision was made for them by paying each member an allowance in money for which no account needed to be rendered. In recent years, individualized needs have increased more rapidly than either social or basic needs and so has the cash economy of the kibbutz. Whether this trend should be allowed to continue unchecked has become a major issue of ideological debate.

It is clear from this account that the satisfaction of basic needs will not for very long remain the sole objective of national development. It is merely a *first target* in societies where the majority of the people fall below an absolute level of poverty. In a comprehensive sense, development may be regarded as a process of individuation. As basic needs are met, social needs appear, and as these, in turn, are satisfied, individualized needs become relatively more significant.

Basic needs must not become a fetish for planners. The object of planning is to create those conditions in the real world that will nourish human beings who are 'rich in needs' (Heller, 1976). This requires the continued development of the productive forces and more particularly the *development of the bases of communal wealth*: land and water, good health, knowledge, and skills.

A short discourse on use value[12]

Most of the world's population are engaged in the production of use values, i.e. in the production of material goods and services that satisfy specific human needs and are available for use without the intermediary role of money. In industrially advanced economies, the most prevalent form of use-value production is in the home and is predominantly women's work: the bearing and raising of children, the preparation of meals, the making and repair of clothing, the beautification of the home, the celebration of festivals, sundry maintenance activities. In agrarian societies, use values are additionally produced in subsistence activities, primarily in fishing and in farming. As a rule, this is both men's and women's work.

The production of use-values contrasts with that of exchange values, or of commodities that become exclusively available through the mediation of money. The relation between use and exchange values is illustrated in

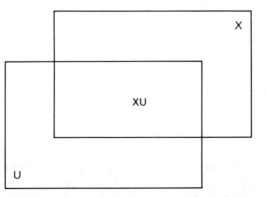

Figure 8.1   Relations between production for use and for exchange.

Figure 8.1 in which two non-dimensional rectangles are shown to overlap. The first, labelled X, stands for the exchange values produced, the second, U, for the production of use values. The area of overlap, XU, represents that part of production in the exchange economy which is also for use, or useful. The remainder of X symbolizes that part of production for exchange in the market which, from a social or more properly speaking, a political point of view, is judged to be *not* useful. Outside of XU, the part of production of pure use values stands for a measure of all the activities that are related to the production of life and do not involve market exchanges.

Determining which values in exchange are predominantly for use and which are not is problematical. Needs are only in a limited sense physiological. In practice, all human needs are culturally mediated: one eats food prepared in certain ways, not merely calories. Basic needs, moreover, may be considered part of a social contract: they arise as a reciprocal claim between individuals and the community in which they live. This reasoning leads to the conclusion that the decision between which commodities and services are needful and which are not is a social one that will require extensive public discussion. Still, some examples of what we mean by the production of exchange values that do *not* appear to satisfy a human need may be helpful at this point. Our candidates would include a weapons arsenal capable of destroying a potential enemy many times over, heroin non-medical uses, advertising that seeks artificially to create a 'need', all products (and services) that satisfy such needs, and a technology which destroys actual or potential use values. Bearing in mind examples of this kind, we conclude that the volume of production unrelated to human needs is probably very large and, especially under capitalism, would appear to be rising.

Expressed in terms of employment at a given level of productivity, the size of the exchange economy is a function of aggregate demand. Insufficient demand, as Keynes has taught us, will lead to a redundancy of labour. On the other hand, the size of the use-value economy, expressed in terms of hours of work performed, is virtually unlimited. Whether the relevant environment is the home, a rural district, or an urban neighbourhood, the amount of work that can, in principle, be done to improve the sense of individual and collective well-being depends on nothing more than the necessary energy and time. This ability of the use-value economy to absorb unlimited quantities of labour time is critically important where unused labour time can be employed in a community for common benefit. We shall return to this point later on.

Production for use is production for what is life-sustaining and enhancing. It is a way of expressing care for the varied qualities of living. In the home, there is always one more thing that can be done: another shirt that needs mending, a special dinner for intimate friends, a celebration on almost any occasion. The same thing is true for the larger environment. In rural areas, irrigation canals can be repaired, trees can be planted, gullies can be lined, new energy sources can be tapped.

None of these things is ultimately valued in terms of the market but for its ability to satisfy a need. To the extent that certain needs are satisfied, higher needs come into being. Needs extend beyond survival; they are conterminous with the meaning of life. But the choice of priorities among competing needs is a collective one.

As suggested in the diagram, the proportional relation between the use and exchange-value economies varies within certain limits. Beyond the level of a primitive subsistence economy, all economies are mixed. A pure exchange economy in which, for example, relations among family and friends would be conducted entirely on the basis of calculated self-interest, is no more conceivable than a pure use-value economy beyond some minimum level of complexity.[13]

Historically, the tendency has been for the exchange economy to gain at the expense of the economy of use values, as when commercial farming supplanted agriculture for subsistence. But, especially in recent decades, the amount of production not for use has probably increased with respect to the exchange economy as a whole. The environmental crisis may be viewed as a result of this long-term trend.

It is characteristic of exchange economies that the production of use values outside the exchange system proper goes generally unrecognized as 'work'.[14] This is quite clear with regard to women's work in the home and with most forms of volunteer work in cities. But in poor agrarian societies, a basic needs strategy for development will have to take the production of use values very seriously indeed. At least initially, most needs will have to be satisfied by expanding the capacity for their production.

This does not mean that the economy of use values will always remain dominant. The production of exchange values is also important, especially for use. Much of this production will initially be earmarked for export and so become a major link between regional and national economies and the rest of the world. At the same time, the expansion of the exchange economy must be strictly controlled so as not to impede the growth of the use-value economy and, at the same time, absorb the maximum number of workers who transfer from the use-value to the exchange economy. We may call this effort at expanding production in the exchange economy, the creation of a *parallel economy*. We shall return to this subject later in this chapter.

Implementing a basic-needs strategy: the agropolitan approach

In the following pages, we attempt to set forth some of the implications of a basic-needs strategy for territorial development. We shall call it the 'agropolitan' approach.[15] The specific setting we have chosen is that of densely populated, agrarian societies characterized by low profiles of social development, high rates of population increase, incipient urban-based industrialization, high external dependency, and rising indices of inequality. Such societies are typically found in Asia and parts of Africa. Outside the appropriate geographical setting for agropolitan development, other forms of territorially-based planned development would be more fitting.

To conclude our history of regional planning doctrines with a projection of a new approach to territorial development is not as unreasonable as it may seem. We propose agropolitan forms as an approach to the development of large segments of the world periphery – the new regions of economic backwardness and dependence which have always been a concern of regional planners. Additionally, our discussion is intended to break the current impasse in regional studies: a new paradigm is needed.

The reader will undoubtedly perceive some similarities between our version of agropolitan development and China's experience over the past twenty years. This is the result, not of a concious effort to hold up the Chinese example for universal emulation, but of structural features that obtain from working within the same framework of assumptions: for instance, that the first-stage objective of development should be the satisfaction of *basic needs*; that development should be organized on a *territorial basis*; that questions of *production and distribution should be jointly solved*; and that the resource base for the development of *productive forces must be continuously expanded*.[16]

Recent discussions of rural development in South America, especially Peru, have led to similar conclusions (Schulz, 1974; Del Risco S., 1975; Roberts, 1975). Papua New Guinea has officially adopted a version of agropolitan development – with a strong ecological bias – as a basis for its national plan (Passaris, 1977). And Bangladesh appears to be moving in the same direction (see Appendix). These instances give us confidence that the procedure we have followed in describing the elements of an agropolitan approach are grounded in a certain logic of structural relations. On the other hand, the actual implementation of an agropolitan form of development under the historical conditions prevailing in China suggests that the approach itself is more than a leap into the void. Our description of salient elements of agropolitan development traces the contours of a *possible* development which confronts directly the need for combing local spontaneity with state organization.

We will discuss the major elements of the agropolitan approach under four headings, including (1) the basic conditions for its realization, (2) the territorial framework, (3) the expansion of production, and (4) the role of the state.

1. The basic conditions

Three conditions are essential to successful agropolitan development:

selective territorial closure, the communalization of productive wealth, and the equalization of access to the bases for the accumulation of social power. They are difficult conditions to fulfill; yet, without them, only limited progress can be made.

Selective territorial closure refers to a policy of enlightened self-reliance at relevant levels of territorial integration: district, region, and nation. This condition flies straight in the face of the ideology of free trade and comparative advantage and the attempts of transnational enterprise to organize a functionally integrated world economy under its tutelage. Selective closure is a way to escape from the fetishism of growth efficiency; it is an expression of faith in the abilities of a people to guide the forces of their own evolution. It means to rely less on outside aid and investment, to involve the masses in development, to initiate a conscious process of social learning, to diversify production, and to pool resources. It means learning to say 'we' and to assert a territorial interest.

The *communalization of productive wealth* is the second condition for agropolitan development. In poor agrarian societies, productive wealth occurs chiefly in the form of land and water. Communalizing this wealth means that the power to determine the ultimate uses and disposition of land and water rests with the appropriate territorial community. In most peasant societies, this is an ancient practice, vestiges of which may be found to this day, as in Mexico's indigenous tradition of the *ejido* (Griffin, 1974; Lehman, ed., 1974).

Communalization may take a variety of forms. All that is asserted here is the *priority interest of the community in the basic conditions of its sustenance.* Whereas individuals seek short-term gains, territorial communities must ensure the long-term survival and well-being of the group. Communalization legitimizes the expression of this interest.

In the context of a basic-needs strategy, communalization is essential. Only the community can guarantee the satisfaction of the basic needs of its members, and to allocate benefits accordingly it must have access to the fruits of its own labour. The full mobilization of available resources, which agropolitan development implies, is possible only where the benefits from such an effort are understood to flow in roughly equal measure to everyone in the community. Where benefits are appropriated primarily for private use, so that the gains accrue unequally, even the initial effort is not likely to be made, and the productive potential of the community will be realized only in part.

The third condition for agropolitan development is the *equalization of access to the bases for the accumulation of social power.* Social power is here conceived as a resource capable of raising the individual's sense of potency. Where access to the use of social power is unequal, the power of the few to dominate the many is enhanced. Where it is more equally distributed, the ground is prepared for entering upon freely co-operative relations.

It is freely co-operative relations that are the well-spring for an active life. They release new energies, generate new ideas in practice, and are capable of transforming what would otherwise be burdensome chores into work that is joyful.

Social power is an inexhaustible resource whose potential capacity increases with use. The long-term development of the human race must be based on this remarkable product that flows more freely the more we use of it. *But it becomes truly available only to those who help to produce it!*

There are many bases for the accumulation of social power. They include:

- productive assets in land, water, and tools
- financial resources
- relevant information
- knowledge and skills
- social and political organization

The next question is more difficult: what is intended by the phrase, 'equalization of access?' In the present context, it means that within territorially integrated communities, everyone is to have an equal chance of gaining access to the use of common resources for production and adaptive use. This emphasis on a probability calculus is intended. Whereas resources of social power may be placed within the reach of everyone, not everyone may wish to use them, or to use them for the same or even similar ends. Complete equality of outcomes can only be enforced by resorting to Draconian measures. Human beings are diverse in their nature, and a mechanical egalitarianism is contrary to the very essence of what it means to be human.[17]

We can also say: 'equalizing access' points to the *production of social power by, for, and of the people.* Real people must be involved in producing, managing, and using social power on a basis of equality and joint decision. This implies a process of production and control that has been devolved to agropolitan districts as the lowest level of territorial integration.[18]

2. The territorial framework

Territorially organized communities may be conceived as arising in the intersection of three abstract spaces, each with its own attributes and describing a different dimension of communal life:

- a common *cultural* space, because the claim to a sufficiency of livelihood implies a moral judgment that will be made only if there exists a tradition of shared symbolic meanings;
- a common *political* space, because the equalization of access to the bases of social power requires a set of political institutions, actors, and roles with respects to which precise criteria of access may be defined;
- a common *economic* space, because the articulation of policies for a sufficiency of livelihood requires a finite set of interdependent productive activities and known levels in the development of productive forces.

Although cultural, political and economic spaces intersect, they do not, as a rule, completely overlap. To the extent that they do, however, they trace the natural habit of a 'community of destiny'. Such areas of overlap may be designated as the primordial units of territorial integration (T) (see Figure 8.2).

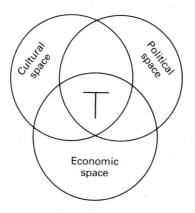

Figure 8.2   Territorial integration in space.

Every major area of overlap, T, may be further divided into component spaces, $t_1 \ldots n$, each of which will display unique characteristics within the common pattern. Agropolitan districts are the smallest of these territorial units that are still capable of providing for the basic needs of their inhabitants with only marginally important resource transfers from outside.[19]

In view of the need for face-to-face encounter in the governance of agropolitan affairs – a form of governance that concerns questions of both production and distribution, and mindful of a population density criterion that would require at least 200 persons per square kilometre of cultivated land – agropolitan districts may be designed to have a total population of between 15,000 and 60,000.[20] The inclusion of a country town within the district would raise their totals by an additional 5–20,000 people. Speaking in rough numbers, we suggest agropolitan districts that would range in population size from 20,000 to 100,000.

This derivation of agropolitan districts applies only to rural areas. In cities, *agropolitan neighbourhoods* may be variously defined within approximately the same overall population limits.[21] According to this procedure, many smaller towns will obviously fall within rural agropolitan districts, while medium-sized cities would constitute districts in their own right.

3. The expansion of production

Applying the principle of territoriality to problems of economic organization means strengthening the territorial economy at all relevant levels, above all, the agropolitan district and the level immediately superior to it, or the region. And strengthening the territorial economy means to encourage self-reliance in the management of economic affairs.[22] From this, a number of correlative principles may be derived:

- development should aim at diversifying the territorial economy;
- development should aim at the maximum development of physical resources consistent with principles of conservation;
- development should encourage the expansion of regional and inter-regional (domestic) markets;
- development should be based as much as possible on principles of self-finance;
- development should promote social learning.

These five principles of a self-reliant territorial development will now be separately discussed.

a. *Diversifying the territorial economy.* In predominantly agrarian societies, diversification has two possible meanings: first, diversifying agricultural production (e.g. food crops where industrial crops are common and vice versa); and, second, augmenting the level of industrial production and service activities in rural areas. (In urban areas, this would take the form of facilitating the growing of agricultural crops and small livestock.)

The diversification of area economies is a way of overcoming the contradictions between city and countryside. It is also a way for making agropolitan districts and regions more capable of dealing with adversity, more ingenious in overcoming difficulties, and also – because more interdependent – more communally oriented.

Michael Goldberg (1975) has argued that the lowest units in a hierarchically structured system tend also to be the most specialized, the least adaptable, and the most readily replaceable units. Although his language is borrowed from ecology, Professor Goldberg is speaking of the small enterprise or firm in a capitalist economy. This firm, indeed, is replaceable. But an agropolitan district with tens of thousands of inhabitants is not; *it must survive.* And if it is to survive, it must diversify its economy; it must become rather like one of Professor Goldberg's 'higher' units where adaptability facilitates resilience to changes in environment. But in stressing resilience, Professor Goldberg fails to mention that the most adaptive human systems are also the most likely to display a high order of creativity in problem-solving. Polivalence in economic structure may thus be highly correlated with innovativeness, social learning, and development.

Diversification in rural agropolitan districts will, at a minimum, require electric energy, radio or telephone communication, regular water supply, drainage, and year-round, all-weather transport to other areas.[23]

Can it be assumed, however, that non-agricultural activities can also be efficiently located in rural areas? Experience in both China and the advanced industrial and post-industrial regions in Western Europe and the United States has shown that the answer to this question is affirmative.[24] Urban-industrial concentrations are an historical phenomenon; they are not necessarily the lowest-cost locations (Gilbert, 1976). For many industries, especially those oriented towards mass markets, generalized labour skills, and agricultural raw materials, decentralized locations may be as economical or more so. The same may be said of convenience services that are best located within walking or bicycling distance from their potential clients. These considerations suggest that the existence of economies of scale (and thus of economies of concentration) has been vastly overstated. The lowest level of areal economy may be efficiency integrated on a pedestrian or bicycle scale, that is, on the scale of a typical agropolitan district.[25]

b. *Maximum physical development constrained by the need for conservation.* The need to develop the physical quality of life is obvious and essential. But physical development is difficult to accomplish, because what needs to be done is often not valued by market economists.

The remuneration of work tasks in the process of production must be evaluated in a social rather than market perspective. Where a sufficiency of livelihood is guaranteed, and labour is not fully used, every contribution to production represents a gain, however slight, to the community. And in an economy in which survival is still the major issue, everything contributing to this objective represents a social gain.[26]

But the maximum development of physical resources does not mean, as it does under industrial capitalism, that resources may be exploited with a view to maximum immediate gain for individuals. *The territorial community has a history that translates forward into time.* Future generations are nearly as important as those living, the only difference being the uncertainty of future knowledge (technical innovations, emergents). For this reason, territorially organized communities tend to value the future more highly than communities which are integrated primarily on a basis of function. This holds as well for agropolitan communities, where resource use must be managed in perpetuity (Gaviria, 1976).

Application of this principle raises the important question of use-value production which we discussed earlier in this chapter. In almost all agropolitan districts, there will be unused time during at least some part of the year (some technological innovations, however, may increase rather than decrease work requirements. Cf. Griffin, 1976). To the extent that work can be mobilized for the production of use values for the community, *in return for a guarantee of basic needs,* the productive base of the community can be expanded. This may be regarded as the classical form of primitive accumulation. Its major initial object in rural areas would undoubtedly be land and water management (anti-erosion controls, small flood control and irrigation projects, land reclamation schemes), the development of local energy resources, transport improvements, and the construction of various social facilities such as schools, clinics, assembly halls, and recreation areas.

c. *Expanding regional and interregional (domestic) markets.* Under the prevailing doctrine of unequal development, the only way to expand domestic markets is something like the following sequence (Paauw and Fei, 1973):

> foreign demand→manufactured exports→expansion of secondary and tertiary employment→increased demand for agricultural products→increased demand for domestic manufactures→increase in domestic production and employment.

In this sequence, everything follows its 'natural' course. The only trouble with the sequence is that it is wrong. Domestic mass markets are created, not by foreign demand for the products of low-cost labour but by increasing the productivity of the masses through agropolitan development! The new industry should be devoted to the production of wage goods, or simple products, including tools in daily use. The variety of such goods is small and the technology of their production is straightforward. Wage goods can be manufactured in small enterprises that are dispersed among agropolitan districts. In this way, people get experience with inventing and with making things. They learn about machines and common business practices.[27]

To build up wage-goods production at home, mass production with advanced technology must be severely limited.[28] Jet planes cannot be matched with gliders in a race!

Successful home production of wage goods will eventually create a demand for machinery and simple transport equipment. This, too, can be produced at home. The new sequence will, therefore, look like this:

> increased agricultural productivity + industrial diversification in de-centralized locations (principally wage-goods production)→ increased occupation of labour→increased demand for wage goods →increased demand for machinery and simple transport equipment →technological and product innovations→enhanced capacity for export of domestic manufactures abroad.

Agropolitan development builds strength from within, based on its own resources, its own skills, its own discoveries and learning. It does not expect a transfusion of strength from 'donor' countries abroad. It does not count on miraculous transformations, nor on results without effort. And so it begins with a development that will satisfy basic needs as, in doing so, it creates new ones.

If the countryside is endowed with basic infrastructure – for instance, if an internal communications and transport network is built up that will connect agropolitan districts and regions with each other – large cities will lose their present overwhelming advantage. The economy will then turn inward upon itself, discover its hidden energies and assets, and, in a 'natural' learning progression, modernize itself from within.

Manufacturing industry will be second in a logical sequence of steps. The first is the continuous upgrading of agricultural productions, starting with overall increases in the physical volume of food and basic fibres, followed, in due course, by increases in the productivity of farm land and the productivity of workers (Mosher, 1976, pp. 46–50).

The development of industry will be tied into this sequence, beginning with agricultural processing and going on to the manufacture of tools and other equipment of use to peasants and workers in their daily lives. Dispersed among the villages and fields, small industries will provide a source of work and income, in a mode of production that is intimately related to the emerging agropolitan structure of society in which the contradictions of industrial capitalism – between city and countryside production and consumption, work and leisure – are progressively resolved.

d. *Following principles of self-finance.* Self-reliance implies some form of self-financing. Yet it is said that poor people, who perforce must provide the bulk of resources, are incapable of saving. Engel's law is invoked to prove this, showing that most of poor people's income is spent on necessities, especially on food. This is true, of course, and not particularly surprising. But if they are properly motivated, even poor people – that is, the great mass of the population in agrarian societies – are capable of extraordinary efforts – witness the remarkable investments in self-built housing through-out the world (Turner, 1977), or the substantial village-bound remissions of money earned by relatives in the city (Johnson and Whitelaw, 1974), or the amounts saved by poor people to finance the education of their children.[29] When poor people do *not* save, it is usually for one of three reasons: because they live below the threshold of subsistence; because family obligations are more immediately pressing; or because what they have managed to put aside is forcibly taken from them – for instance, when the government bulldozes self-constructed housing in shanty towns, landlords extract exorbitant rents, moneylenders collect astronomical interest payments, or the terms of trade with the city are rigged by govern-ment against the countryside.

The first and foremost rule of self-finance is therefore this: to establish conditions that will secure for the benefit of oneself and one's family the effort saved out of present consumption. Peasants are not more altruistic than other people (Galjart, 1975). Yet they are capable of exceptional sacrifice if the benefits to them, including improvements in the territorial community that yield a *common* benefit, are clear and direct.

To ensure that effort given up to the community results in benefits to the masses, the basic conditions of agropolitan development must be ful-filled: selective territorial closure – to prevent the outbound transfer of resources; the communalization of wealth – to prevent the appropriation of communal benefits for private gain; and the equalization of access to the bases of social power – to prevent the accumulation of social surplus in the hands of those whose access is privileged.

A further condition for self-finance is that the employment of local resources in different tasks should be left, as much as possible, to the decisions of the appropriate institutions at district and regional levels. Not only is the central allocation of resources for local benefit a virtual impossibility, but the democratic doctrine that the people have a right to share in the decisions that involve the collective use of their own resources must be respected. In principle, local, regional, and national plans should be dovetailed into each other. But particularly at district and sub-district levels, what the people want, as opposed to what the state would like to happen, constitutes a proper subject for discussion between them and, indeed, for extensive negotiation. Agropolitan planning, along with other forms of planning, requires a substantial margin of uncertainty.[30]

e. *Promoting social learning*. Social learning occurs whenever the institutions comprising the agropolis show an enhanced capacity for dealing with the problems that confront them. It is not, strictly speaking, a descriptive term, referring to a modality of institutional performance. The social learning approach to problem-solving points instead to both structural forms of social relations and to specific practices that will promote it (Friedmann and Abonyi, 1976; Friedmann, 1978).

The practice of group evaluation and self-criticism is an especially valuable technique. So are campaigns whose principal purpose is to encourage social learning. Such campaigns would be conducted periodically with the full panoply of group discussions, field observations, experimental trials, and interdistrict contests. Suitable topics would include improved irrigation practices, environmental sanitation, youth culture, small livestock production, group decision-making, marketing, infant care, afforestation, and water management. Follow-up work would be done by local cadres. For the idea is not to teach some set of abstract skills, but to induce new practices. And for this local village cadres are essential. They will provide the link to supporting central services and encourage those innovative practices through which effective learning will occur.

Care should also be devoted to the design of channels for the routine exchange of information among agropolitan districts themselves. Some information exchange will happen spontaneously, of course, as limited functional relations develop among districts and regions, but special measures to promote the sharing of information on relevant local experiences will make this evolutionary process more effective. Officers might be appointed for each district to develop information networks and to facilitate cross-district learning. For example, regular visits to neighbouring districts might be organized to observe livestock breeding techniques, the results of new hybrid strains, bio-conversion technology, solar energy production, improved methods of grain storage, and so forth. The inauguration of a new school, or the completion of an irrigation or small hydro-electric project might be cause for region-wide celebration, dramatizing the event and encouraging its emulation. The object of all these activities would be to improve actual practice and to teach the general principle that development is not 'imported' but produced through one's own efforts.

4. The role of the state

Each agropolitan district is a self-governing unit whose authority over its own productive and residentiary activities, considered jointly, is restrained only by the concurrent needs of all other districts and the combined needs of the larger community of which they form a part. This limitation on autonomy is balanced by the requirement that the level of development of productive forces across all districts shall be approximately equal.

Self-reliance requires self-finance, and self-finance calls for self-government. The political autonomy of agropolitan districts is a fundamental principle and may be exercised through assemblies, with delegates sent by component functional and territorial units, representing productive and residentiary interests respectively. Planning and other technical personnel should be attached to the assemblies in order to bring all possible formal knowledge to bear on their decisions.

But even though they are autonomous, agropolitan districts are not sovereign units. They are parts of a larger territorial system – the nation – that, in turn, is linked into the all-embracing functional system of the world economy.

In social formations that are organized on the basis of agropolitan principles, the role of the state is at once protective, developmental, facilitative, regulatory, and redistributive. It is *protective* by securing territorial boundaries against outside, predatory forces and keeping the peace among the constitutive units of the state. It is *developmental* by co-ordinating national policies for both structural change and growth, and by undertaking projects of common benefit which exceed the ability of agropolitan districts. It is *facilitative* in that, through its own resources, it stands prepared to support agropolitan districts (and regions) in the realization of their own projects. It is *regulatory* by maintaining those critical balances within the system of social relationships that will permit both change and growth to occur without excessive disruption of the system as a whole. And it is *redistributive* in that it takes surplus resources from rich districts to equalize redevelopment possibilities in less favoured areas.

In agropolitan society, the central state is a strong state. Increased power at district and regional levels requires a growth of power at the centre. It follows that a system of agropolitan governance is not without its own sources of conflict. Although corporate power is made subservient to territorial power, the contradictions between them have not been successfully resolved. Conflicts will arise among territorial units (districts and regions), each with its special interests to defend, and there will always be differences in local and/or personal viewpoint. But agropolitan governance is not intended to sublimate conflicts into a greater harmony; *it is to provide a legitimate forum for articulating conflicts and searching for appropriate means of resolution.*

Absence of agreement, however, has nothing to do with the logic of structural relations. Where conditions of equal access to the bases of social power are established, as they would be in agropolitan society, a community may rightfully express a general, or territorial interest. *The territorial interest, then, becomes in every case controlling over subordinate, including corporate, decisions.* This holds true for all levels of territorial integration. But the division of territorial powers between centre, region and district will continue to be charged with tension, as each asserts the authority of a political will that corresponds to its own level, without recourse to objective standards of arbitration among them. The reach of territorial authority is indeterminate and only checked by the opposing territorial power of other units.

The parallel economy

The foregoing description of the agropolitan approach to development is an attempt to set forth the conditions of a better life for the billions of peasants and urban workers in the periphery of the world economy. It is an approach that tries to bring together questions of production and distribution in the same solution by shifting the bulk of developmental activities to where the people are, an approach which stresses a development *from within* in which human energies are released in freely cooperative relations. Starting with basic needs, it is also a development which, in parallel with the general development of productive forces, allows for the gradual emergence of individual needs.

It is therefore necessary to point out that the agropolitan approach is not intended to achieve a maximum level of self-sufficiency, or to expand the use-value economy to the virtual exclusion of values in exchange, or to oppose an urban-based industrialization at all costs. In emphasizing those elements which have been overlooked or neglected in traditional doctrine, we do not wish to suggest that they become the only elements.

Nor does an insistence on selective territorial closure mean an hermetic isolation from the world economy. The world economy exists, and if its further integration along functional lines is to become workable, the urban-based, corporate economy must be restricted to a non-competitive and, if possible, complementary realm. Corporate industry is noncompetitive when it produces commodities that do not substantially duplicate the production of decentralized agropolitan industries. It is complementary where it develops backward and forward linkages with the thousands of small industries in agropolitan locations.

So long as corporate industry and business exist – and they will not only continue to exist but will probably expand – the movement of people from rural districts to the cities will also continue. (Once they are there, however, they would be settled in self-governing agropolitan districts. See note 21.) The agropolitan approach is not meant to freeze the existing pattern of settlement. Its sole purpose is to make possible a development that is geared to the satisfaction of evolving human needs.

Over time, cities that are organized on agropolitan principles will grow, extending their reach over vast areas. But instead of destroying rural life, they will absorb it and, in absorbing it, transform it. And even though the exchange economy will expand relative to the economy of use values, at least for a time, the production of use values will continue to contribute importantly to national development. The agropolitan approach is a dynamic form of development. Except for a few basic principles, it does not follow any formulae but pursues the logic of its own evolution in specific settings.

The historical process will not be without continuing internal contradictions between territorial and functional forces of integration. The struggle to achieve an agropolitan form of development in the teeth of world-wide trends towards greater functional order will be a protracted one. But no civilization has ever attained to greatness without such a struggle.[31]

Concluding remarks

Agropolitan development has been described as an early stage in modern social evolution, as a beginning, not a terminus. Starting with an emphasis on basic needs – a sufficiency of livelihood – its ultimate purpose is to facilitate the satisfaction of emerging social and individualized needs. Only the initial conditions have been specified. Once begun, agropolitan development will pass through its own historical transformations.

For regional planners schooled in the older traditions of spatial development, the agropolitan approach will at first seem unfamiliar. Accustomed as they are to deal as specialists with the structuring of the single dimension of *functional space*, they will have difficulty in accepting the realization of agropolitan development in its more technical aspects as the substance of their craft.

Because its starting point is the principle of territorial integration, agropolitan development stresses the importance of political decision-making, governance and management. Policies for institutional change form an integral part of the entire approach and cannot be separated from it for the dubious virtue of 'simplifying' the problem.

Being holistic in conception, is agropolitan development therefore a utopian construct? Holistic designs that are meant as something other than a mere extrapolation of the past require a *tabula rasa* for their realization. Since in the real world clean slates do not exist, and even revolutions cannot wipe out historical accretions, what uses can be made of this scenario?

The scenario is for countries of the world periphery. Yet it would be foolish to believe that a single model of development could apply to all of them. The agropolitan approach is not a model in this sense. Rather, it represents a working out of two principles whose actualization under prevailing conditions in Asia and Africa appears to be feasible: the recovery of a territorial interest in the face of transnational hegemony and the implementation of a doctrine of equal development.

Although it is holistic in design, agropolitan development is derived from and consistent with a variety of national experiences. The most complete form, of course, is China's. But partial features may be detected in Viet Nam, the Republic of Korea, Sri Lanka, Bangladesh, Pakistan and Tanzania. To describe these varied experiments would have taken us beyond the scope of the present essay, but, in one way or another, they are all attempts to institute a form of rural development that will directly benefit the masses of the people.

Our scenario does not negate the necessity of world integration. It argues instead for the subordination of functional, exogenous interests to those of a territorially integrated society. This, however, calls for the kind of political leadership that is often desired but rarely encountered. Agropolitan development is thus more likely to evolve in response to particular historical opportunities than as a result of technocratic planning.

Agropolitan development may be viewed as the central thrust of an emerging social movement (Castells, 1976). Incipient beginnings can be found in both Europe and North America, as in Spain's regional movement or the struggle for territorial autonomy in Quebec. In chapter 7 we saw how a number of development streams are beginning to come together, loosely grouped under the general concept of territorial integration. Basic-needs strategies, espoused by the ILO (International Labour Office, 1977), and ecodevelopment (Sachs, 1974, 1976) are striking examples. Both have a potentially powerful backing and, in turn, are linked to the movement for greater self-reliance (Illich, 1975; Vanek ed., 1977; Morris and Hess, 1975; Pugwash Symposium, 1977). But if these strategies are to be translated into effective practice, an appropriate territorial framework will be required. This the concept of agropolitan development seeks to provide.

As outlined in this chapter, the agropolitan approach is specifically designed for agrarian societies. We may ask whether it has any relevance for industrialized societies as well. A number of historical trends suggest that this may well be the case. Most important is the growing recognition among western politicians that national-territorial and transnational-corporate and bureaucratic interests do not always coincide. With major cities, themselves the headquarter enclaves of transnational corporations, sliding into bankruptcy (New York); with entire national economies, such as Holland and Great Britain's, at the mercy of transnational concerns; and with massive unemployment threatening the most industrialized countries of Europe, partly as a result of transnational 'flight' into the low-cost labour markets of the Third World, political pressures for the territorialization of development are mounting. These tendencies are reinforced by the growing self-consciousness of many European regions, from Catalunya to Brittany, from Scotland to Bavaria, from Flanders to Sicily. What these regions claim is more than merely attention to their economic plight. They desire a greater measure of autonomy within the national and international field of forces in which they share.

A successful response to these pressures will require concerted action on a world-wide bases. For the first time in history, this conjunction establishes something like a common, if transitory, interest between rich and poor nations and creates an opening for major social changes in the countries of both the core and the periphery. These changes will obviously be imposed by the prevailing logic of territorial integration. The enthusiasm with which agropolitan ideas are already being advocated by some western planners for implementation in the Third World may prove to be infectious and coincide, at certain moments, with specific political currents in the West.

Traditional regional planning will no doubt continue for many years. But the cutting edge of professional thinking and practice already lies elsewhere – wherever the interests of territory are being asserted over those of function in the Herculean task to reverse more than two centuries of attrition of territorial integrity throughout the world.

Notes

1. The designation of *spatial* development planning which mirrors a functional principle of integration (i.e. the node-linkage model) came only slowly into general use. The older language of *regional* planning was preferred because it recalled, however fleetingly, the familiar notion of a *territorial* space. Its continued use during the transition eased the pain of loss.

2. Superficially, it made sense to treat questions of production separately from questions of distribution, so long as the relevant calculations were carried out in an *exchange* economy. Since money is the common fiduciary medium in such an economy, it was natural to regard it as both infinitely convertible (everything has a price and can be expressed in terms of any other value) and infinitely mobile. (However, as Fred Hirsch (1976) has pointed out, the principle of convertability has limits even in a market economy. Thus, the functioning of the market economy is vitally dependent on the existence of a *public* economy whose behaviour is governed by principles other than self-interest.) The politically chosen welfare function could therefore always be achieved – at least in theory and so long as it remained within the total resource availabilities – if one was willing to make the necessary 'trade-offs' against potential economic growth. Economists, of course, argued unanimously that growth was always preferable to any form of redistribution. But if there had to be redistribution for *political* reasons, it should conform to two principles: (1) income should be redistributed and not

productive wealth; and (2) redistribution should be made out of the annual increments of growth and not total income (Chenery *et al.*, 1974). Politicians readily concurred, the more so as they found it altogether more convenient to let the rich get richer than to give to the less rich. The practice of the doctrine of unequal development was always: inequality.

3. This formulation recalls the designation of backward regions as 'little economies' (Gilmore, 1960). Prosperity was viewed, as is typical in an exchange economy, as a function of *scale*. The assumption was that *the larger the scale of integration, the higher would be the level of attainable production.* Following national market integration would come successive stages of multi-national and finally global integration. What was not yet generally understood in the mid-sixties, however, was that in the case of the developing countries, even *national* integration was at least partly the handiwork of transnational forces that sought, step by step, to lay the foundations for a global economy (Peccei, 1969).

4. In the case of the TVA, the original planning region was a major river basin. This was an engineering concept, but it retained vestiges of territorial thinking. As the production of electric energy became the dominant activity of the agency, however, the region was redefined in terms of a purely functional criterion of the market area in which TVA power was sold. This area, of course, extended considerably beyond the original boundaries of the river basin.

5. The transnational ideology, whose foremost exponent, perhaps, is Peccei, is a post-capitalist, managerial ideology. The problem is seen as increasing production and maintaining world stability so that production can increase further, even though it would benefit only a minority of the world's population. This ideology was first formulated by the Catholic philosopher, James Burnham, whose book, *The Managerial Revolution*, caused a sensation when it was published in 1941. Unrepentedly elitist, Burnham in 1943 published a second volume, *The Machiavellians*, which he subtitled 'Defenders of Freedom'. In it, he reviewed the tradition of Italian political thought, from Dante to Pareto, which, as it happens, is also the tradition shared by Aurelio Peccei, who almost certainly would be proud to be counted among 'the Machiavellians'.

   It is interesting to trace the intellectual history of Burnham's ideas in American thought. As Richard Gillam (1977) points out, present-day neo-conservatism, represented by figures such as Irving Kristol, Daniel Bell, Nathan Glazer, Daniel Moynihan and Peter Drucker, are direct descendants of Burnham's managerial philosophy. The tremendous appeal of the Club of Rome's way of thinking can thus more easily be understood. The world has become too complex for politicians. What is needed are charismatic statesmen on the model of, shall we say, Charles de Gaulle, who, together with their cadres of world planners, are trying hard to run the life-support system on which everyone depends. For the moment, neither Russia nor China are members of the Club of Rome. But Peccei's idea of inviting them to join is not unreasonable. The International Institute for Applied Systems Analysis in Laxenburg, Austria, which is headed by a Russian and whose manager is an American, may well be a forerunner of the kind of institution we are likely to encounter with increasing frequency.

6. Peccei (1969) had allowed for the hegemony of what he called the Great Four: America, Europe, the Soviet Union, and Japan. This combination never worked, of course, and Tinbergen quite correctly makes his sovereignty restraint binding on *all* nations, including his own. Still, it must be admitted that most transnationals continue to have their headquarters in the United States. Although we would argue that this is merely an historical coincidence, Americans still believe that transnationals are basically *American* companies committed to working for America's 'best interests'. In a study of the Joint Economic Committee of the US Congress (1977) we may read (pp. 29–30):

> With billions of dollars invested in the Third World, the United States has a substantial stake in the financial flow of earnings and royalties and, particularly, in the extractive industries, the flows of specific commodities. Serious limitations

on US capital abroad could reduce present and future gross national product or, in the case of raw materials, actually lead to a disruption of production because of shortages of supply. The most likely outcome appears to be more host country controls on foreign investments, and increase in the national ownership of the multinational firms. The developing world is caught between political aspirations for economic independence and economic aspirations for future growth. If economic aspirations predominate, the multinational will continue to play an active role.

How real the benefits are for the United States, no one seems to know for sure. But they are certainly not taken for granted. As the Joint Economic Committee Study points out: 'The evidence on the overall impact of investment and technology flows on the US economy is simply not all in' (p. 30).

West Europeans have been quicker to perceive a possible divergence between transnational corporate and national political interests. The IMF has dictated terms to Great Britain. A group of transnationals headquartered in Holland has done much the same to the Dutch government. The 'German' textile industry is abandoning Germany. The general disregard of transnational corporations for national sovereignty in the case of the weaker Third World countries is too well known to need documentation. Even heads of state are known to have been on the payrolls of transnational corporations!

7. For an application of Johnson's approach to national regional planning, see Taylor, 1974.

8. The 'broad consensus' emerging from the 1976 World Employment Conference is ambiguous about the meaning to be attributed to basic needs. It appears that the use of basic needs as a strategy for *welfare planning* carried the day. As an alternative approach to *territorial development*, the use of basic needs was mainly championed by the poorer countries of the Third World and certain socialist countries (International Labour Office, 1977).

9. This obviously excludes the very young, the very old, the infirm, and others who are precluded by their physical condition of engaging in useful work.

10. It is important to point out that basic needs do not refer to physiological minima. All needs are culturally mediated and will consequently vary among societies and according to the level achieved in the development of their productive forces.

11. In formal terms, this is an expression of the principle of commutative justice.

12. The concepts of use and exchange value are borrowed from Marx (*Capital*, Vol. I, ch. 1). The following discussion is, however, only loosely related to Marx's own conceptualization.

13. A pure use-value economy is charmingly portrayed in a famous chapter from the *Tao Te Ching* (Lau, tr., 1963, ch. LXXX):

> Reduce the size and population of the state. Ensure that even though the people have tools of war ... they will not use them; and also that they will be reluctant to move to distant places because they look on death as no light matter.
>
> Even when they have ships, they will have no use of them; and when they have armor and weapons, they will have no occasion to make a show of them.
>
> Bring it about that the people will return to the use of knotted rope, will find relish in their food, and beauty in their clothes, will be content in their abode and happy in the way they live.
>
> Though adjoining states are within sight of one another, and the sound of dogs barking and cocks crowing in one state can be heard in another, yet the people of one state will grow old and die without having had any dealings with those of another.

14. A research project of the Max Planck Institut at Starnberg near Munich has devised a model for measuring use values according to the time budget method (Reid *et al.*,

1976). Time budget accounts would complement but not replace traditional methods of reckoning GNP. For a still more adequate accounting system, of course, the method of calculating GNP would itself have to be revised in order to reflect both distributive values and social costs. Work along these lines is currently underway in a number of research institutions.

15. An earlier version of the agropolitan concept was presented in Friedmann and Douglass (1975).

16. For details of China's development experience, especially with a view to its territorial base, see Schenk, 1974; Gurley, 1975; Joint Economic Committee, 1975; Salter, 1976; and Paine, 1976. One of the best overall formulations of Mao Tse-Tung's thoughts on China's development is found in his 1956 speech, 'On the Ten Great Relationships', which also forms the basis of Paine's (1976) analysis (Schram, ed.; 1974).

17. Formal equality of *results* is a Procrustean bed. Only the most iron social discipline would be able to enforce it, right down the line, for every member of a social group. See Harich, 1975.

18. Major inequalities in resource endowment among agropolitan regions must be compensated by the action of higher-level authorities. At the same time, these authorities must strive to prevent predatory aggrandizement of one social unit at the expense of another. *A rough equality of access to social power must be maintained over the whole of the territorial system.*

19. Under agropolitan conditions, the primary spatial system arises from the intersection of cultural, economic, and political attribute spaces. A secondary system of nodal structure is superimposed upon this pattern, reflecting functionally integrated activities that co-exist but are subordinate to territorial interests. See the section on the parallel economy later in this chapter.

20. According to common practice in the United States, an area is considered *urbanized* when it lies adjacent to a city of at least 50,000 people and has a minimum settlement density of 100 housing units per square mile. Using the 1970 average size of household of 3.17, this translates into a population density of 120 persons per square kilometre. At the older ratio of 4.0 persons per household, the density would be 152 per square kilometre.

    A proposed agropolitan density of 200 per square kilometre of cultivated land is thus an arbitrary standard which does, however, suggest an 'urban' density pattern. Variations of these dimensions can obviously be used. It might be noted, however, that with the proposed size-density function, the entire agropolitan area would be accessible by bicycle within, at most, one hour.

21. Urban agropolitan districts would be self-governing areas which would be designed for a reasonable mix of industrial, agricultural, and residentiary functions. Their densities would tend to be higher than rural districts, requiring more careful land use and environmental planning. One important objective of urban planning for agropolitan development would be the reduction of average travel time within the city, especially the journey to work.

22. Self-reliant development was the subject of the 24th Pugwash Symposium which was held at Dar-es-Salaam, Tanzania, 2–6 June 1975 (Pugwash Symposium, 1977).

23. Recent studies have explored the variety of energy sources that can be tapped for rural development. See Somil (1976) and National Academy of Sciences (1976).

24. The case of China's rural industrialization has been the most thoroughly documented of any experience outside the industrial West. See Sigurdson, 1975.

25. According to Dandekar and Brahme (1977, pp. 23–4), who base their conclusions on a series of carefully executed village surveys in Maharashtra State (India):

> It is unrealistic to conceive of building up rural industries that utilize local products to meet local demand. Just as the urbanite's preferences lead him to buy imported goods wherever possible, so also the villager's preferences lead him to buy the product of the city wherever possible. From our case studies, it is apparent

that with the growing integration of the rural-urban economy, the traditional industries are on the decline. . . . To succeed, a rural industry has to latch into the urban economy and make a profit from urban money. There is either not enough surplus in the village to allow the industry to thrive or what surplus there is, is already largely flowing to the city. One must therefore accept that a successful rural industry may not develop many forward or backward linkages in the villages around it and come to terms with the limited role that rural industries can play in rural development.

This gloomy conclusion is not, however, justified. The 'industries' described by the authors include not only the traditional village but also the raising of livestock (chicken, pigs, milch cows). To accept the statement that rural 'industries' have only a 'limited role' to play in rural development is, therefore, tantamount to saying that the livestock has no future in the region studied by the authors, unless it is organized by corporate (urban) interests. By the same perverted logic, one could say that a *national* industry has to latch into the *international* economy and make a profit from *international money*.

Conclusions such as these are not convincing. If traditional rural industries do not succeed in India, it is because very little effort has been made to diversify the rural economy, building up the rural infrastructure in ways that will permit diversification to occur. A solution where half the males are earning money in distant cities, leaving their villages to women, children, and old men is not a satisfactory solution from a territorial (basic-needs) point of view. It is, of course, entirely acceptable to corporations.

26. The introduction of use values into the development calculus would automatically put an end to the vicious practice of 'pricing' work performed outside the market economy according to the current subsistence rate for labour. If the myth can be disestablished that wage rates accord with productivity 'at the margin', then also the concept of an 'industrial reserve army' would disappear, as the production of use values in the community could simply not be *reduced* to an exchange-relation, whatever the artifice. See Stuckey, 1977.

27. Because they are important to alternative development approaches, a good deal has been written about small-scale entrepreneurs. Among the more important studies are Buchele, 1972; Dinwiddy, 1974; Hart, 1969–70; Kaplan and Huang, 1976; Kilby, 1965; Marris and Somerset, 1972; and Nafziger, 1972. The broader question of the viability of small-scale enterprise is discussion by Bienefeld, 1975, and McGee, 1975, among others.

28. This does not mean that modern (i.e. western) technology should be forbidden. It does not mean that its use should be carefully planned so as to *protect* the wage-goods sector of the agropolitan economy against unreasonable competition from the corporate (national and transnational) sector. One way to do this would be through social pricing of imported machinery and raw materials and through the elimination of subsidies to the corporate sector.

29. In India and Pakistan, for instance, rural savings rates of 4–13 per cent are reported, and this is without counting the enormous income unjustly transferred to landlords and the corporate urban sector (Griffin and Khan, 1972, p. 203).

30. Essays on economic planning in China are extremely instructive on this point. See Donnithorne, 1972, 1976; Lardy, 1975.

31. See Appendix to chapter 8 for a recent effort to define an agropolitan policy for Bangladesh.

Bibliography

Bienefeld, M. 1975: The informal sector and peripheral capitalism: the case of Tanzania. In Oxenham, J., editor, 1975, 53–73.

Buchele, R. B. 1972: The development of small industrial entrepreneurs as a tool of economic growth. Working Paper no. 31. Honolulu, Hawaii: East–West Technology and Development Institute.

Burnham, J. 1941: *The managerial revolution: what is happening in the world.* New York: the John Day Co.

    1943: *The Machiavellians: defenders of freedom.* New York: the John Day Co.

Castells, M. 1976: Theoretical propositions for an experimental study of urban social movements. In Pickvance, C. G., editor, 1976, 147–73.

Chenery, H., *et al.* 1974: *Redistribution with growth.* Oxford University Press.

Cornelius, W. A. and Trueblood, F. M., editors 1975: *Urbanization and inequality.* Vol. 5: *Latin American urban research.* Beverly Hills, Ca.: Sage Publications.

Dandekar, H. and Brahme, S. 1977: Role of rural industries in rural development. Prepared for the Binational Interdisciplinary Seminar on Rural Development, Gokhale Institute of Politics and Economics. MS. Poona, India.

Del Risco S., F. E. 1975: Elementos para la definición del rol del sector agrario en el Perú. *Revista Interamericana de Planificación* **9**, 36–48.

Dinwiddy, B. 1974: *Promoting African enterprise.* London: Overseas Development Institute.

Donnithorne, A. 1972: *The budget and the plan in China: central-local economic relations.* Contemporary China Papers, no. 3. Canberra: Australian University Press.

    1976: Centralization and decentralization in China's fiscal management. *The China Quarterly* no. 66, 328–39.

Friedmann, J. 1966: *Regional development policy: a case study of Venezuela.* Cambridge, Mass.: the MIT Press.

    1975: A spatial framework for rural development: problems of organization and implementation. *Économic Appliquée* **28**, 519–44.

    1978: The epistemology of social learning: a critique of objective knowledge. *Theory and Society* **6**, 75–92.

Friedmann, J. and Abonyi, G. 1976: Social learning: a model for policy research. *Environment and Planning A* **8**, 927–40.

Friedmann, J. and Douglass, M. 1975: Agropolitan development: towards a new strategy for regional development in Asia. In United Nations Centre for Regional Development, 1975, 333–87.

Galjart, B. 1975: Peasant cooperation, consciousness, and solidarity. *Development and Change* **6**, 75–84.

Gaviria, M. 1976: *Ecologismo y ordenación del territorio en España*. Madrid: Cuadernos para el Dialogo.

Ghai, D. and Alfthan, T. 1977: Methodology of basic needs. A Working Paper. Geneva: International Labour Office.

Gilbert, H. 1976: The argument for very large cities reconsidered. *Urban Studies* **13**, 27–34.

Gillam, R. 1977: Intellectuals and power. *The Center Magazine* **10**, no. 2 (May/June), 15–30.

Gilmore, D. R. 1960: *Developing the 'little' economies: a survey of area development programs in the United States*. Supplementary Paper no. 10. New York: Committee for Economic Development.

Goldberg, M. 1975: On the inefficiency of being efficient. *Environment and Planning A* **7**, 921–39.

Griffin, K. 1974: *The political economy of agrarian change: an essay on the green revolution*. London: Macmillan.

1976: A comment on labour organisation in rice production. Conference on Economic Consequences of New Rice Technology. International Rice Research Institute, Los Banos, Laguna, Philippines, 13–16 December.

Griffin, K. and Khan, A. R., editors 1972: *Growth and inequality in Pakistan*. London: Macmillan.

Gurley, J. G. 1975: Rural development in China 1949–72, and the lessons to be learned from it. *World Development* **3**, 455–71.

Harich, W. 1975: *Kommunismus ohne Wachstum? Babeuf und der 'Club of Rome'*. Hamburg: Rowohlt.

Hart, K. 1969–70: Small-scale entrepreneurs in Ghana and development planning. *Journal of Development* **6**, 104–20.

Heller, A. 1976: *The theory of needs in Marx*. London: Allison & Busby.

Helman, A. 1974: *The distribution and allocation of consumer goods in the kibbutz*. Ph.D. dissertation. London School of Economics and Political Science.

Hirsch, F. 1976: *Social limits to growth*. Twentieth Century Fund Study. Cambridge, Mass.: Harvard University Press.

Hoyle, B. S., editor 1974: *Spatial aspects of development*. London: John Wiley & Sons.

Illich, I. 1975: *Tools for conviviality*. London: Fontana/Collins.

International Labour Office 1977: *Meeting basic needs: strategies for eradicating mass poverty and unemployment*. Geneva, ILO.

Johnson, E. A. J. 1970: *The organization of space in developing countries*. Cambridge, Mass.: Harvard University Press.

Johnson, G. E. and Whitelaw, W. E. 1974: Urban-rural income transfers in Kenya: an estimated remittances function. *Economic Development and Cultural Change* **22**, 473–9.

Joint Economic Committee, Congress of the United States 1975: *China: a reassessment of the economy*. Washington, DC: Government Printing Office.

1977: *The United States response to the new international economic order: the economic implications for Latin America and the United States. A study.* Washington, DC: Government Printing Office.

Kaplan, P. F. and Huang, C. H. 1976: The industrial modernity of Filipino small-scale industrial workers. *Economic Development and Cultural Change* **24**, 799–814.

Kilby, P. 1965: *African enterprise: the Nigerian bread industry.* Stanford: Stanford University Press.

Lardy, N. 1975: Economic planning in the People's Republic of China: central-provincial fiscal relations. In Joint Economic Committee, Congress of the United States, 1975, 94–115.

Lau, D. C., translator 1963: *Lao Tsu: Tao Te Ching.* London: Penguin Books.

Lehman, D., editor 1974: *Agrarian reform and agrarian reformism. Studies of Peru, Chile, China, and India.* London: Faber and Faber.

Lindberg, L. N. and Scheingold, S. A., editors 1971: *Regional integration: theory and research.* Cambridge, Mass.: Harvard University Press.

McGee, T. G. 1975: *Hawkers in selected Southeast Asian cities.* A report to be presented at a conference on the 'Role of marginal distribution systems in development'. Kuala Lumpur, Malaysia. 23–26 September.

Marris, P. and Somerset, A. 1972: *The African entrepreneur. A study of entrepreneurship and development in Kenya.* New York: African Publishing Co.

Morris, D. and Hess, K. 1975: *Neighborhood power: the new localism.* Boston: Beacon Press.

Mosher, A. T. 1976: *Thinking about rural development.* New York: Agricultural Development Council.

Nafzinger, E. W. 1972: South-Indian industrialists: a profile of entrepreneurs in Coastal Andhra. Working Paper no. 34. Honolulu, Hawaii: East–West Technology and Development Institute.

National Academy of Sciences, 1976: Energy for rural development. Report of a panel of the Advisory Committee on Technology Innovation. Washington, DC: NAS.

Oxenham, J., editor 1975: *Human Resources Research.* Special issue of *Bulletin* **6**. Institute of Development Studies, Sussex University.

Paauw, D. S. and Fei, J. C. H. 1973: *The transition in open dualistic economies. Theory and Southeast Asian experience.* New Haven: Yale University Press.

Paine, S. 1976: Balanced development: Maoist conception and Chinese practice. *World Development* **4**, 277–304.

Passaris, S. 1977: Ecodevelopment in Papua-New Guinea. *Ecodevelopment News* (Paris) no. 2 (May), 2–14.

Peccei, A. 1969: *The chasm ahead.* London: Collier-Macmillan.

Pickvance, C. G., editor 1976: *Urban sociology: critical essays.* London: Tavistock Publications.

Pugwash Symposium 1977: The role of self-reliance in alternative strategies of development. *World Development* **5**, 257–66.

Reid, U., Sonntag, P. and Holub, H. 1976: Probleme der Volkswirtschaftlichen Gesamtrechnung und ein Erweiterungsvorschlag: die Arbeit-Konsum-Rechnung. Draft MS. Starnberg: Max Planck Institute.

Roberts, B. R. 1975: Center and periphery in the development process: the case of Peru. In Cornelius, W. A. and Trueblood, F. M., editors, 1975, 77–106.

Rondinelli, D. A. and Ruddle, K. 1976: *Urban functions in rural development: an analysis of integrated spatial development policy*. Prepared for the Office of Urban Development, Technical Assistance Bureau, Agency for International Development, US Department of State.

Ruttan, V. W. 1975: Integrated rural development program: a skeptical perspective. Staff paper 75-4. New York: Agricultural Development Council.

Sachs, I. 1974: Environment and style of development. *African Environment* (Dakar) **1**, 9–34. Also in *Economic and Political Weekly* (Bombay) **9**, 828–37.

1976: Ecodevelopment. *Ceres* (Rome), no. 42, 8–12.

Salter, C. 1976: Chinese experiments in urban space: the quest for an agropolitan China. *Habitat* **1**, 19–36.

Schenk, H. 1974: Concepts behind urban and regional planning in China. *Tijdschrift voor Economische Sociale Geografie* **65**, 381–88.

Schram, S., editor 1974: *Mao Tse-Tung unrehearsed. Talks and letters*: 1956–1971. London: Penguin Books.

Schulz, O. 1974: Estrategias del dessarrollo de las comunidades rurales. *Revista Interamericana de Planificación* **8**, 23–33.

Sigurdson, J. 1975: Rural Industrialization in China. In Joint Economic Committee, Congress of the United States, 1975, 411–35.

Somil, V. 1976: Intermediate energy technology for China. *World Development* **4**, 929–37.

Stuckey, B. 1977: The spatial distribution of the industrial reserve army. MS. Starnberg: Max Planck Institute.

Taylor, D. R. F. 1974: Spatial aspects of Kenya's rural development strategy. In Hoyle, B. S., editor, 1974, 167–87.

Tinbergen, J., co-ordinator 1976: *RIO: reshaping the international order*. A report to the Club of Rome. New York: E. P. Dutton.

Turner, J. F. C. 1977: *Housing by people. Towards autonomy in building environments*. New York: Pantheon Books.

United Nations Centre for Regional Development 1975: *Growth pole strategy and regional development planning in Asia*. Proceedings of a seminar. Nagoya, Japan: UNCRD.

Vanek, J., editor 1977: *Self-management: economic liberation of man*. London: Penguin Books.

Wallerstein, I. 1974: The rise and future demise of the world capitalist system: concepts for comparative analysis. *Comparative Studies in Society and History* **16**, 387–415.

Wriston, W. B. 1976: *People, politics, and productivity: the world corporation in the 1980s*. London: Citicorp.

Appendix:
Economic development through people's participation on a self-help basis: lessons from Ulashi (Bangladesh)

by Qazi Kholiquzzaman Ahmad and Mahabub Hossain*

The following document is reproduced as an example of how agropolitan ideas may look in practice. The country is Bangladesh, and the occasion is an in-depth review of an important 'self-help' experience involving the construction of a large-scale drainage and irrigation project. This is a new approach to national development in Bangladesh, which is here set down by the authors, based on the consensus which seemed to emerge from the discussions referred to in the preface below. It is expected that large-scale mobilization on a self-help basis, essentially along the lines suggested here, will form the cornerstone of development policy in Bangladesh, from 1978 onwards.

Preface

A one-day seminar was held in Dacca on the Ulashi–Jadunathpur project† on the theme 'lessons from Ulashi', under the auspices of the Bangladesh Economic Association and the Bangladesh Institute of Development Studies (BIDS), on Saturday, 29 October 1977. It was inaugurated by Dr M. N. Huda, Member, President's Council of Advisers, in charge of the Ministry of Planning, at 8.45 am; and its deliberations continued up to 8.00 pm. The number of participants in the seminar was about 100. They included presidential advisers, government officials, professional researchers, teachers and social workers.

The seminar was followed by an intensive discussion session held at BIDS on Sunday, 30 October 1977 at 3.00 pm. It lasted for over four hours, and there were eighteen participants.

* The authors are, respectively, Senior Research Economist and Research Economist at the Bangladesh Institute of Development Studies, Dacca. In addition, Dr Ahmad is General Secretary of the Bangladesh Economic Association. The document reproduced in this Appendix with the kind permission of Dr Ahmad was drafted in November 1977.

† The project is located in Jessore district, and is about 150 miles from the capital, Dacca. A brief description of the project is given in section V of this paper.

This report has been prepared by the undersigned, in the light of recent thinking in development economics in the context of rural development and new national economic order* and in the light of the deliberations in the discussion meeting. While they feel that the ideas, analyses, and proposals presented in this report, mainly in sections VI and VII, represent the consensus of the participants in the intensive discussion session, they recognize that the primary responsibility for this report lies with themselves.

Q.K.A.
M.H.

I. The conventional approach to development

The conventional framework of economic development focused on increased per capita GNP as the main objective of development. This was to be achieved through accumulation of capital, the scarce resource, and its investment in industrialization, modernization and urbanization through a 'top down' process of central planning and control. The potential for internal accumulation of capital was recognized to be limited; and the gap in the capital required for desired growth was to be met by a flow of resources from the developed countries (i.e. foreign aid). It was assumed that the question of distribution would be taken care of automatically in the development process, or through fiscal policies. More recently there has been some attempt to incorporate the idea of distributive justice and a measure of democratic participation (through co-operatives, for instance) into the process of development planning. But the basic philosophy and the framework of development remained unchanged.

II. Outcome of the conventional approach

The outcome of pursuing the conventional approach to development in Bangladesh is well known. This 'urban-biased', 'top-down' planning process has failed to bring about a significant increase even in the per capita GNP, perhaps mainly because of population pressures. But, more important, its benefits have mainly accrued to urban elites and larger landowning groups. The relative position of the masses in relation to income and opportunities has deteriorated. The ever-increasing human resources have not been properly utilized, further accentuating the disparities in income and opportunities. Reformists' attempts at reducing disparities failed because the rich could always influence the process in the long run, even though they might face temporary setbacks. A considerable proportion of the population suffers from inadequate

* For some discussion of the new thinking in development economics in the context of rural development and new national economic order, see, for instance, Haq, Mahbubul, *The Third World and the International Economic Order*, Overseas Development Council, Washington, DC, September 1976; and Wignaraja, Poona, 'From the Village to the Global Order: Elements in a Conceptual Framework for *Another Development*', unpublished, United Nations Asian and Pacific Development Institute, Bangkok, 1977.

food, shelter, clothing, medical care, etc.; that is, their basic needs are not being met. The dependence on foreign aid has accumulated over time, and the debt-servicing burden is fast assuming alarming proportions.

III. The new approach

A consensus has been strongly emerging in recent years that the conventional approach is irrelevant to the needs of developing countries, and that both the objectives of development and ways of achieving it have to be redefined. The new approach may be articulated as follows:

(i) The goal of development is the enrichment of the quality of life, through the fulfilment of both the spiritual and the economic aspirations of all the people.

(ii) It is to be recognized that the development is for man, and that he is also the principal factor around whom developmental efforts are to be planned. Hence, the vast human resources are to be harnessed and adequately developed to be put to appropriate productive use.

(iii) A 'bottom-up' planning process is to be followed, so that a sense of participation in the development process is created among the masses, and the urban bias in development planning removed. The mobilization of the people is to be based on the self-reliant approach, so that they can use their creative energies to improve their lot, and, hence, that of the country as a whole.

(iv) The village-based development approach is to include all rural activities such as agriculture, small and cottage industries, and small trading.

(v) Solidarity among different interest groups is to be fostered through promotion of economic and other interests of all groups by means of mutual co-operation and collaboration. Interests of disadvantaged groups should receive adequate attention.

(vi) The new approach should aim at (a) gradually decreasing the disparities in income and opportunities; (b) fulfillment of the basic needs of all groups of people within the shortest possible time; and (c) the progressive reduction, and the eventual removal, of dependence on foreign aid.

(vii) While the new approach emphasizes rural development, it must recognize that large-scale industries, transport and modern sector activities must receive adequate attention in order that development should not become lopsided and create another kind of dependence on foreign countries. Priorities should be given to capital-goods industries, especially to industries producing machinery and inputs for the agricultural sector, and also to agricultural processing industries.

(viii) As people's participation is the crucial element in the new approach, their proper mobilization is the key to the success of this approach. But the poor, illiterate masses cannot participate in the development process on their own. It is necessary to motivate, prepare and activate them. Who will do this? That is, who are the 'change agents'? This is the crucial question. The transition from the present situation to the new order is crucially dependent upon the change agents. The other important element in the approach is that it must be flexible enough to accommodate regional and local differences in resource endowment, attitude towards life, and economic aspirations.

(ix) It is recognized that unless the new approach is based on a sound political process and is built around a fundamental land reform programme, there will be difficulties in bringing about the new economic order. But, it is felt, as these two dimensions of the development process may not be satisfactorily fulfilled in the near future, the best thing is to start the process of development through people's participation. One may hope that the process itself will lead to the desirable political structures and land reforms.

IV. Scope of development in Bangladesh through the new approach

In Bangladesh there exists vast scope for starting the process described above by undertaking water conservancy and water utilization projects. Other types of projects which may perform the same basic role include road building, construction work, and so forth. The projects need not be large. Small projects may serve equally well as the catalyst for development. Indeed, small projects may be more suitable for implementation through people's participation.

A large component of such projects will be financed by local resources through people's participation and utilization of un- and under-utilized human resources. Indeed, the labour component, which may be one-half or so, can be expected to come fully from local resources. It is also likely that income created in local areas in the wake of projects and related activities will generate savings for investment in projects which are to be implemented later.

Projects undertaken under the new approach will help achieve self-sufficiency in food and hence will lead to a reduction in depencence on foreign aid. The strategy adopted in relation to the sharing of benefits by different groups of people should ensure the gradual reduction in the disparities in income and opportunities which now characterize the economic structure of the country.

It is recognized that the projects cannot be implemented without substantial public financial support. This, however, may be gradually reduced as rural incomes rise and generate more and more savings. But it is felt

that adequate public investment should be directed towards supporting these projects if only to reduce the present urban bias in development
planning.

V. Ulashi as an experimental model of development

The Ulashi–Jadunathpur project and the subsequent *swanirvar* (self-help)
movement in the area has succeeded in motivating and stabilizing rural
people to participate in the development process. It also has a great
symbolic value in relation to the new approach to rural development in
Bangladesh.

The first phase of Ulashi was a self-help canal-digging project, involving
an earthwork of 16.5 million cubic feet, which was to help both drainage
and irrigation. It was conceived by the Water Development Board, but
could not be implemented, because of the paucity of funds, unless it was
dug with human labour on a self-help basis. There was a public investment
of only Taka 0.849 million. The completion of the canal created confidence
in their own abilities among the people of the area and opened up both
the possibility of further development in this area and the initiation of
development activities elsewhere through people's participation. People
of 119 adjoining villages formed *swanirvar* committees, surveyed local
resources, identified local problems and formulated local development
plans with support from the Deputy Commissioner (head of district civil
administration), Jessore, following a 'bottom-up' approach. About 52 per
cent of investment in this plan is expected to come from local resources
on a self-help basis. The planning process adopted here may be taken
as an example of micro-level planning following a 'bottom-up' course,
and an approach to development planning in Bangladesh may be built
around it.

On 30 April 1977 the canal digging was completed on schedule. Several
critical factors contributed towards the success of the project, which should
be borne in mind when trying to repeat this type of self-help project in
other areas:

(i) The initiation of the project came from above. It was undertaken
according to the instruction, and with the approval, of the chief executive
of the country, whose continued support and encouragement were instrumental in creating and sustaining the enthusiasm of local people and
government functionaries in implementing the project. In case of widespread replication of this 'model', such help from above may not be
feasible.

(ii) A part of the workload of the project was distributed amongst
potential beneficiaries according to a somewhat arbitrary assessment of
benefits receivable by landowners. Such contribution obviated the possibility of social discontent in the local area and sustained mass support for
the project. It is recognized that the project would not have been com-

pleted if the workload had not been distributed amongst the potential beneficiaries on a progressive scale. However, this was done by the Deputy Commissioner without legal backing, and may not be accepted by people everywhere. Legal provisions contained in the Local Government Ordinance 1976 for community taxation may be applied in all such cases by appropriate Local Government Authorities.

(iii) Close supervision and adequate motivation, coupled with an effective monitoring and reporting system by the Deputy Commissioner and his staff, have provided the momentum for the success of the project so far. In view of the shortage of skilled administrative inputs in Bangladesh, it is doubtful whether adequate administrative support would be available in the case of widespread replication of the project.

It has also to be noted that in the cases where the Deputy Commissioner or any other officer provides the leadership, his transfer may jeopardize the progress of the project – this has happened in the past. Hence, the involvement of people at all stages is a must for a successful continuing process of development.

VI. Institutions for development through the new approach

The main lesson that can be learned from Ulashi is that it may lead to the evolution of a viable model of development, if it can be ensured that project selection and implementation are not imposed from above. The way in which Ulashi was started was not ideal, and may not be feasible in other cases. There should be a locally based organizational process to conceive and implement such projects (through a 'bottom-up' planning process). To ensure that, proper institutions have to be established in rural areas.

These institutions can be built around the present *swanirvar* movement and the local public organizations in the following fashion:

(i) The existing Thana Training and Development Centre (TTDC) may be extended down to the village through Union* Training and Development Centre (UTDC) and Village Training and Development Centre (VTDC). The need for government investment for building the necessary physical structures is likely to be minimal. The government has already decided to establish the following organizations at the union level; (a) a family welfare centre, (b) an agricultural sub-station, (c) a branch of a bank, and (d) a sub-health centre. These organizations should cluster around the UTDC. At the village level, the primary schools can be used as a base for the VTDC. In villages where there are no government schools, the private schools may be recognized (and supported) by the government, and in cases where no primary schools exist such schools may be established.

* *Union* is an administrative unit composed of a number of villages. *Thana* is the next higher administrative unit, followed upwards by sub-division, district and division.

(ii) In villages, unions and thanas there should be people's organizations (councils) where all interest groups are proportionally represented. These councils* should have committees, such as the following, with representatives from different interest groups:

    (a) Law and Order Committee
    (b) Agricultural Committee
    (c) Health and Family Planning Committee
    (d) Education Committee
    (e) Planning Committee

The Planning Committee will initiate and be responsible for formulating village plans through surveys of village resources and identification of problems and projects. Technical assistance may be sought from upper levels and from appropriate government agencies in cases of project formulation. The committees should also determine the distribution of the workload of the self-help elements of the projects.

In the village, there should, in addition, be a *Gram Shava*,† with all adult members of the village participating, and the village plans should be approved by this *Shava*.

The village plans will be sent to upper levels for incorporation in union- and thana-level plans. The union- and thana-level committees will mainly function as co-ordinating bodies. The thana plans will be co-ordinated at the level of districts by the District Council which will liaise with the Planning Commission at the centre.

The Planning Commission may allocate resources up to district level and the District Council may co-ordinate allocation of resources at lower levels. Once incorporated in the national plans, local plans will be implemented by village committees. Special implementation committees may be formed for individual projects.

(iii) Social organizations representing different functional groups should be formed (e.g. landowners' committee, landless' committee, women's committee, youth committee, etc.) to provide forums for these groups to (a) discuss their problems, (b) to send representations to the village-level committees about their interests, and (c) to oversee the functions of the village-level committees.

(iv) The *muktangon* school system‡ provides a framework which can be used to generate interest and commitment among the villagers in village

* These people's organizations may be conceived as 'governments', and each functional area as a 'ministry' headed by a 'minister'. There is a growing support for this approach. Experiments are going on in the country with alternative forms of people's organizations, and the most effective approach will hopefully emerge soon.

† Gram Shava means village assembly.

‡ The primary objective of the *maktangon* (open) school system is to provide students with work- and life-oriented education, such as village surveys, agricultural activities, handicrafts and other economic and social activities for village development. Also, it has the objective of using the school establishment as a centre of various group activities and as an adult-education centre, one after another following school hours.

programmes. For example, the women's centres may be attended by the union-level family-planning workers and the workers of the voluntary health squad; and the programmes of health, education, and family planning can be discussed in these forums. Similarly, the young people in the *muktangon* may be encouraged to become acquainted with, and to review, local problems, especially those regarding the implementation of development programmes.

(v) The Village and Union Councils should be given the responsibility of supervising the activities of local government officers, such as primary school teachers and family-planning workers. The Union Council should also be entrusted with the responsibility for disbursement of salaries to these officials so that they can more effectively exercise their supervision.

(vi) If they can be mobilized as such, young people may act as change agents. The education system must be appropriately modified to serve as a base for such mobilization.

Given their training and background, it would appear that bureaucrats cannot perform a change-agent role.

VII. Government policies and actions

The following government policies and actions are needed:

(i) It is strongly felt that in order for the new approach to succeed, the government must take a policy decision to give priority to those projects which are conceived and initiated by people's organizations. In other words, the government must announce its commitment to development through people's participation.

(ii) The government must give adequate attention to rural development and increase the allocation of funds for it from the development budget.

Contrary to public pronouncements, it has been noted that the rural sector is not receiving adequate allocation of funds. During recent years, public allocation of resources to the rural sector has actually been going down in real terms. If the new approach is to succeed, it is imperative that adequate public resources be allocated to the rural sector.

(iii) The government must create facilities and conditions for the change agents to be identified and organized. Young people are a possible target group.

(iv) The government must give priority to the expansion of primary and life-oriented education.

(v) The mass media should be used for spreading informal education and the new approach to development.

(vi) The government must maintain constant vigilance to ensure that more powerful groups do not control the activities and appropriate benefits, and to facilitate progress towards spontaneous mass participation in development activities and egalitarian distribution of benefits.

(vii) In cases of distribution of *khas* land to the landless, appropriate measures should be taken to ensure tenurial security and provision of logistic support.

(viii) An effective delivery system must be established for timely supply of credit and other inputs to rural areas. Facilities for marketing of agricultural and non-agricultural products must receive due attention.

(ix) For reorientation of civil servants, a well-designed training programme for rural development must be developed, which, among other things, must include training for the preparation and management of projects.

Afterword

In many parts of the Third World, regional planning is being moulded into territorial forms of agropolitan development. The case of Bangladesh is only the most recent example. But the territorial approach to regional development need not follow agropolitan lines. There are other possibilities.

The dominant doctrine of both national and regional economic development has until recent times been functional. But once the contradictory consequences of its application became visible – human redundancy, resource destruction, growing inequalities – many scholars and planners were led to examine the theoretical bases of their policy prescriptions. The rediscovery of territorial approaches to development was the result.

For the sake of achieving greater clarity, let us restate the major characteristics of both functional and territorial doctrines as they apply to subnational area development.

Functional, or spatial, development planning is assumed to have universal validity. Typically, its formulation is mathematical and its specific spatial expression is modelled as a network of nodes and linkages that extends beyond regional and national boundaries to encompass, at the limit, the entire world. Spatial planning emphasizes the location of economic activities. Each location is considered as a point on a topological surface representing such single-function variables as costs of production or access to markets. From the standpoint of a local area economy, location decisions are determined *exogenously*, either by firms seeking their optimal location or by the state pursuing interests of its own.

Territorial planning, on the other hand (whether on the scale of cities, regions, or nations), has reference to historically defined populations inhabiting specific places. Often these populations enjoy a substantial measure of political autonomy. Territorial planning is therefore an endogenous activity. It searches for historical continuities, seeks a general improvement in the quality of living for all the people in the area, and strives for the full development of their productive potential. Its method is holistic, multi-level and complex.

Despite their obvious differences, functional and territorial planning co-exist with each other, but their typical relation is conflictive. This can be demonstrated with reference to a simple example.

Imagine a cement plant that chooses to locate at point X, the point at which its total costs of production are lowest. (For our purposes, it is indifferent whether the plant is privately owned or not.) At this location, which is optimal from the standpoint of the enterprise, it will employ, say, 100 workers who are drawn from the surrounding rural area. Prior to finalizing its decision, however, the firm may bargain for such additional benefits as a local tax exemption and other subsidies, for instance public investments in access roads and plant facilities. Supposing it is successful in these negotiations, and the plant is now constructed and in operation, additional costs will be imposed upon the community in the form of pollution that will cause deteriorating health conditions among the local people, the destruction of aquatic life and recreational pleasures, and significant material damage. These costs will almost entirely be borne by the community within which the cement plant is located but to which its only *functional* relation is, on the one hand, the employment of local men and women and, on the other, the surplus which it extracts through the systematic destruction of territorial values (local resources, quietness, beauty). Since the location of the cement plant is an exogenous decision, however, the choice needn't be confined to this particular locality. Should the community bargain too harshly, the plant may look for a location in a more benign political environment.

Cement plants are indispensible, of course, a modern economy cannot do without them. Clearly, then, they must be located somewhere, and wherever this is, injuries to territorial values will result. The most that can be expected is that the balance of costs and benefits will somehow be redressed in favour of the local community, but this will require appropriate action by the state. The state has indeed the power to shift the incidence of costs from the community to the producer (and so to the general consumer of the final product), but the extent to which it will do so will depend on such variables as the nature of the activity concerned, the existence of alternative locations, the ownership of the capital in question, the economic needs of the localities, the nature and size of the social costs generated in production, and others. Moreover, such a shift is likely to impair the overall rate of economic growth. The extent to which this represents a relevant, not to say, decisive consideration can only be determined from a territorial point of view.

The determination of social costs and their incidence requires territorial planning. Territorial needs must be carefully articulated, and the territorial base in resources must be considered. Just as regional planning during the sixties and seventies was dominated by location specialists, so the planning of the eighties and nineties is likely to be dominated by specialists in resource management, much as it had been a half-century earlier when regional planning first appeared in the United States. The time is ripe for the containment of functional power and its subordination to a territorial will.

Index